D1187598

BUCK PRIVATES

(Including the Original Shooting Script)

By Ron Palumbo

Foreword by
Tom Smothers

Introduction by
Leonard Maltin

Series Editor
Philip J. Riley

UNIVERSAL FILMSCRIPT SERIES
FIRST EDITION

Published by
BearManor Media
P.O. Box 1129
Duncan, OK 73534-1129
bearmanormedia.com   Tel. 580-252-3547

Copyright ©2013, Ron Palumbo

Reproduction in whole or in part is prohibited without the written permission of the copyright holder.

Photographs, filmscript and other production materials used with the permission of and by special arrangement with Universal Studios.

The film BUCK PRIVATES Copyright ©1941 by Universal Film Company, Inc. Renewed 1968 by Universal Pictures. All rights reserved.

The purpose of this series is the preservation of the art of writing for the screen. Rare books have been a source of enjoyment and an investment for the serious collector, and even in limited printings there were usually a few thousand produced. Scripts, however, numbered only fifty at most, and we are proud to present them in their original form. Some are final shooting scripts and some are earlier drafts, so that students, libraries, archives and film-lovers might, for the first time, study them in their original form. In producing these volumes, we hope that the unique art of screenplay writing will be preserved for future generations.

The opinions expressed in this series are those of the individual authors and not the publisher.

Front cover poster courtesy of Bob Furmanek.
Back cover art courtesy Ron Palumbo.

Manufactured in the
United States of America

To my mom and the memory of my dad,
with fond remembrances of "The 1940s Room."

Contents

Foreword
by Tom Smothers

My brother Dick and I have been working as a comedy team for the past fifty years, and as youngsters Abbott and Costello were a huge part of our comedy upbringing. Along with Laurel and Hardy, Burns and Allen, and Martin and Lewis, they defined for us and a generation of Americans what was genuinely funny.

Working in comedy with a partner was unique and grabbed our collective attention. Because it was a relationship between two people, it carried an even greater import. There are undercurrents of real disagreement, along with genuine affection. As Dick puts it, "Working in a comedy team is like an old marriage: a lot of fighting and no sex."

What was so perfect about Abbott and Costello was that they were such different, absolutely contrary personalities, yet you sensed there was a personal, intimate relationship beyond the comedy routines. I don't know if Bud and Lou were together long enough to really appreciate their roles; did Lou ever really understand how important Abbott was, and vice versa? I think in their hearts they really did.

Of course, as a kid, I could not help but like Abbott and Costello. But I became a big fan later on, when I saw reruns on TV. We studied Bud Abbott; he's Dick's favorite straight man in the history of the world. He never got a break, never got the girl, and was just the meanest sucker in the world, always try-ing to screw somebody. Yet that's what made him so interesting. In our act, if Dick gets too nice to me, I'll remind him, "Think of Bud Abbott." When the audience turns on my brother, and they start to boo him, that's when I know the act's really working. Bud Abbott had that gift with Lou Costello.

The historical setting has defined many artists. Dick and I were pretty anti-military during Vietnam, but if we had been around in Abbott and Costello's time, we'd have taken the same position they did. Our dad was a West Pointer who was killed in World War II. We always said that that war was the last righteous war. Abbott and Costello and *Buck Privates* and their other service comedies reflected the consensus of the righteousness of that war. Like a lot of people, Dick and I perceived Vietnam as unjust, and we reflected it. The time was right for us to do that. And I wonder, if Abbott and Costello had been raised in the same generation we were, what their viewpoint would have been regarding Vietnam. It'd be interesting to know if Abbott and Costello would have been motivated like we were at the time and been anti-establishment comics.

Hollywood in Abbott and Costello's era is such a magical period in our imaginations. This book is the next best thing to going back and watching them make *Buck Privates*. Any student of comedy, or anybody who loves comedy and comedy teams, is going to be thrilled with this book.

Introduction
by Leonard Maltin

Too many people who write about film history do so with blinders on. They miss the important part of the story they're trying to tell: context.

This is what sets Ron Palumbo's account of *Buck Privates* apart from most other considerations of Abbott and Costello's career. There isn't a facet of this film's history that he hasn't explored in detail, from the wave of service comedies that flooded the screen in the early 1940's to the popularity of boogie-woogie music, so well represented by the Andrews Sisters.

He also documents the careers of Bud and Lou's collaborators: studio executives, writers, co-stars and crew.

The result is not just a thorough look at one milestone movie, but a rich serving of Hollywood history.

Palumbo also knows how to navigate the muddy waters of anecdotes. So much that has been written about Abbott and Costello is colored by hazy memories and self-serving stories, it's vital to decide which anecdotes have the ring of truth and which need to be taken with the proverbial grain of salt.

One truth has never been questioned: *Buck Privates* was a sensational hit. It made overnight

movie stars of Bud Abbott and Lou Costello and launched a decade of incredible activity for the duo. It bolstered the fortunes of Universal Pictures, which made A-picture profits with a film that was shot as a B.

That Abbott and Costello's routines are just as funny today as they were in the 1940's is a tribute to the timelessness of their humor, and the tremendous skill they brought to their performances; that expertise was refined over many years' time, in front of audiences in burlesque houses, radio studios, and Broadway theaters. No wonder they were so good in their first movie appearances.

Abbott and Costello were great comedians, and *Buck Privates* was their springboard to success in Hollywood. This book does them both justice.

Leonard Maltin first wrote about Abbott and Costello in his 1970 book, Movie Comedy Teams. *Since then he has become better known for his appearances on* Entertainment Tonight, *and his paperback reference,* Leonard Maltin's Movie and Video Guide. *He serves as film critic and columnist for* Playboy *magazine, and teaches at the University of Southern California.*

Acknowledgements

I would like to express my deepest gratitude to Bob Furmanek, my collaborator on the book *Abbott and Costello in Hollywood* and other projects. His diligent research for that volume provided more than a sturdy foundation for this one; it provided the first few floors. Thanks, Bob.

Of course I am much obliged to Phil Riley for originating the Universal Filmscript series; to Ben Ohmart at Bear Manor Media for reviving it; and Michael Stein and John Conforti at MagicImage for initiating this book.

I am also greatly indebted to the Abbott and Costello families: the late Bud Abbott, Jr.; Vickie Abbott Wheeler and Don Wheeler for giving us unprecedented access to Bud's scrapbook; Paddy Costello Humphreys for permitting unlimited access to Lou's scrapbook; and an extra special thanks to Chris Costello for donating hours of interviews she conducted with Betty (Mrs. Bud) Abbott, Maxene Andrews, Pat Costello, Alex Gottlieb, Joe Kenny and Arthur Lubin, for her own terrific book, *Lou's On First*. Thanks, Chris.

I have also drawn from interviews conducted for *Abbott and Costello in Hollywood* with Arthur Lubin, Patty Andrews, and Pat Costello. In supplementing that original research, I had the pleasure of interviewing the children or spouses of many of the principal participants in this film. Each provided invaluable information, photographs, or interviews. Many thanks to Ruth Frazee Krasna's daughter, Jane Bates; Jane Frazee's son, Tim Tryon; Dean Collins' wife, Mary; Dean's colleague, Rudy Linan; Alan Curtis' nephew, Chris Ueberroth; and Don Raye's wife, Dorothy. Special thanks to the late Dann Cahn

for sharing memories of his father, his perceptive insights into filmmaking at Universal in the early '40s, and his enthusiasm for this project.

Many thanks to the staffs of the Academy of Motion Picture Arts and Sciences Margaret Herrick Library (Los Angeles) and the Billy Rose Theater Collection of the New York Public Library at Lincoln Center (New York) for their assistance in providing access to biographical files, still photographs, clippings, and back issues of *Daily Variety*, *The Hollywood Reporter*, and the *Motion Picture Herald*. A special thanks to Ned Comstock, who, on short notice, arranged for me to review files in The Universal Collection at the USC Cinema-Television Library and Archives of the Performing Arts.

I would like to acknowledge the invaluable assistance of Nancy Pearce and Jan-Christopher Horak when they were at Universal Studios Archives and Collections; and Lisa Lippman and Cindy Tenamoto at Universal Music Publishing.

I am further indebted to Ray Faiola, Garry Garnet, Bill Honor, Scott MacGillivray, Don Morlan, Jim Mulholland, Carl Palumbo, Jonathan Reichman, and Ron Sarbo for providing support, advice, or material that made my task easier and the book better. Extra thanks to Ray for providing copies of the sheet music.

Thanks also to Jimmy Siegel and Eliot Riskin, who made it possible for me work at and visit Universal Studios in the course of our real jobs.

Finally, thanks to my wife, Karen, and our daughter, Vienna, for their ongoing patience, love and support.

—Ron Palumbo

Say Good-bye to Hollywood

Lou Costello stuffed a $5 bill into the gloved hand of the doorman of Hollywood's Knickerbocker Hotel and climbed into the car his brother Pat was driving. The doorman closed Lou's door. "Thank you, Mr. Costello," he said. "Have a safe trip back to New Jersey."

Lou thanked the doorman, but that innocent remark had stung him. Costello had come to Hollywood three times in his quest to become a movie star, and each time the result was a trip back to New Jersey.

Louis Francis Cristillo was a gifted athlete as a kid, and even won the New Jersey State basketball foul shooting championship. But his burning ambition was to be a movie star. "From the very beginning, my father was both an athlete and a ham," his daughter, Chris, wrote in *Lou's On First*, a biography of her father. "Dad always wanted to be in show business. From the time he was four years old, he play-acted with his friends or alone in front of a mirror. Nobody knows where he got it; there were no actors on either side of the family."

Born in Paterson, New Jersey, on March 6, 1906, Lou fell in love with the movies. He and Pat would cut school to spend their lunch money on westerns or Charlie Chaplin shorts.

A younger and trimmer Louis Cristillo.

"He absolutely idolized Chaplin, and it was Chaplin, indirectly, who influenced my father to change his course in life. Instead of a dramatic actor, he wanted to be a comic," Chris writes.

When he was twenty-one, Lou felt he was ready to try his luck in Hollywood. Reluctantly, his parents consented. But after more than a year in Hollywood, all he could get was occasional work as a laborer, extra or stunt man. His timing couldn't have been worse. Talkies were coming in, and stage actors were hot commodities in Hollywood. He was advised to return to New York and get theatrical experience if he wanted to work in movies.

So he left Hollywood and headed back to New Jersey.

Midway across the country, Costello's tiny bankroll ran out. "There was a burlesque show in St. Joseph, Missouri, that wanted a Dutch comedian," Lou recalled on *This is Your Life* in 1956. "I was never on the stage, but I told the fellow I was a Dutch comedian." ("Dutch" was a corruption of *Deutsch*, the German word for "German." The comic performed with a German accent, as popularized by the immensely successful comedy team of Weber and Fields around the turn of the century.) Perhaps because the Empress Theatre was desperate, Lou was hired.

On Lou's first trip to Hollywood, he worked as a stunt man and extra in MGM's Trail of '98 *(1928).*

Earliest known photograph of the team, working in a burlesque show for the Minskys in May, 1936.

In his autobiography *This Laugh Is on Me,* burlesque graduate Phil Silvers cited two myths about burlesque. "The first is that burlesque was a great training ground for comedians. That's true. But the other myth, that all burlesque comics were great, wasn't true. That's why they stayed in burlesque. The ones who rose out of it were able to build creatively on the basics they had learned. Witness Abbott and Costello, Bert Lahr, Jackie Gleason, Bobby Clark, Ed Wynn, Red Skelton, Eddie Cantor, and Fanny Brice." And Phil Silvers.

There was a canon of about two hundred burlesque sketches and gags that had been inspired by or adapted from the Greek comedies, the Italian *Commedia dell'arte,* English music halls, and American minstrel shows. After a year on the burlesque circuit a good comic knew them all and freshened them up with ad-libs. Later, a comic learned how to knit several old bits together to create a whole new routine. Lou worked at the Empress for about a year, and then did a stint at a burlesque house in St. Louis before returning home to New Jersey.

For the next two years he toured with shows on the Mutual Burlesque wheel. When Mutual folded in 1931, performers scrambled for jobs in stock burlesque. Lou worked at Minsky's flagship Republic

Theater on 42nd Street and the Orpheum in Paterson, among many others. While Costello's reputation as a comic was building, he hadn't forgotten his dream of becoming a movie star. In the summer of 1932, with a few years of "stage" experience under his belt, he jumped at a chance to appear in stock burlesque in Los Angeles and take another crack at Hollywood. His notices at the Follies and Arcade theaters were good, but after ten weeks in Los Angeles a second shot at movies never came.

Again, he left Hollywood to return to Paterson.

Over the next two years Costello would meet both his life partner and business partner in stock burlesque. His wife, Anne Battler, was a chorus girl in a Minsky show headlined by the legendary Ann Corio. They married in January 1934.

A year later Lou crossed paths with an acclaimed straight man known as Buddy Abbott. Born to a show business family on October 2, 1897 (not 1895) in Asbury Park, William Alexander Abbott had been around burlesque most of his life. His father, Harry, was an advance man for shows on the reputable Columbia wheel from about 1902 to 1922. Bud started as an assistant treasurer in 1917, became a small-time producer, and then moved on stage around 1923. Bud developed an act with his wife,

2

Performing the "Drill" routine in Hollywood Bandwagon *late in 1937.* Variety *called it "hilarious." The soldier on the left is Vic Parks, who, coincidentally, became Lou's stunt double in the 1950s.*

Betty—a versatile, well-known performer in her own right. They worked for Mutual for several years then transitioned to stock burlesque with Minsky's and their competitors. Bud quickly became one of burlesque's best straight men and producers and worked with veteran comics like Harry Steppe and Harry Evanson. Show business critic Joe Laurie Jr. once wrote, "A good straight man can make a fair comic look good, and a great comic look better."

Although Abbott and Costello had been in the same burlesque shows with other partners, it wasn't until early in 1935 at the Eltinge Theater on 42nd Street that they had the opportunity to perform together. Betty Abbott recalled, "They worked wonderfully together. People started to say, 'Why don't you team up?'"

Early in 1936, they made it official.

The new team went to work for the Minskys, who had several burlesque theaters in New York City and the eastern United States. But despite their surroundings, Bud and Lou always kept their act clean. "An audience may laugh at you for off-color jokes when they're in the theater," Bud once explained, "but when they get outside and talk it over, their opinion of you is pretty low." This philosophy was instrumental in Abbott and Costello's later success in bringing bawdy burlesque routines to a mass audience.

That spring, the primary booking agent for the Steel Pier in Atlantic City, Eddie Sherman, caught the boys' act and offered them a spot in the Pier's minstrel show for the summer. According to Bob Thomas

in *Bud & Lou,* Costello was eager to take the gig while Abbott was loath to trade burlesque for minstrelsy. Yet Bud certainly knew that he wasn't giving up much, since bookings in stock burlesque were never as long as they were on the old wheels. Although the minstrels had worked in blackface since the Pier opened in 1898, the show was by now a streamlined vaudevillian revue re-branded as the "Modern Minstrels," with only the end men in blackface. A postcard from 1936 explained, "The Minstrel offerings today are thoroughly modern, the age demands the finest in mirth and melody. Each week a complete change is undergone; song, skits and dances are new to please the Steel Pier patrons." Still, to persuade the reluctant Abbott, Costello reportedly offered him an extra $10 a week from his salary. Curiously, however, the team was listed on the Steel Pier handbills as "Costello and Abbot" [sic].

The Modern Minstrels was an opportunity for the team to keep honing the act and, more significantly, test material on middle class audiences. The boys returned to burlesque in the fall and continued to develop their timing and routines by doing four shows a day, six days a week. They also began refining an old bit called "Who's the Boss?" that had been transposed to the baseball diamond years earlier. Betty Abbott once explained, "Bud had done the baseball bit a long time before he worked with Lou. That was public domain. He did it with some comic—I don't remember who it was—and it was a little different, because he and Lou put an awful lot of stuff

With the unsung third member of the team, comedy writer John Grant. A former burlesque straight man and producer, Grant had an uncanny ability to freshen up and recycle the old routines.

in it, a lot of new material. Eddie Sherman had them copyright it."

Early in 1937 the team celebrated its first anniversary. Burlesque, however, didn't have long to live. Abbott and Costello worked at the Star Theater in Brooklyn for just two days before Mayor Fiorello LaGuardia ordered all the burlesque theaters in New York closed. It was the team's last performance in burlesque. Bud and Lou had no choice but to go legitimate. Fortunately, Sherman had already booked the boys for a second summer at the Steel Pier...with a $5 raise.

After the Steel Pier, Abbott and Costello joined a traveling vaudeville unit with the prophetic title "Hollywood Bandwagon." Bud and Lou performed the "Drill" routine and "Who's On First?," which, according to *Variety*, was the big hit of the show.

After the tour, Eddie Sherman became their manager. A booker for the Loew's circuit caught their act in Washington, D.C., and signed them for a stage show at Loew's State in New York, just blocks away from the old burlesque houses they had played. Henny Youngman, then a regular on radio's *Kate Smith Hour,* urged Kate's manager and producer, Ted Collins, to see Abbott and Costello perform. Collins did, but wasn't sold: the "Drill" routine was too visual for radio, and he disliked "Who's On First?" Sherman turned to the William Morris Agency to join the lobby to persuade Collins to hire Bud and

Lou. Collins agreed to give the team a one-shot on February 3, 1938, doing their "Mudder/Fodder" bit. The boys didn't miss a week on the show after that. Seven weeks later, on March 24, 1938, a national radio audience heard "Who's On First?" for the very first time. It was an instant smash.

But not many burlesque bits were purely verbal and right for radio. A week later, an old acquaintance from burlesque named John Grant was hired as the team's writer. Grant (1891-1955) had an encyclopedic knowledge of burlesque and could recall every version of every routine, including ones that even veterans like Abbott and Costello didn't know. It was the start of a mutually beneficial association that would last seventeen years and take the trio through radio, Broadway, movies and television.

In late June, *Variety* reported that MGM screentested Abbott and Costello for the musical *Honolulu*. It was eventually released in 1939 with George Burns and Gracie Allen in comedic support.

Early in 1939, Bud and Lou were signed for their only Broadway show, *Streets of Paris*. Veteran comic Bobby Clark headed the cast, which included Brazilian import Carmen Miranda. When the musical opened at the Broadhurst Theater on June 19, 1939, legendary *New York Times* theater critic Brooks Atkinson welcomed "the hilarious team of Lou Costello and Bud Abbott, who carry laughter to the point of helpless groaning...Both men work themselves up into a state of excitement that is wonderful to behold."

After 274 performances, *Streets of Paris* closed on February 10, 1940, then went out on a limited tour that included Washington, D.C. President Franklin D. Roosevelt enjoyed the show and invited Abbott and Costello to entertain at the White House press correspondents dinner. Later that spring, Mike Todd mounted a streamlined version of *Streets of Paris* at the World's Fair starring Abbott and Costello and another famous burlesque alumnus, Gypsy Rose Lee. To top things off, NBC signed Bud and Lou to be Fred Allen's summer radio replacement.

Around this time, three movie studios courted Abbott and Costello for upcoming musicals. The William Morris agency brokered a deal with MGM for the team to do a couple of routines in *Ziegfeld Girl* for $17,500. But Eddie Sherman thought Bud and Lou could do a lot better. On their own initiative, Bud, Lou, and Eddie made a deal with Universal vice president Matty Fox for the team to appear in a musical for $35,000. Eddie reasoned that Bud and Lou would have a better chance of being noticed at the smaller studio. MGM was notorious for signing talent and then having it sit idle. By the time MGM released *Ziegfeld Girl* in April 1941, Abbott and Costello were shooting their fourth film at Universal.

The musical Universal had on the boards was *One Night in the Tropics* (then called "Riviera"), with songs by the legendary Jerome Kern. The cast included Allan Jones, Robert Cummings, Nancy Kelly, and Peggy Moran. Shooting started on August 26, 1940, with Eddie Sutherland directing.

Lou Costello took his third trip to Hollywood. This time it was with a partner, Bud Abbott.

One Night in the Tropics had been in development for months when word came down from the front office to integrate two burlesque comics into the script. John Grant went to Hollywood with the team and suggested routines that might be shoehorned into the film's dizzy plot. Even though Bud and Lou performed several of their best bits (including "Who's On First?"), and the soundtrack featured five Kern songs, the picture was a mess. Producer Leonard Spigelgass (1908-1985) groused, "It was absurd to put Abbott and Costello in the picture. You had a story; you had all that Jerome Kern music. You add a third external element, and the story just disappears. I had to work all night with the writers to try to give them some semblance of a reason for being in the picture—and there wasn't any. We also had an absolute maniac named Jerome Kern who went out of his mind whenever he saw Abbott and Costello. I don't think he ever met them, but oh God, he did not approve of them. He almost tore my hair off."

With Allan Jones and Robert Cummings in One Night in the Tropics *(1940), Bud and Lou's film debut.*

Lou and older brother Pat (1903-1990) on the set of One Night in the Tropics.

When *Tropics* wrapped on September 30, Bud and Lou thought they were finished with Universal—and perhaps motion pictures, too. Lou's brother, Pat, recalled, "After we saw [a screening of] *One Night in the Tropics*, we thought that it was the end of Abbott and Costello's movie career."

Co-star Peggy Moran laughed, "Bob Cummings and I always referred to it as 'One Night in the Flopics.'"

So on this particular October day in 1940, as he and Pat drove away from the Knickerbocker Hotel, Lou Costello wanted to visit Universal City one last time. "We went back to the studio because Lou wanted to go around and thank everybody and say good-bye to the people we had met," Pat recalled.

On the way, Lou thought about the ten-week vaudeville tour Eddie Sherman had arranged for them. They'd be on stage again, performing in front of a live audience. That's where they thrived. Making movies—which required repeating a routine over and over in multiple takes until the element of surprise was gone, in front of a cast and crew that were forbidden to laugh—just wasn't natural. When they

got back to New York, several Broadway producers would be eager to talk to them about upcoming shows. They'd have their pick of the lot.

Still, Lou Costello was crushed by the results of his latest trip to Hollywood.

The car turned down Lankershim Boulevard, and in a few moments Lou and Pat Costello passed through the gate at Universal. Lou may have wondered if he'd ever make it onto a Hollywood lot again.

Pat Costello continued the story. "Lou said, 'Pat you stay in the car, I'll go in and say good-bye, and then we'll go.' I said fine, and I stayed in the car.

"Now, I would say I waited about an hour for Lou, because I was in and out of the studio commissary several times, getting cups of coffee. Well, Lou finally came out, and he was as white as a ghost! I had never seen him so rattled. I said, 'Lou, what's the matter?'

"He said, 'We've got to get a hold of Bud right away—we've got to find Abbott!' I said, 'What for?'

"He said, 'They want us to do two more pictures!' I said, 'What?!'

"He said, 'They want us to do two more pictures!'"

A New Team at Universal

Lou had met with Matty Fox (1911-1964), a former theater chain executive, nephew of studio president Nate Blumberg, and currently a Universal vice president. An industry innovator, Fox was later the first to syndicate old movies to the new medium of television, and pioneered subscription TV in the 1960s.

Costello recalled this pivotal meeting in an interview with the Associated Press in 1954. "I once had been a stunt man, carpenter and extra in the movies," he explained, "and I knew I wanted to stay in the movies. I had nothing to lose, so I went over to see Matty Fox at Universal.

"I said, 'Matty, I just came over to say goodbye before I go over to Paramount.' Matty got up from his chair and said, 'What are you going to do over at Paramount?'"

What followed was the most important ad-lib of Lou Costello's career.

"I told him they wanted to see me about some story ideas I had for Abbott and Costello. Fox got interested right away and said Universal would like to hear about the ideas. This caught me off guard because I had no story ideas and in fact I didn't even know anyone at Paramount.

"So I enacted two old burlesque routines that

Abbott and I had done many times. Matty held his sides laughing. He called in the other top studio brass. I had a bunch of laughers, so I really gave out with the routines."

Lou auditioned the "Drill" and "Moving Candle" bits. The "Drill" was particularly timely. Three weeks earlier, President Roosevelt had signed the Burke-Wadsworth Bill authorizing the first peacetime draft in U.S. history. The vast majority of Americans still opposed any policy that might drag the country into another European war. But after the fall of France that June, a Gallup Poll found that 64% of American men and their families approved of a peacetime draft to shore up the country's frail military. Soon, more than sixteen million men between the ages of twenty-one and thirty-five would register for selective service. At the end of the month, a draft lottery would determine who among them would be the first 800,000 to be inducted and spend a year in training camps.

Costello continued, "They not only signed us, but they bought the routines as original stories." The "Drill" would form the centerpiece of *Buck Privates*, and the "Moving Candle" inspired *Hold That Ghost*.

Lou couldn't believe what had just transpired. He kept a poker face in Fox's office, but by the time he

With their longtime manager, Eddie Sherman.

Matthew Fox, the Universal exec who signed the boys.

reached Pat, he was in a daze.

Pat continued, "Lou said, 'We've got to get a hold of Bud right away—we've got to find Abbott!' Well, I don't know how many phone calls I made trying to find Bud, but we couldn't locate him anywhere. Finally, we gave up, and we were driving out the studio gate, saying good-bye to the guard, when a cab pulls up. And who gets out of the cab? Bud Abbott. Lou said, 'Christ, we've been calling all over for you! They want us to make two more pictures!'"

A different version of this story—with Bud and Eddie Sherman also in the meeting with Fox—first appeared in Bob Thomas' book *Bud & Lou,* and all subsequent biographies. There are several possible explanations for this. Sherman was the source of the anecdotes in *Bud & Lou* and he simply may have embellished his role. Or, he just may have mixed up his meetings. Bud, Lou, and Eddie met with Matty Fox when the team signed for *One Night in the Tropics* in July. Back then, the boys really were considering offers from other studios, and may have run through some routines for Fox.

But Pat Costello's version—that Lou bluffed Fox into a deal all by himself—corroborates an account in *Collier's* magazine in 1947, and Lou's in 1954.

Within days, Louella Parsons' column on October 12, 1940 carried the news: "Abbott and Costello have so pleased Universal that their protracted vaudeville tour has been melted down to a lone appearance. After this engagement, they will return to the lot for another film assignment."

Meanwhile, in preview screenings in Los Angeles,

audiences were enjoying Bud and Lou but little else about *One Night in the Tropics.* A letter from one theater owner to the *Motion Picture Herald* complained, "Terrible still won't describe this one. Abbott and Costello helped. Without them, the picture would have been an absolute flop. Played no business, as expected."

Critics would concur. *Variety* summed up, "It's a slim story that fails to hold together with any sustaining degree, and the music by Jerome Kern fails to reveal one tune that will be remembered. Only the comedy of Abbott and Costello, neatly spotted for periodic appearances, saves the picture from general tediousness...Fast-talking and slapsticky in turn, the team clicks solidly with six specialties for solid laughs in each instance."

Co-star Allan Jones reflected, "It made stars of them. They'd have become stars in any picture they put them in. It just happened to be *my* picture."

Later on, Bud and Lou preferred to ignore *One Night in the Tropics* and say that *Buck Privates* was their first film.

The world premiere of *One Night in the Tropics* was scheduled for New Orleans. But when Costello told Matty Fox that he was going back to Paterson for an annual benefit for his parish church, St. Anthony's, Universal moved the premiere to Paterson. It was held on October 30, the day after the national draft lottery.

A few days later, Bud and Lou arrived at Universal's New York headquarters at 1250 Sixth Avenue to negotiate their contract. Two of the top executives

Left to right: Universal's president, Nate Blumberg; head of production, Cliff Work; and Deanna Durbin, the studio's biggest star from 1937 through 1940. The studio let her contract expire in 1949.

from the William Morris agency joined them: Abe Lastfogel, an office boy who rose to become its president in 1932, and Sam Weisbord, his eventual successor. Abbott and Costello signed with William Morris in 1938 after Weisbord helped get them on the Kate Smith radio show. (In 1941, however, Bud and Lou fired the agency, claiming that it had packaged the team with other stage acts without consent; refused to represent them in a dispute with the Edgar Bergen-Charlie McCarthy radio show; and, incredibly, advised movie executives that the comedians "were not cut out to be motion picture stars.")

Eddie Sherman recalled, "We sat down, Abe Lastfogel, Sam Weisbord, Bud, Lou, and myself, and I think Universal started by offering us $35,000 a picture and four pictures per year. There was a question of either $5,000 or $10,000 more per picture, and I said, 'I will forego that and rather have ten percent of the profits.' Well, nobody ever heard of percentage deals in those days. But I had a crazy idea about it because I thought those pictures would be great. It was up to $40,000 or $45,000 per picture and I said, 'No. We'll take the ten percent.'"

Sherman continued, "Now, Abbott and Costello were adding this up in their heads and saw maybe $40,000 more a year if we took a higher salary per picture. Lou called me out into the hall. I said, 'Lou, take the deal I suggest. I think those pictures will make you a hell of a lot of money percentage-wise. I'll make you a deal right now. If you don't make at least the $10,000 difference on each picture, you don't

have to pay my commission.' Lou said, 'If you feel that strongly about it, I've got to go along with you.'

"Universal was tickled to death to take the percentage deal rather than pay the extra money. As it turned out, the *least* Abbott and Costello made on any of the first four pictures was $250,000—their percentage amounted to that much. So it was almost a difference of $1 million a year."

As Sam Weisbord put it, "That $5,000 cost Universal millions and millions."

(Universal made profit participation deals with Bing Crosby, Mae West, and W.C. Fields in 1939. Admittedly, they were all established stars at the time. Crosby and the studio equally split the production costs and the profits of *East Side of Heaven*. West's agreement for *My Little Chickadee* called for twenty-five percent of the net profits. Fields got twenty percent of the gross over $600,000 for *You Can't Cheat an Honest Man*.)

And so, on November 6, 1940, Bud and Lou signed their second contract with Universal. The deal called for two pictures—*Buck Privates* and *Oh, Charlie!*—over a period of twelve weeks. They would receive a flat $35,000 per picture, plus ten percent of the gross over 170% of the production cost. For example, if a film cost $250,000 to make, the team's profit participation kicked in after the film earned its first $425,000. Later, if the studio wished to exercise its option and keep the team, the boys would get $3,500 per week the first year, for no more than four pictures per year, with salary increases each year for up to seven years. They couldn't have known it then, but with extensions, re-negotiations, and raises, this contract would last fourteen years.

Following that meeting, Bud and Lou made personal appearances with *One Night in the Tropics* in other cities, including Buffalo, Detroit, Chicago and San Francisco. According to the *New York Post,* they were scheduled to return to Hollywood on November 15 to, in their words, really "get down to the business of making pictures." Universal, the newspaper reported, was working on a "timely script."

When Universal signed Abbott and Costello, the studio was on its way to its best year since 1926. For the fiscal year ending October 31, 1940, Universal posted a profit of nearly $2.4 million—double that of 1939—and enjoyed its second consecutive year in the black after four straight years of losses.

The turnaround might be credited to Universal's latest management team. President Nate Blumberg and head of production Cliff Work replaced Robert Cochrane and Charles R. Rogers on January 1, 1938. Cochrane and Rogers had replaced Universal's founder, Carl Laemmle Sr., and his son, Carl Jr., in 1936 after they defaulted on a loan and lost control of the studio.

Before joining Universal, Blumberg (1894-1960) was the vice president and general manager of RKO's theater chains. Work (1891-1963) was his West Coast division manager. They brought in other former theater managers to produce Universal's films and run the studio. Screenwriter Edmund L. Hartmann (1911-2003) recalled, "The studio executives were all theater exhibitors, owners, and operators. They knew nothing about the technique of making movies, but they knew what to put on the marquee to bring in a crowd. So they would assign contract people to do something in a picture that had nothing to do with the story at all—just to be able to use that person's name on a marquee. And they never talked about movies; you could talk about football, you could talk about horse racing. But if you talked about movies,

they looked at you like you were some kind of nut."

A nine-man executive committee made every decision related to production at Universal City. In daily meetings that started at 8:30 a.m. and ran about half an hour, they discussed films in production, scripts, casting, contracts, talent, and so on.

But Universal had something far more influential on its bottom line than the new management. It had certifiable box office gold in teenage songstress Deanna Durbin. Between 1937 and 1940, Durbin's eight hit musicals grossed about $16.5 million. The infusion of cash allowed Blumberg and Work to increase production from 47 films in 1938 to 55 in 1940 and expand the studio's talent roster. W.C. Fields, Mae West, Edgar Bergen and Charlie McCarthy, Hugh Herbert, Olsen and Johnson, and the Ritz Brothers all joined Universal during this period. The studio that practically owned the horror genre in the 1930s was now stockpiling vaudevillians, reflecting the sensibilities of its new management.

Cliff Work assigned executive producer Milton Feld to oversee the two Abbott and Costello films. Feld (1893-1947) started out as the manager of the Newman Theater, one of Kansas City's grandest movie palaces. In one interview, Walt Disney said that Feld commissioned the fledgling animator's seminal *Laugh-O-Gram* cartoons for the theater in 1921. Feld migrated to Hollywood in 1925, where he managed theaters and produced stage shows. In the mid-1930s he was hired as an assistant to Darryl F. Zanuck and became an associate producer at 20th Century-Fox. Feld joined Universal in 1938 as one of five executive producers responsible to Cliff Work.

The executive committee also decided that Abbott and Costello's army picture would be a comedy with music. This was standard practice for comedies of the era and a way for the studio to hedge its bets, since Universal wasn't sure if Bud and Lou could act, let alone carry a film.

The question for the committee was, with whom do we team Abbott and Costello?

A Duo Gets a Trio

By late October, reviews were coming in on a mediocre little Universal musical called *Argentine Nights,* which featured the Ritz Brothers and marked the screen debut of the Andrews Sisters. *Variety* called it "a strong program attraction that will give a good account of itself at the wickets. Film debut of the Andrews Sisters will catch many of the trio's platter following, and provides a chance for exploitation to add to theater grosses."

LaVerne (1911-1967), Maxene (1916-1995), and Patty (1918-2013) were better known across the country than Bud and Lou at the time. The children of Greek and Norwegian immigrant parents, the Andreos sisters were born in Minneapolis and learned to sing by imitating the popular Boswell Sisters. "We couldn't read music," Maxene explained, "but when we heard a song, we heard it in harmony."

Patty sang lead, Maxene soprano, and LaVerne alto.

During the Depression the sisters dropped out of school and began singing with various dance bands and touring with the likes of Ted Mack, Leon Belasco, and comic bandleader Larry Rich. The family moved to New York and Decca signed the girls in 1937. Their second release was the popular standard "Nice Work If You Can Get It," but it was the disc's B side, "Bei Mir Bist Du Schoen," a reworking of a number from the 1933 Yiddish musical *I Would If I Could,* that became the first of their unprecedented nineteen gold records.

In April 1940, with eight top ten hits to their credit, the girls signed their first contract with Universal. Patty explained, "Jack Kapp [who formed Decca in 1934] knew Nate Blumberg, the president of Universal. It was through him that we got our break."

The studio put the sisters into *Argentine Nights.* The requisite romantic leads were Constance Moore and George Reeves (later TV's classic *Superman*). Before shooting began in May, however, Universal added the Ritz Brothers to the cast, and production was delayed a month while the script was reworked. Maxene recalled, "I found out later that Universal had a deal they had to do with the Ritz Brothers; so to get the studio off the hook with them, they put us in the picture together."

The Andrews Sisters hated *Argentine Nights* for three reasons: "Because it was our first picture," Patty recalled, "and [because of] the Ritz Brothers, who were very experienced doing pictures, and they made it rough for us." Maxene added, "It was incredible. They were overbearing and rude. They pulled every

Appearances to the contrary, LaVerne, Patty and Maxene were not having fun with co-stars Jimmy, Harry and Al Ritz in Argentine Nights *(1940), the girls' screen debut.*

trick in the book to upstage us."

The third reason the girls hated the film was their garish make-up. "We looked like the Ritz Brothers in drag," Patty cracked. "We looked so ugly on screen that we walked back to Manhattan from the Bronx premiere, and Maxene was in tears all the way."

The *Harvard Lampoon* voted the girls "Most Frightening" in its annual list of Film Worsts.

Universal showed no further interest in the trio. "The studio was so sure *Argentine Nights* was a flop that they dropped our contract; they didn't want us any more," Maxene recalled.

The girls returned to the recording studio and live appearances. They were soon consoled by their latest release, "Ferry Boat Serenade," which charted on October 12 and moved steadily higher.

A hit record, favorable trade reviews for *Argentine Nights,* and the need for a musical act to complement Abbott and Costello all piqued Universal's interest in the Andrews Sisters again. "At that point, Universal still wasn't sure if Bud and Lou could carry a picture alone—or whether the Andrews Sisters could either," Patty said. "But they knew with the two commodities they had something. That's how we got into *Buck Privates.*"

Although Abbott and Costello were offered a two-picture deal, the Andrews Sisters' contract, signed on November 10, called for one film with options for more. The girls received between $12,000 and $15,000 for *Buck Privates.*

A few days after signing their contract, the trio recorded "I'll Be With You in Apple Blossom Time" and "Scrub Me Mama (With a Boogie Beat)" at Decca's studios in New York. On November 28, the very day the Andrews Sisters reported to Universal City, "Ferryboat Serenade" reached No. 1 on the charts. It remained in the top spot for the next three weeks—well into filming of *Buck Privates.*

With Bud and Lou winning good reviews and the Andrews Sisters riding a hit record, Universal issued a press release: "The Andrews Sisters and Abbott and Costello have been retained by Universal for a special production, 'Buck Privates.' Decision to feature all five artists in one picture followed the spectacular success of both star combinations in their initial films. Both fans and exhibitors are clamoring for them. They will start production within thirty days after principals return from east where they're making stage appearances."

How'd You Like to be a Producer?

On October 31, 1940, the day after *One Night in the Tropics* premiered in Paterson, a screenplay titled "Buck Privates" was delivered to Universal. In the script, two buddies outrun a cop who later turns up in boot camp as their sergeant; there's a comic drill routine; and the story climaxes in war games between the Red and Blue armies. What's more, the script suggests Shemp Howard for a supporting role as a rookie soldier.

But this screenplay was *not* written for Abbott and Costello. It was another in a series of Richard Arlen and Andy Devine programmers produced at the studio between 1939 and 1941. It was written by Maxwell Shane (1905-1983), who adapted the most recent Arlen-Devine opus, *The Leather Pushers* (1940). Born in Paterson, New Jersey, Shane later was one of the producers of *M Squad,* the hard-nosed detective series that made Lee Marvin a star.

Milton Feld had another screenwriter, Harold Shumate (1893-1950), working on a story specifically for Abbott and Costello and the Andrews Sisters. A prolific if not outstanding writer, Shumate had, by 1940, accumulated seventy screenplay or story credits dating back to the silent era. After a seven-year tenure with Columbia's B unit, he landed at Universal. Many of the Austin, Texas, native's screenplays were westerns, like *When the Daltons Rode* (1940). Later in 1941, Shumate wrote the adaptation for Abbott and Costello's western spoof, *Ride 'Em Cowboy.*

Shumate submitted his twenty-two page treatment, clinically titled "Abbott & Costello Conscription Story," within days of Shane's script, on November 4, 1940. (This was two days before Bud and Lou signed their contracts.) Since *Buck Privates* was conceived as

a musical, Shumate wrote a backstage drama to allow for all the songs. The story was loosely based on Pygmalion. Bob Trent, a wealthy bachelor and gifted songwriter, discovers Judy Gray, a talented but inexperienced singer, and sets about transforming her into a great vocalist. Their goal is to land jobs with the famous Ted Sherman orchestra. Sherman, a vain and marginally talented bandleader, not only tries to steal Judy from Bob (who eventually realizes that he loves her), but Ted also tries to steal Bob's masterpiece, "the next great Army marching song." Of course, by the end of the script Bob receives proper credit for the song, he and Judy reunite, and Ted sees the error of his ways.

Shumate cast the Andrews Sisters as vocalists with Ted's band, while Abbott and Costello were inept talent agents who somehow manage to get Judy an audition with the bandleader. For conveniences of the story, the Andrews Sisters, Abbott and Costello, and other vaudevillians live in Bob's spacious Manhattan penthouse. Apparently Bob is a sucker for any act that's down on its luck. Even Judy moves in for her intensive training. Halfway through the script, all the male cast members are either drafted or enlist. Abbott and Costello, while avoiding a collection agent, duck into a movie theater that's being used as an enlistment center and accidentally sign up. In a running gag, the boys also antagonize a civilian neighbor who predictably turns up as their commanding officer in boot camp. (The Production Code Administration, Hollywood's censor board, later suggested that the boys' nemesis be a sergeant, not an officer.)

The girls put in more appearances on visitor's day

Far left: Executive Producer Milton Feld supervised all of the Abbott and Costello films at Universal through 1947. Associate producers like Alex Gottlieb (near left) reported to Feld. Alex went on to produce eight A&C films at Universal, the team's two color films, and the first few episodes of the boys' classic TV series.

and during the camp show finale. Shumate summarized the picture's rousing finale: "This is to be our biggest number, and as has been suggested, will be in the spirit of 'Over There' and the feeling of 'God Bless America.' It must be sung by a huge male chorus, there must be marching men, Judy singing, the Andrews Sisters backing her up, and the camp must really be lifted off its feet for a while...And as the number moves to its conclusion, we get special effects—glimpses of drafted men marching to camp singing this new song—of transports pulling out with bands playing the same number—a nation marching off to prepare itself for defense of God and country..."

Shumate's treatment was passed on to John Grant, who suggested additional routines for Abbott and Costello. The boys could do their "Dice" routine on the train en route to camp; a run-in with a sergeant could lead to "Go Ahead and Sing"; and the "Prize Fight" sketch could be part of the rec hall sequence. There was an opportunity for still another cross-talk routine during the camp show finale. Two more musical ideas were also generated: a big farewell song to be performed by the Andrews Sisters at Grand Central Station; and a tune for the hapless Costello like Irving Berlin's "Oh, How I Hate to Get Up in the Morning."

Shumate incorporated Grant's routines and these musical ideas, changed the title to "Sons o' Guns," and met with Feld and possibly Grant four days later. More ideas were tossed around. In Shumate's first draft, Bob also aspired to work for Ted's band. But by

Shumate's final draft, Bob was a crack arranger for Ted, and the two men make a bet when Bob claims he can transform any girl with raw talent into a top vocalist. Abbott and Costello, who were talent agents in the first draft and unemployed vaudevillians in the second, were cast as sidewalk necktie salesman in the third. In each of Shumate's versions, Bud and Lou inadvertently enlist in a movie theater that's used as an enlistment center. This may have been inspired by Buster Keaton's service comedy, *Doughboys* (1930). Buster inadvertently enlists at an employment office that serves as a recruitment center.

When Shumate delivered these changes on November 11, Feld told him to start writing the actual screenplay. Milton and the executive committee, however, clearly had doubts, and decided to put another writer on the project. Feld summoned 34-year-old Alex Gottlieb to his office. Born in Russia and raised in Kansas, Gottlieb (1906-1988) graduated from the University of Wisconsin, where he majored in journalism. After he relocated to New York, he worked as a reporter for the *Brooklyn Eagle*. In 1929 he ghostwrote an article for a female classmate, and the byline led to a job for the girl. In appreciation, the girl's brother, an executive with Paramount, offered Gottlieb a job as publicity director of the Rialto Theater. That executive was Milton Feld.

"I came out to Hollywood in 1937," Gottlieb recalled. "I'd been advertising director for United Artists and Columbia Pictures. I was publicity director for Walter Wanger until he went broke. I had some friends at Republic, so I went to work as a screenwriter at Republic, then Universal, writing little B movies. I'd become a fair writer."

And a prolific one. Gottlieb also wrote radio scripts for Al Jolson, Edgar Bergen and Charlie McCarthy, and the *Big Town* series. He collaborated on a comedy called *Separate Rooms* that was then running on Broadway. A second collaboration, *World Premiere,* was set to open on Broadway in 1941. At Universal, Gottlieb co-wrote *Ex-Champ* (1938), *Gambling Ship, Mystery of the White Room,* and *Inside Information* (all 1939). Most recently he scripted *Meet the Wildcat* and *Dark Streets of Cairo.* The two films received polar opposite reviews. *Variety* called Gottlieb's *Wildcat* script, which was about an art thief in Mexico City, "careless" and "absurd." But *Cairo,* a tale of jewel thieves, was met with praise: "Alex Gottlieb has concocted enough new plot wrinkles to sustain interest."

Gottlieb recalled, "Milton Feld said, 'How'd you like to be a producer?' Naturally I said I'd like to move up from writer to producer. He said, 'We've just signed a comedy team from burlesque, Abbott and Costello. They were on radio with Kate Smith. Have you ever heard of them?' I said, 'Yes, I saw them in *Streets of Paris* in New York and laughed my fool head off.' Milton said, 'We want to make a series of B pictures with them, and we want a writer/producer, somebody who can write scripts behind John Grant.' I asked why he picked me. He said, 'You are the twenty-seventh [or seventeenth or twentieth, according to other sources] writer I've talked to. Everyone else turned it down. They're all ambitious. They all want to be producers, too. But they all said that these are a couple of cheap burlesque comics who will never get *anywhere.* You'll make a few pictures with them and that's the last we'll hear of them.'"

One other producer on the lot accepted an Abbott and Costello assignment: Burt Kelly (1899-1983) was put on *Oh, Charlie!,* which was being developed simultaneously. But unlike most of the studio brass, Gottlieb had actually seen Abbott and Costello perform, and witnessed the remarkable effect they had on an audience.

"I told Milton, 'Those twenty-seven writers are all wrong, and the studio is all wrong. I saw Abbott and Costello on Broadway with a crowd that paid a lot of money to see them, and those people never stopped laughing. I couldn't believe the amount of laughter. I kept looking around. They appealed to every kind of audience. They had found a common denominator of humor. Milton, I will bet you that within a year they rate Number One at the box office. You can make the pictures cheap, but I guarantee that they'll be that popular.'

"And Milton said, 'We don't want that. We just want to make a series of B pictures to round out our program.' I said, 'You can plan anything you like. But I will be the star producer on your lot, I will make Universal rich, and I'll make stars of Abbott and Costello.'

"Milton thought I was crazy."

Screenwriter Stanley Roberts (1916-1982), who wrote the screenplay for *Who Done It?* (1942) and later shared an Academy Award for the screen adaptation of *The Caine Mutiny* (1954), explained, "They put Alex in charge, who'd never produced a picture before. They really didn't care what happened."

Universal may not have expected much within its executive suite, but publicly the studio gushed over the boys. Louella Parsons' column on December 9 reported, "My old friends Abbott and Costello have gone over like a million at Universal, where they believe that the comedy zanies of the radio are the biggest discovery in the field of comedy since Charlie McCarthy...Universal feels with a little brushing up Bud and Lou will be among their biggest stars."

Gottlieb went to work on a screenplay based on Shumate's story. On November 18, Alex turned in the first forty-one pages of his version, while Shumate delivered sixty pages of his script. The project was now being called "Buck Privates," and annotated, "Screenplay by Harold Shumate; Abbott and Costello Material by John Grant."

Reviewing both screenplays, the executive committee became convinced that Shumate's story wasn't right for *Buck Privates.* The love triangle between Bob, Judy, and Ted took up too much time at the expense of Abbott and Costello and the Andrews Sisters. What's more, only half of the script took place in the army camp. But budget considerations, rather than plot or character development, guided story conferences at the miserly studio. Shumate's scenario—with its penthouse, cafe, and nightclub sets, big band orchestras, and various vaudeville acts—would cost more than Feld was willing to spend.

Pressure was mounting at Universal. On the day before Shumate and Gottlieb turned in their scripts, the *New York Times* reported that five other studios planned draft comedies. Paramount was readying *Caught in the Draft* for Bob Hope, while Warner and RKO were bickering over the title "You're in the Army Now." Columbia announced "Pack Up Your Troubles," and Fox planned "Rise and Shine." The trade publication *Motion Picture Exhibitor* reported, "They say that the first Army camp [picture] will get the money." Universal couldn't afford to be last in what might turn out to be a short-lived novelty trend. Cliff Work reminded Feld that they wanted to start filming *Buck Privates* by December 2 or 3.

Feld called Arthur T. Horman (1905-1964), who was one of the writers on *Argentine Nights*. Horman had just finished writing a service comedy for Warner Bros. called "Navy Blues." (It wasn't put into production until well after *Buck Privates* was released.) Horman's current screen credit was *Give Us Wings*—a Dead End Kids vehicle directed by Charles Lamont. A *New York Times* reviewer hailed *Give Us Wings* as "so bad it is often quite amusing," and believed it was a "formidable contender for the title of the year's best bad picture."

Feld paired Horman with Gottlieb and sent them off to come up with a new treatment for *Buck Privates* with certain guidelines. Probably the first consideration was to set the action in an army camp and depict some of what the new soldiers could expect. Second, Abbott and Costello and, to a lesser extent, the Andrews Sisters, must be featured more prominently. Also, Shumate's story was elitist; it followed two privileged men—a famous bandleader and a rich songwriter; the army camp was superfluous. The new story should demonstrate the breadth and equity of the draft. Meeting these goals would have the added benefit of streamlining any romantic subplot.

Five days later, on November 23, Horman and Gottlieb had outlined a new story that retained the routines specified by John Grant and some of the musical numbers previously discussed.

Their story opens with Abbott and Costello's necktie pitch, and proceeds like the *Buck Privates* we know: the boys flee from a cop (Officer Mattson), duck into a movie theater, and accidentally enlist. The other characters, depicting the scope of the draft, are introduced during the Grand Central Station sequence: spoiled playboy Parker Randolph Jr.; Bob Martin, a worker in one of the Randolph factories; Dick Burnette, a sensitive pianist and composer;

camp hostess Judy Gray, daughter of World War I hero Capt. Arnold Gray; and the Andrews Sisters, who sing the film's first song, a "farewell ditty," during this sequence.

Abbott and Costello's "Dice" routine takes place on the train. At camp, Officer Mattson turns up as Sergeant Mattson, and Bud and Lou do their "Money Exchange" and "Drill" routines. Meanwhile, Parker and Bob not only compete for Judy, but for the rank of corporal. Bob looks like a sure bet when he outshoots Parker on the rifle range, but Parker prepares for the written exam by sewing cheat sheets into his shirtsleeves. Abbott and Costello foil the playboy's plan by switching his shirts, and Bob wins the promotion. When Parker wangles a date with Judy, Bob becomes jealous and they nearly come to blows in their tent. The sergeant blames Costello for the ruckus and assigns him stable duty. (Apparently the studio had a mule act under contract, and even Shumate tried to work it into his versions!) Dick Burnette, meanwhile, begins composing a stirring march on the piano.

During visitor's day, Bud and Lou do their "prize fight routine," Bob and Judy's romance blooms, and the Andrews Sisters perform a second, unspecified song. But when Parker passes a crack about Judy, Bob hits him and is arrested for striking a private. Judy consents to a date with Parker if he agrees not to press charges against Bob. Abbott and Costello inform the Captain that Parker provoked the fight, and the Captain releases Bob and rescinds Parker's pass. Bob and the boys drive into town to retrieve Parker. In a little cafe, where the Andrews Sisters perform another number, Bob is shocked to discover Parker on a date with Judy. Of course, Bob gets the wrong idea, and Judy can't explain for fear that Parker will bring charges against Bob. Rather than tell her the charge against him was dropped, Bob storms back to camp to seethe. When Parker finally returns from his date, Bob is waiting up, and slugs him again. The next day, Judy still doesn't explain to Bob why she was out with Parker, and Bob thinks the worst.

That night, Parker and Dick are assigned guard duty at the munitions dump. Parker cavalierly lights a cigarette, then absentmindedly tosses the match into the munitions chamber. As a small fire spreads toward the powder kegs, Parker flees in a panic. Dick summons the courage to dive on the fire and put it out, but not before a small explosion seriously injures

Universal Studios in 1943. The sixteen soundstages on the front lot were separated from the back lot's town and village facades by a hillside. Over the years, the hill was razed and another sixteen soundstages were added. The hills on the right of the photograph are now the site of the studio's sprawling theme park.

him. Bob catches Parker, then carries Dick out of the chamber. Incredibly, Bob decides to take the blame to save Parker for Judy's sake. But Parker's story—that Bob was responsible for the explosion—doesn't sit right with Abbott and Costello. The boys discover one of Parker's monogrammed cigarette butts at the crime scene. Parker's tent mates hold a kangaroo court and confront him with the evidence, but Parker appears unmoved. Bob's court-martial is about to begin when Parker interrupts and humbly confesses everything.

At the finale, the camp orchestra plays Dick's patriotic march; Bud and Lou perform their "Hole in the Wall" routine; the Andrews Sisters sing another number; Bob and Judy reunite; and Parker vows to take the army seriously.

Reviewing this scenario, the studio realized it suffered the same flaw as Shumate's—too much emphasis on the competition between Bob and Parker for Judy. More troubling, however, was how Parker's dereliction nearly kills another soldier, and the inade-

quacy of his confession to depict a sincere change in his attitude. To portray Parker's negligence less fatally, Horman and Gottlieb hit upon the idea of reworking the rifle match. Parker evades the important contest and betrays his squad. Parker's reformation must be proven by action, not words. The writers replaced the munitions dump sequence with a sham battle where Parker could properly redeem himself. Parker fails his first test, the rifle match, but rises to the occasion in the war games when it counts most. In addition, the battle would show America's new army in action and, possibly more important, save Universal money by using stock footage.

Meanwhile, John Grant added more Abbott and Costello bits to the script. "Go Ahead and Play the Radio" was inserted to further antagonize Sergeant Mattson, and the routines "Hole in the Wall," "You're 40, She's 10," and "What Are You Doing in the Depot?" were placed in the finale. The "Drill" routine, however, was altered for the worse. Abbott and Costello had been performing the sketch on stage for a few years, with Bud as the sergeant and Lou the hapless trainee. Perhaps in deference to military protocol, the writers called for Sergeant Mattson to drill Abbott and Costello, plus ten other men. This switch on the routine endured through each subsequent draft of the screenplay, including the final shooting script in this book. Of course, it was filmed the way Bud and Lou usually performed it, and became the standout sequence in the film.

The Andrews Sisters were set for three songs, but at this point only one of them was mentioned by name: "Boogie Woogie Bugler" [sic]. The sisters' other numbers were the "farewell ditty" at Grand Central Station and the big, patriotic number in the finale. As it turned out, these wound up being the same song, "You're a Lucky Fellow, Mr. Smith," but at this point the script called for two different numbers. The producers also decided that the "farewell" number would carry over onto the train as a call-and-response song like "Hit The Road," which Raye and Prince had written for *Argentine Nights*. "Hit The Road" (not to be confused with "Hit The Road, Jack") appeared on the flip side of "Ferryboat Serenade."

Over the next week, Horman and Gottlieb wrote two more drafts, refining their story. By turning Bob into Parker's long-suffering chauffeur, the writers quickly set up their relationship, stressed the equity of the draft, and created a competition between classes that underscores one of the themes of the film. Horman was also told to integrate Abbott and Costello throughout the sham battle sequence and make room for a fourth song, "Bounce Me, Brother, With a Solid Four." This new number was intended for the bandleader, Dick Burnette.

About this time, Milton Feld became ill with a particularly bad flu that swept through Hollywood. The *Motion Picture Herald* reported that the epidemic disrupted production all over town. Approximately 500 stars and studio workers were stricken, including seventy at Universal—Deanna Durbin and Feld among them. This may have contributed to the delay in the start of filming *Buck Privates*.

Over the long Thanksgiving weekend the screenplay began to fall into place. A draft dated December 3 is quite close to the final shooting script. The writers made some minor refinements, such as transposing Parker Randolph's name to Randolph Parker, III. But the most significant changes involved the musical numbers. An effort was made to space the songs evenly throughout the script. In addition, "You're a Lucky Fellow, Mr. Smith" grew even more elaborate. The number started with a spoken introduction, broke into a bouncy upbeat tune in Grand Central Station, and carried over to the train with call-and-response passages. Someone then suggested developing the number in the style of "Beyond the Blue Horizon," from the Ernst Lubitsch film *Monte Carlo* (1930), where the chugging of the train echoes the melody.

Costello's novelty number, "When Private Brown Becomes a Captain," first conceived as far back as Shumate's second draft, now occurred in the "Play the Radio" scene, not during KP.

Don Raye, Hughie Prince, and Vic Schoen wrote a fifth song, "I Wish You Were Here." This ballad for separated lovers was originally intended for the Andrews Sisters. Their version, taken from a playback disc, was issued by Universal on a special promotional record with "You're a Lucky Fellow, Mr. Smith." But someone realized that the song could further the plot's love triangle. So, Jane Frazee sings "I Wish You Were Here" in the film.

Gottlieb and his collaborators also attempted to redefine the Abbott and Costello screen characters by making Bud more devious and Lou more innocent than they were in *One Night in the Tropics*. To further polarize them, the boys received descriptive character names; Abbott would be "Slicker Smith," and Costello the more nebbish "Herbie Brown." That tradition continued through all their films, and was later adopted by Martin and Lewis.

Milton Feld and Universal's executive committee were not the only ones insisting on changes to the script. Every draft of every screenplay was sent to the Production Code Administration, where Joseph I. Breen's staff of censors pored over screenplays for anything remotely offensive. "There were pages and pages of things you couldn't do or say," screenwriter Edmund Hartmann explained. "It's a wonder pictures were made at all." Director Arthur Lubin mused, "Wouldn't Breen turn over in his grave if he knew what was going on today?" From the very first draft of Shumate's screenplay, Breen urged Feld to "secure competent technical advice as to the military angles involved in this story in view of the present critical conditions and the situations of this country involving the Army. It would be especially important

Poster artwork was usually created before the script was finalized. After reviewing an early draft of the screenplay, the Production Code Administration suggested that the boys' nemesis be a sergeant, not an officer.

that the finished picture be not subject to unfavorable criticism or possible legal action by the War Department."

Arthur Lubin made service comedies with Abbott and Costello in the Forties and Francis the Talking Mule in the Fifties. He explained, "You can't do an army, navy or air force picture where you need the help of the government without their okay, and usually they provide one or two technical advisors to be on the set at all times."

The technical advisor on *Buck Privates* was Captain Jack Voglin (1904-1982), a VMI graduate who had served three years in the Army. In 1936, when Universal planned to make a film about the New York Hippodrome, once the world's largest theater, the studio hired Voglin as a technical advisor. His father was the Hippodrome's managing director, and Jack had worked there. The film was never made and the Hippodrome, long in decline, was demolished in 1939. Voglin stayed in Hollywood and worked as an extra and stunt man. When the war broke out in Europe he was assigned to the Motion Picture Producer's Association as official Army technical advisor for all selective service films. At one point Voglin was working for four different studios. During World War II he was briefly recalled to the

Army, then returned to the motion picture business, where he worked as an assistant director or production manager in films and TV for the next twenty-five years. Voglin married Abbott and Costello's favorite leading lady, Hillary Brooke, in 1943, but they divorced in 1948.

Cliff Work now planned to start *Buck Privates* on Wednesday, December 11. Horman and Gottlieb labored to complete the final shooting script by December 10, and continued refining their screenplay as the picture was shooting. Screenwriter Robert Lees and his partner, Fred Rinaldo, were writing Abbott and Costello's next film, *Oh, Charlie!*, when they were tapped to work on scenes for *Buck Privates*. Lees could not recall any specific contributions to the screenplay, and no studio documentation survives. Six years later, however, Lees and Rinaldo wrote the screenplay for the sequel, *Buck Privates Come Home.*

Gottlieb was in his office working on the script when he had his first meeting with Lou Costello. Alex recalled, "Lou told me a little bit of his history and then he got real serious. He said, 'Alex, I only have one ambition in life, and if you help me fulfill that ambition, anything you want me to do, I'll do.'

"I asked him what it was, and he said, as if he was a little boy, 'I wanna be a *star.*'"

I'm Sorry, I'm Not a Dance Director

While Gottlieb and Horman were honing the script, Milton Feld and Cliff Work considered directors. Universal had two on staff whose comedy credentials went back to the silent era: Eddie Cline and Eddie Sedgewick.

Cline (1892-1961) started as one of the Keystone Kops and then graduated to directing at Mack Sennett's studio. He co-directed and co-scripted many of Buster Keaton's shorts in the 1920s. At RKO he directed Wheeler and Woolsey, a popular comedy team that worked a little like Abbott and Costello. Most recently at Universal, Cline had helmed the W.C. Fields classics *My Little Chickadee* and *The Bank Dick* (both 1940). He wound up directing Universal's other comedy teams—the Ritz Brothers and Olsen and Johnson—and the C-budget features of the Andrews Sisters.

Sedgewick (1892-1953) was a former circus and vaudeville performer in a family act, "The Five Sedgewicks." He also started in silent films as a comedian and made the transition to directing in 1921. Sedgewick also directed Buster Keaton in the late 1920s and early 1930s, including Keaton's service comedy, *Doughboys* (1930). He later directed Laurel and Hardy in *Air Raid Wardens* (1943).

Neither Cline nor Sedgewick was assigned *Buck Privates*.

Instead, when 41-year-old Arthur Lubin reported to the studio's executive offices on November 27 to sign a new, long-term contract, he was told that he was going direct a musical about the peacetime draft starring Abbott and Costello and the Andrews Sisters. Even though his latest film, *Where Did You Get That Girl?*, included musical numbers, the director was baffled by his new assignment.

"I was honest," Lubin recalled. "I said, 'I'm sorry, but I just don't feel I'm the right director for this project. I'm not a dance director.' They all looked at me with puzzled expressions. One of the men said, 'Dancing? What do you mean?' I replied, 'There's a troupe at the Figueroa Theater called the [Merriel] Abbott Dancers. Isn't that who we're talking about?' Everybody laughed. Then they explained who Abbott and Costello were."

Lubin, who has been lauded in several recent books about gay Hollywood, was born in Los Angeles on July 25, 1899. Comedian Harold Lloyd, a family friend, recommended the boy for a scholarship to the San Diego School of Expression. After briefly serving in the navy, Lubin graduated from the drama school of Carnegie Tech in 1922. He soon began acting on Broadway. One of his earliest roles was in *The Red Poppy* with another newcomer, Bela Lugosi. Lubin recalled helping the Hungarian actor learn his lines phonetically. (Later, Lubin directed Lugosi and Boris Karloff in *The Black Cat* [1940]).

Lubin also began producing and directing theater in New York and Los Angeles. These productions included *This One Man*, starring Paul Muni; *When the Bough Breaks*, starring Pauline Fredericks; and *Her Man of Wax*, starring Lenore Ulric. In 1926, he and his fellow actors were arrested in Los Angeles for putting on what was then considered an obscene play: Eugene O'Neill's *Desire Under the Elms*.

Lubin entered silent films as an actor during this period. In the drama *His People* (1925), he played Morris, an ambitious Jewish law student who, ashamed of his humble family background, pretends to be an orphan after falling in love with a judge's daughter. *The New York Times* wrote: "Arthur Lubin deserves great credit for his work as Morris." Lubin also played King Louis XIII in *Bardelys the Magnificent* (1926); coincidentally, Lou Costello worked as an extra or stunt man in the film.

But Lubin was less successful on screen than he had been on stage. "Whatever personality I had on the stage certainly wasn't photogenic," he confessed. Lubin began to prefer producing and directing. He joined Paramount as an assistant to producer William LeBaron. "My first big break was becoming assistant to William LeBaron. Afterwards, I went to MGM where I was lucky enough to be chosen with Henry Hathaway as a protégé of Paul Bern." Lubin worked on the production end of two Mae West pictures, *Night After Night* (1932) and *She Done Him Wrong* (1933), and became friends with her. In 1934 he directed his first feature, *A Successful Failure* (1934), at Monogram, followed by *The Great God Gold* (1935). He joined Universal in 1936.

"I was the first director signed by Universal when Charlie Rogers and a new production team came in 1936," Lubin recalled. "That was due to his assistant, who knew of my work directing on the stage in New York and out here, and the little reputation I had with Monogram and Republic in making pictures quickly. I don't think Charlie Rogers was at Universal more than two years. Most of the pictures he made were not very good, and then new management came in, a group of theater owners. Nate Blumberg became the president of the studio. But I remained under contract to Universal almost thirty years, through the various regimes that took over the studio."

Lubin's first credit at Universal was *Yellowstone* (1936). The following year he directed John Wayne in the action pictures *California Straight Ahead, Adventure's End, The Idol of the Crowds,* and *I Cover the War* (all 1937). "Duke was a joy to work with," Lubin recalled. "We became close personal friends. But after our last picture together, he left Universal still waiting to hit the big time." That would come two years later in John Ford's *Stagecoach* (1939).

Over the next three years Lubin helmed numerous mystery and gangster films with titles like *Prison Break, Midnight Intruder, Secrets of a Nurse, The Big Guy, Big Town Czar, Call a Messenger, Risky Business, I'm Nobody's Sweetheart Now,* and Alex Gottlieb's *Meet the Wildcat.*

Arthur Lubin helmed five A&C films in ten months.

By the time he was tapped for *Buck Privates,* Lubin had over thirty film credits, including eight as an actor. Yet the studio never considered him for its better productions. Speaking about this period in his career, Lubin reflected, "I was very happy. I was working regularly, and I had a lovely office at Universal. It was a small studio, and everyone was charming, both Mr. Rogers and later Mr. Blumberg and Cliff Work. I went on directing these B pictures until I got a break with Abbott and Costello."

With his background in B-movie melodrama, why was Lubin chosen to helm the first film by two burlesque comics? Lubin explained, "I've never considered myself a great director. I consider myself a good director. Producers liked me because I am not temperamental. I got along well with the actors and the production department. I bring it in on schedule and on budget, but I enjoyed my work. So I had a reputation of doing pictures quickly and bringing them in on schedule."

Lubin's selection confirms that the studio put the budget ahead of art. "They warned me they didn't

Before he directed five Abbott and Costello films in 1941, Arthur Lubin directed four John Wayne films in 1937—and none were westerns. Above left: Wayne in Adventure's End. *Above right:* Idol of the Crowds.

want to spend much money on *Buck Privates*," Lubin said. "I don't think Universal had much faith in the outcome of the picture. They weren't sure how the audience would take the gags."

Of course, Lubin ultimately proved to be the right choice. Patty Andrews recalled, "I loved Arthur Lubin. A delightful, delightful man. He was a joy to work with because he was always up and happy and enthusiastic. He gave you encouragement. Everything a good director should do."

To acquaint himself with Abbott and Costello, Lubin screened *One Night in the Tropics*. "My feeling was that they would be wonderful. Then it was a mutual love affair between the three of us," Lubin recalled. "My first meeting with them was at Bud's house—I think possibly the first week of shooting *Buck Privates*. Bud was trying to impress upon me how important he was and how Lou couldn't do without him. Then he brought out a photo album filled with naked women. I asked him, 'Who are they?' And he said, 'Oh, this is my wife. Look, dear, here are all your pictures.' They were strip teasers in a period when strip teasing was a good occupation. It was a little strange."

Lubin often said that the *Buck Privates* screenplay baffled him because the Abbott and Costello routines were indicated by writing, "The Drill Routine here" or "An Abbott and Costello routine here." Yet none of the drafts of the screenplay are formatted that way. What Lubin may have seen was Gottlieb's November 23 "Step Outline," a terse summary of the script that concentrates on the story but abbreviates the song numbers and comedy routines. Horman's first draft, dated November 26, includes all the dialogue in all

the routines. Even so, anyone would be hard-pressed to understand how each routine was performed. So Lubin asked the boys to demonstrate. "When we came to their scenes in the script I'd say, 'Well, boys, let me see it first.' I would rehearse with them and would ask them not to give me everything but just to show me where they were going to go," he explained. "Then from that I would say, 'We'll take a close-up here, and a two-shot here,' and we'd shoot it. I never interfered, because no one could direct their routines as well as they. There was nothing I could do, because these were tried and true old burlesque routines."

Universal's production manager, Martin Murphy, began to assign the other principal members of the crew, including cinematographer Milton Krasner and film editor Phil Cahn.

By 1940, the Brooklyn-born Krasner (1904-1988) had been a full-fledged cinematographer for seven years, refining his craft on more than sixty B-movies. He shot one of Lubin's first films, *The Great God Gold* (1935), as well as Lubin's first at Universal, *Yellowstone* (1936). Krasner photographed the W. C. Fields comedies *You Can't Cheat an Honest Man* (1939) and *The Bank Dick* (1940), as well as the noir classics *The Woman in the Window* (1944), *Scarlet Street* (1945), and *A Double Life* (1947). He won an Academy Award for *Three Coins in the Fountain* (1954), and was nominated for *Arabian Nights* (1942), *All About Eve* (1950), *An Affair to Remember* (1956), *How The West Was Won* (1962), *Love With the Proper Stranger* (1963), and *Fate is the Hunter* (1964). Krasner's last feature credit was on *Beneath the Planet of the Apes* (1970), after which he shot the TV series *McMillan and Wife* at Universal.

Film editor Philip Cahn (seated) is shown here editing Buck Privates *as his son, Dann stands by. (Courtesy of Dann Cahn.)*

Midway through filming, Krasner was switched to the melodrama *This Woman is Mine* (1941), starring John Carroll and Carol Bruce. Jerry Ash (1892-1953) completed photography on *Buck Privates*. Usually a second unit cameraman, Ash was the cinematographer on Universal's *Flash Gordon* serial.

Editor Philip Cahn (1894-1984) had cut three of Lubin's previous films, including *Where Did You Get that Girl?* and *Black Friday* (1940). Before entering the film business, Cahn tried raising chickens on a ranch in North Hollywood. One night, however, the electricity went out and his incubators failed. His stock of 2,500 baby chicks died. Phil soon joined his brother, Edward (1899-1963), as a film editor at Universal in the late 1920s. Phil became a founding member of Film Editors' Local 776 and a charter member of the American Cinema Editors (A.C.E.).

Phil cut one of Universal's biggest hits, *Imitation of Life* (1934), but for the most part he was assigned to run-of-the-mill melodramas. He wound up cutting all five of Lubin's Abbott and Costello films, and two important later A&C films, *In Society* (1944) and *The Time of Their Lives* (1946). He also edited *Eagle Squadron* and *Arabian Nights* for producer Walter Wanger in 1942. Many of Phil's editing credits are in the horror genre, and include *The Mummy's Hand* (1940), *House of Frankenstein* (1944), *House of Horrors* (1946), *The Brute Man* (1946), *The Lost Continent* (1951) and *Bela Lugosi Meets a Brooklyn Gorilla* (1952). Cahn also worked as a producer-director in Universal's B unit. In the 1950s he moved into television, and was most proud of his long association with Loretta Young and her series.

Cahn's son, Dann, began his apprenticeship as an editor at Universal in 1941, and appeared as a sailor in the "Sons of Neptune" routine in *In The Navy*. Dann later edited every episode of *I Love Lucy*, and became head of post-production at Desliu. He also worked with Alex Gottlieb in 1955 when Alex produced the TV series *Dear Phoebe*, starring Peter Lawford. In 1978 Dann edited the TV movie *Bud & Lou*, which cast Harvey Korman and Buddy Hackett as Abbott and Costello. Editing is clearly in the family genes, because Dann's son, Dan, is an editor.

Say, What Kinda Beat is That?

arly in November, while Harold Shumate was writing his first story treatment, Don Raye and Hughie Prince began working on the songs for *Buck Privates*. In fact, Raye and Prince were signed before the Andrews Sisters. Each man had composed a hit for the girls; Raye wrote "Well, All Right," and Prince wrote "Yodelin' Jive." Together, they wrote "Rhumboogie" (another hit) and "Hit The Road" for *Argentine Nights*.

Raye (1909-1985) was born Donald MacRae Wilhoite, Jr., near Norfolk, Virginia, where his father was a navy officer. An outstanding dancer as a kid, Raye won the Virginia State Dancing Championship, and performed in vaudeville as a teenager, often writing the songs for his act. "He was a great 'hoofer,'" his widow, actress Dorothy Gilmore, recalled, "and a very athletic and acrobatic dancer." While working for Lou Levy at Leeds Music in 1935, Raye contributed lyrics to "Rhythm in My Nursery Rhymes" alongside Sammy Cahn, Saul Chaplin and bandleader Jimmie Lunceford.

He amassed over 270 song writing credits, including standards like "I'll Remember April," "Irresistible You," and "You Don't Know What Love Is," as well as "Down the Road a Piece," which was later covered by Chuck Berry and the Rolling Stones. Dorothy reflected, "Don was a very humble man. I don't know if it was a result of his upbringing or what, but he never talked about his work. He was very modest."

Hughie Prince (1906-1960), who was born in Greenville, South Carolina, has over fifty song writing credits, including "Sweet Mollie Malone," "Pipe Dreams," "Let George Play It," "Rock A Bye the Boogie," and "Sadie Hawkins Day."

In retrospect, Raye and Prince were perfect for *Buck Privates*. Raye was in top patriotic form in 1940. Dorothy recalled, "The bandleader Fred Waring asked Don to write a patriotic anthem as an alternative to 'God Bless America.' Don wrote beautiful lyrics, and Fred thought they were terrific, but they couldn't find anyone to write the music. Then Fred got Al Jacobs to write the melody." The result was the classic "This Is My Country."

In November, another Raye/Prince tune, "Beat Me Daddy Eight to the Bar," charted for both the Andrews Sisters and the Will Bradley-Ray McKinley orchestra. The song, about a renowned syncopated piano player, provided the model for "Boogie Woogie Bugle Boy" and inspired the title "Bounce Me Brother With a Solid Four."

Even so, the songs required work. A reporter tagged along when Raye and Prince presented a novelty song they had written for Lou Costello to an unidentified Universal producer. While Prince took the piano, Raye explained, "It's about this trumpet player in Chicago. His number comes up and he is gone with the draft. The song goes, 'Three cheers for the red, white and Private Jones.' So now that he's in

Maxene, Patty and LaVerne with lyricist Don Raye (left) and composer Hughie Prince, who wrote Boogie Woogie Bugle Boy *and three other songs for the film.*

the army, he plays reveille in swing." The producer was unconvinced. The reporter left while Raye was still pitching and the producer remained unmoved. Of course this sounds like an amalgam of "Boogie Woogie Bugle Boy" and "When Private Brown Becomes a Captain." Fortunately, the two songs were eventually untangled and fleshed out.

Raye and Prince had worked closely with the Andrews Sisters' arranger, Vic Schoen, for years. Schoen (1916-2000), a Brooklyn native, played trumpet in local nightclubs when he was in high school. Self-taught as an arranger, he was in his late teens when he began arranging for Count Basie, and twenty years old when he teamed with the Andrews Sisters. Their first hit together was "Bei Mir Bist du Schoen." Schoen and his orchestra accompanied the girls on their records almost exclusively until 1951. Gossip columns in 1940 reported that Schoen and Patty Andrews would marry, but her father disapproved. Schoen later wed and divorced singers Kay Starr and Marion Hutton. Vic also arranged for Bing Crosby, Glenn Miller, Tommy Dorsey, Harry James, Jimmy Dorsey, and Benny Goodman. He wrote and arranged for the films *The Road to Morocco, The Road to Rio,* and *The Court Jester.* Vic is also revered for his "Bachelor Pad" arrangements on late Fifties albums. He and bandleader Les Browne conceived a suite for two big bands, which they recorded on the album

Impact! Band Meets Band (Kapp).

As the patriotic theme "You're a Lucky Fellow, Mr. Smith" took shape, Universal's musical director, Charles Previn, hired Joseph Francis (Sonny) Burke (1914-1950) to arrange the number. Earlier in 1940, Burke inherited Sam Donohue's band when Donohue left to join Gene Krupa's outfit. But Donohue soon left Krupa, and asked Burke for his band back. Sonny obliged, and began a successful career as chief arranger for Jimmy Dorsey and Charlie Spivak. He became one of the West Coast's leading arranger-conductors, crossbreeding the styles of two of the greatest swing bands, Jimmie Lunceford and Count Basie.

Universal turned over all of *Buck Privates'* original songs to Lou Levy (1911-1995). Sometimes referred to as the "fourth Andrews Sister," Levy was also the girls' manager and often selected their material. He and Maxene eloped in July 1941 but kept their marriage a secret for two years to avoid her father's wrath. Levy, an ex-hoofer, formed Leeds Music in 1935 with the help of Sammy Cahn and Saul Chaplin. A subsidiary of Decca, Leeds later published Bob Dylan's first songbook; the Beatles' first American hit, "I Want to Hold Your Hand"; and Henry Mancini's early songs.

Levy was a member of the board of directors of ASCAP from 1958 to 1970, and received the Songwriter's Hall of Fame Abe Olman Award for excellence in music publishing in 1987.

The Cast Signs Up

In the era when *Buck Privates* was made, few directors had any say in the pre-production and post-production of their films. B-movie workmen like Arthur Lubin certainly didn't.

"In those days, the director had no rights," Lubin explained. "The head of the music department selected the music. A director had no right to see his picture cut until it was finished. I had nothing to do with the casting. The leads were usually cast before the script was finished. The casting director and the producer would get together and say 'I think we ought to cast so-and-so and so-and-so. Let's see what Lubin thinks about it.' If I had no objection, that would be it. If I would say, 'Well, I think so-and-so would be better,' they would consider it. But usually the final say was always the producer in those days."

Universal's casting director, Dan Kelley, arranged to borrow Lee Bowman from MGM for two pictures. Bowman had recently completed an uncredited role in *Go West* (1940) with the Marx Brothers. It was playing in theaters when *Buck Privates* was shooting. Following his role as Randolph Parker III, he joined the cast of *Model Wife*, again as a playboy.

Born in Cincinnati on December 28, 1914, Bowman sang on local radio stations while studying law at the University of Cincinnati. One source claims that although he started his career as a radio singer, his singing voice was too deep for motion pictures. He became a member of the school's Fresh Painters drama group and left law school to study at the American Academy of Dramatic Arts in New York. He was cast in *Berkley Square* on Broadway, spotted by Paramount talent scouts, and signed to a studio contract. His first film was either *Swing High* or *Internes Can't Take Money* (1937).

Bowman spent a year at Paramount and then moved briefly to RKO before signing with MGM, where he remained for four years. He was usually cast in second leads and frequently loaned out to other studios. Between 1937 and 1940 he appeared in more than two dozen films, including *Last Train From Madrid* (1937), *Having Wonderful Time* (1938), *Lady and the Mob* (1939), *The Great Victor Herbert* (1939), *Third Finger Left Hand* (1940), *Florian* (1940), and *Wyoming* (1940). He also played Irene Dunne's fiancé in Leo McCarey's classic *Love Affair* (1939).

Off screen, Bowman seemed to live up to his playboy roles. Louella Parsons called him "one of the most popular bachelors to hit Hollywood in a long time." He dated Dorothy Lamour, Sylvia Sidney, Anne Shirley, Rochelle Hudson, and Eleanor Whitney. But just weeks after completing his roles in *Buck Privates* and *Model Wife*, Bowman eloped with Helene Del Valle, daughter of veteran director silent film director Arthur Rosson, and stepdaughter of Victor Fleming. They had been dating for about six months.

For the role of Bob Martin, Parker's long-suffering chauffeur, the studio signed Alan Curtis, a freelancer who had just completed *High Sierra* with Humphrey Bogart. It was released a week before *Buck Privates* in January 1941.

Curtis, who was born Harold Ueberroth on July 24, 1909, in a Chicago suburb, began his career as a model. Noted advertising, magazine and pin-up illustrator Bradshaw Crandall, who also used Norma Shearer before she broke into films, recommended Curtis to the famous Johnny Powers modeling agen-

Lee Bowman and Jane Frazee. Lee was on loan from MGM for two pictures. After Buck Privates *he joined the cast of* Model Wife *(1941).*

Former model Alan Curtis with Joan Crawford in Mannequin *(1937), which also starred Spencer Tracy.*

cy in New York. Powers helped Curtis get a screen test with RKO, where he was cast in a bit part as a model in *Smartest Girl in Town* (1936) and as a sailor in *Winterset* (1936).

Curtis was relegated to small roles and walk-ons in his next ten films until Joan Crawford saw his screen test and wanted him to play her con-artist boyfriend in *Mannequin* (1937). Although the studio argued that Curtis was too inexperienced for the part, Crawford took him under her wing and, with the help of director Frank Borzage, coached him.

Curtis appeared in six films between 1938 and 1940, including two with Nat Pendleton: *Shopworn Angel* (1938) and *Burn 'Em Up O'Connor* (1939), an auto-racing programmer. He was one of the title characters in *Four Sons* (1940), an update of a 1928 tearjerker about a German family split by its attitude toward Nazism. It was the start of a string of war-themed films for Curtis that included *Buck Privates*.

In 1937 Curtis married the first of his five wives, actress Priscilla Lawson (1914-1958). She is probably best known for her role as Princess Aura, Ming's daughter, in Universal's *Flash Gordon* serial. They divorced in 1940. Not long before production began on *Buck Privates*, Curtis became engaged to Hungarian singer-actress Ilona Massey (1910-1974).

Like the Andrews Sisters, Jane Frazee hailed from Minnesota and was part of a sister vocal act. She was

born Mary Jane Frehse on July 18, 1918, in either Duluth or St. Paul. Jane and her older sister, Ruth, sang and danced in vaudeville, nightclubs, and on radio. They migrated to Hollywood in 1939 and appeared in a musical short, *Arcade Varities*, for RKO. But the act split up in 1940 when Ruth married writer-producer Norman Krasna. MGM offered Jane a contract, but she signed with Republic for a leading role in *Melody and Moonlight*. When the film was released in October 1940, *Variety* called Jane, who was blonde in the film, "a nifty looker who seems slated for better things if her extreme likeness to Lana Turner doesn't step in the way."

Universal took notice and signed her to a term contract at $250 a week. At the time, Jane's brother-in-law, Norman Krasna, was writing the Deanna Durbin films at Universal. Jane's first studio assignment was *Buck Privates,* as camp hostess Judy Gray.

Milton Feld and Alex Gottlieb realized that they needed an imposing character actor to play Sergeant Collins and were having a tough time filling the role. Then, late in 1940, MGM dropped Nat Pendleton's contract. He had just completed *Flight Command* (1940) playing a chief petty officer. (The film was in release when Nat was working on *Buck Privates*.) Universal offered the role to the 6-foot, 215-pound Pendleton, whose 44" chest and 17 3/4" biceps earned him the nickname "The Hollywood Hercules."

The Frazee Sisters. Ruth (right) quit the act after she married producer Norman Krasna.

Nathaniel Greene Pendleton was born on August 8, 1895, in Davenport, Iowa, and grew up in Cincinnati, Brooklyn, and Englewood, New Jersey. "The stage and screen were more or less in my blood, I guess," Pendleton explained in an interview in the May 1940 issue of *Physical Culture*. "I became a child actor back in Philadelphia at the age of 14—though I guess if anybody had called me a 'child' in those days I'd have wanted to knock his block off. I used to take parts somewhat like those Jackie Cooper plays now. It was my uncle, Arthur Johnson, who got me in. He was a big star in those days, and was Mary Pickford's leading man. He was also a director of the old Lubin Company [no relation to Arthur]. So you see the deck was more or less stacked as far as I was concerned. I was conditioned to the stage and screen."

Other Pendleton ancestors reportedly included Francis Scott Key, the author of "The Star Spangled Banner." "He was the brother of my great-great-grandfather," Pendleton explained. "I also come down from General Nathaniel Green, a hero of the Revolutionary War. He was my great-great-great uncle. That's why they called my father Nathaniel, I suppose, and me Nat."

While majoring in economics at Columbia University, Nat captained the school's wrestling team and won the National Intercollegiate wrestling championship. "Later I won the A.A.U. national championship as a member of the New York Athletic Club, and the Metropolitan A.A.U. championship," he

recalled. Pendleton competed on the U.S. Olympic Wrestling team that won a Silver Medal at Antwerp, Belgium in 1920. He later won the world amateur heavyweight championship in Amsterdam.

Pendleton's entree into stage acting was playing wrestlers on Broadway in *Naughty Cinderella* and *The Gray Fox*. He didn't give up wrestling professionally, however, and reportedly once raced between the theater and the old Madison Square Garden to wrestle in a match between acts of *Naughty Cinderella*. In 1925 Pendleton not only became wrestling's world professional heavyweight champion by defeating Robert Roth in Paris, but also made his adult screen debut in *The Hoosier Schoolmaster*.

Hollywood kept him busy playing dumb gangsters, jocks, bouncers and chauffeurs. According to *Physical Culture*, "One thing that irks him is that he does dumbbell parts so well that Hollywood never lets him show any intelligence in a picture if it can help it. Thus the parts he plays often represent the opposite extreme from what he really is." His early credits include *The Big Pond* (1930), *Star Witness* (1931), *Blonde Crazy* (1931), Cecil B. DeMille's *The Sign of the Cross* (1932), *Lady for a Day* (1933), *I'm No Angel* (1933), *Death on the Diamond* (1934),

A former Olympic and professional wrestler, Pendleton was nicknamed "The Hollywood Hercules." He played a grappler in Deception *(1932), which was based on his story idea.*

Veteran character actors Nella Walker; Douglas Wood; and Samuel S. Hinds (with Lee Bowman).

Fugitive Lovers (1934, which included Ted Healy and His Stooges), *Manhattan Melodrama* (1934), *The Cat's-Paw* (1934), *Reckless* (1935), *Baby Face Harrington* (1935), *The Garden Murder Case* (1936), *Life Begins in College* (1937, with the Ritz Brothers), *Swing Your Lady* (1938, in which he played a wrestler with Humphrey Bogart as a promoter), *It's a Wonderful World* (1939), and *Northwest Passage* (1940).

According to some sources, Pendleton was considered for the role of Tarzan before Johnny Weismuller won the part. That year, Nat had a starring role in *Deception* (1932), which was based on his own story idea about a wrestler who battles an unscrupulous promoter. Pendleton had a small part in the Marx Brothers' *Horse Feathers* (1932), and a featured role as the strong man Goliath in *At The Circus* (1939). He may be best remembered for his recurring roles as Lt. John Guild in *The Thin Man* (1934) and *Another Thin Man* (1939), and as Joe Wayman, the dumb but likable ambulance driver in nine Dr. Kildare films—three of which were released in 1940.

Rounding out the *Buck Privates* cast were veteran character actors Nella Walker as Mrs. Parker; Douglas Wood as Mr. Parker; and Samuel S. Hinds as Major General Emerson.

Walker (1886-1971), Hollywood's perennial society matron, had been part of a vaudeville team with her husband, Wilbur Mack, but the marriage ended

soon after she began working in films. Nella also appeared in *Back Street* and *Hellzapoppin'* at Universal in 1941. Later, she worked with Laurel and Hardy in *Air Raid Wardens* (1943) and played Mrs. Van Cleve in *In Society* (1944). In 1954, Walker was cast as Humphrey Bogart and William Holden's mother in *Sabrina.*

Douglas Wood (1880-1966) was the son of 19th century stage actress Ida Jeffreys. After a long stage career, Wood entered films in 1934, usually playing a lawyer, judge or elected official. He turned up in three of 1941's biggest war-themed films: *Buck Privates, Sergeant York* and *In The Navy* (as an admiral). In 1942 Wood, Nella Walker, and Lee Bowman appeared in *Kid Glove Killer.*

Samuel S. Hinds (1875-1948), a former New York attorney, was a founder of the Pasadena Playhouse and appeared in more than 200 films. Hinds made 15 films with Nat Pendleton, including several in the *Dr. Kildare* series, where Hinds played Kildare's father. Early in 1941, Hinds had roles in *Back Street, Buck Privates* and *Man Made Monster,* which were also shooting on the Universal lot. In 1942, he was cast in three Abbott and Costello films: *Ride 'Em, Cowboy* (as Sam Shaw), *Pardon My Sarong* (as Chief Kolua) and *It Ain't Hay* (as Col. Brainard). Hinds may be best remembered for his role as Peter Bailey in *It's a Wonderful Life* (1946).

We Had a Lot of Fun on that Picture

Although the start date for *Buck Privates* had been pushed back, Bud, Lou and the Andrews Sisters were kept busy. The girls spent some time on Universal's scoring stage recording five songs for the film. Abbott met with studio make-up artist Jack Pierce, who designed a hairpiece to cover Bud's thinning crown. Bud wore hairpieces in the team's movies for the next seven years, up to *Mexican Hayride* (1948).

On December 2, the day they were originally scheduled to start filming, Abbott and Costello donned uniforms and performed "Who's On First?" for 450 conscripts at Fort MacArthur in San Pedro. The boys were made honorary buck privates and were documented by Ralph Staub's *Screen Snapshots* newsreel. (Charlie McCarthy was made an honorary lieutenant in the same outfit.)

Patty Andrews said the sisters hadn't met Abbott and Costello prior to *Buck Privates,* yet they'd heard the boys on the Kate Smith program. However, they may have met at the Steel Pier in Atlantic City in 1938. On December 4, 1940, the two teams did a special show for the marines at Camp Elliott in San Diego. In what may have been something of dress rehearsal for *Buck Privates,* Bud and Lou did three routines and the Andrews Sisters sang five songs, including "Scrub Me Mama (With a Boogie Beat)." Abbott and Costello also performed at Fort Ord in Monterey, and reportedly buried a time capsule that included the *Buck Privates* screenplay in the cornerstone of the camp's new recreation hall.

Patty, Maxene and LaVerne turned up on Edgar Bergen and Charlie McCarthy's radio program on December 8. Just before *Buck Privates* started shooting, Universal picked up the option on the Andrews Sisters' contract, and announced that the girls would appear in three pictures per year.

Universal's president, Nate Blumberg, arrived from New York on December 2 for ten days of studio conferences and sales meetings. He no doubt took the time to visit the sets of the films in production. Shooting on the lot were *Back Street,* starring Charles Boyer and Margaret Sullavan; *Nice Girl?,* starring Deanna Durbin; *Man Made Monster,* with Lon Chaney, Jr., in his first role in the genre; *Six Lessons From Madame LaZonga,* with Lupe Velez and Leon Errol; the serial *Sky Raiders;* and *Buck Privates.*

During the studio president's visit, Alex Gottlieb made the same prediction to Blumberg that he made to Milton Feld. "I told Nate Blumberg the same thing—that within a year Abbott and Costello would rate Number One at the box office. He thought I was crazy, too. He said, 'Do anything you want with them, just make the pictures and don't spend too much money.' I said, 'You won't have to spend a lot of money to get audiences to laugh at Abbott and Costello.'"

Buck Privates was budgeted at $233,000 on a twenty-day shooting schedule. By comparison, *Back Street,* Universal's prestige production for early 1941, was budgeted at $679,000, while *Man Made Monster* was allotted $86,000.

Finally, on Friday, the 13th of December, Arthur Lubin rolled film on *Buck Privates.* If they were superstitious, Abbott and Costello didn't show it; in fact, they could hardly contain their enthusiasm. "From the first day of shooting they were on the set hours ahead of time," Lubin recalled. "Everything

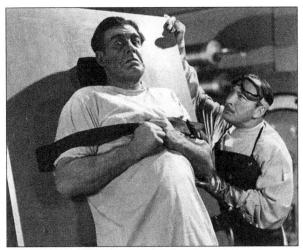

Also shooting on the Universal lot: Back Street, *starring Margaret Sullavan and Charles Boyer, and "The Mysterious Dr. R," released as* Man-Made Monster, *with Lon Chaney Jr. and Lionel Atwill.*

was magic to them. They would walk around the set and look at the scenery or the camera as if they were in a daze. They would point up at a grip and say, 'What's he doing?', or 'Why is that person doing that.' Everything was new and strange to them."

It was, however, an unlucky day for a young assistant director named Joe Kenny (1911-1985). That morning, Kenny drove to the studio during a torrential downpour and wound up in a serious accident. His car was totaled and he landed in the hospital with a broken neck and back. Crewmembers took turns visiting him at the end of each day. One afternoon, Lou Costello showed up. "I was totally surprised," Kenny recalled. "I had only met him once on the set of *One Night in the Tropics.* He brought me a box of fruit, cigarettes and booze, put it all on a table and then turned around and said, 'Come on, get your ass

out of bed!' That was very funny, because I was in a body cast!" Kenny later worked on the majority of the Abbott and Costello films at Universal and had a great rapport with the team. Veteran assistant director Vernon Keays replaced him on *Buck Privates.*

Although precise records no longer exist, we can piece together a rough production schedule. One thing is certain: *Buck Privates* was not shot in sequence. Even though the weather was miserable, it's doubtful that Lubin planned to begin with the film's opening exteriors, anyway. He certainly couldn't start on the "Necktie Pitch" sequence because Nat Pendleton hadn't been signed.

Instead, Lubin shot on a sound stage on Friday and Saturday, starting with the movie theater interiors, medical exam rooms, and camp clothing depot. These scenes included Smitty and Herbie's entrance

One of the first scenes filmed had the boys collect their uniforms and bedding from the supply depot. It was later cut from the finished film.

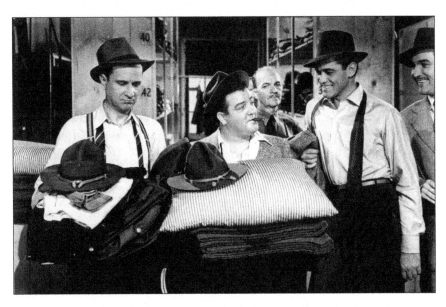

The boys shot their classic Dice routine on the first day. Smitty lures Herbie into the game, but begins to realize that Herbie is not the novice he claims to be. Prolific bit player Eddie Hall is standing at left; Leonard Elliot, in bowtie, leans forward on the right.

in the theater foyer, up to their accidental sign-up. Also covered was a scene where bandleader Dick Burnette (played by Don Raye) reports for service (Sc. 4), but it was ultimately cut from the film.

More significantly, Lubin shot the boys' "Dice" routine on the first day, using the train washroom set (Sc. 72). Lubin may have taken a page out of director Eddie Sutherland's book by shooting a routine as early as possible in the schedule. Sutherland started A&C with "Who's On First?" in *One Night in the Tropics*. The Breen censors warned that some local censor boards deleted scenes with money in connection with gambling, and advised that the money "be suggested rather than actually shown." Lubin simply avoided showing money in his close-ups.

Leonard Elliott (1904-1989), a stage actor and nightclub comedian, plays the recruit wearing a bow tie during the dice game. Elliot made his Broadway debut in 1938 in *Right This Way* with Joe E. Lewis, and portrayed Judas in *Family Portrait,* which starred Judith Anderson, in 1939. He had recently appeared in the Yiddish-language melodrama *Overture to Glory* (1940). Elliott signed a term contract with Universal, and after *Buck Privates* he appeared in *It Started With Eve* (1941), starring Deanna Durbin. He returned to Broadway and well-reviewed nightclub work, but landed few film roles. Elliott appeared in *Weddings and Babies* (1960), a Cannes Film Festival winner starring Viveca Lindfors, and the Italian horror classic *Lo Spectro* (1963), a sequel to *The Horrible*

Dr. Hitchcock (1962). His last film credit was *Diary of a Mad Housewife* (1970). His small role as "Briggs" in *Buck Privates* gives us no opportunity to judge his abilities. A later scene in the rec hall, where Elliott performs an unspecified specialty number wearing a mop as a wig, was cut from the film (see page 44).

The dice game is longer in the film than in the script. Smitty lures Herbie into a crap game, but is astonished when Herbie begins dropping gambling slang like "Fade that," or "Let it ride" at precisely the right moments. Curiously, there is no indication in the script for the physical abuse that Smitty inflicts on Herbie after each gambling phrase. Here is where Abbott and Costello's remarkable teamwork shines. The boys embellish the routine with repetition, slaps, pauses, and overlapping dialogue. Rhythm is so crucial to the team's interplay; you not only laugh at what Bud and Lou say, but how they say it. In the shooting script, Herbie claims he learned the jargon at "the Cigar Counter." The boys changed it to "Clubhouse," which affords more humor in its rhythm. (In the Columbia short *Shot in the Escape* [1943], Billy Gilbert and Cliff Nazarro recreated Bud and Lou's "Dice" routine almost verbatim, but used "Lunch Wagon" instead of "Clubhouse.")

There are several ad-libs that don't appear in the script, like Herbie's line, "I play jacks. I'm up to my fourzees." When Smitty inquires if Herbie ever played dice at the Clubhouse, Herbie says the other boys wouldn't let him because he's too young. Then, in an ad-libbed aside, Costello adds, "Startin' Tuesday I'm going out with girls." Without missing a beat, Bud replies, "Well, I don't blame you," and keeps the routine moving along. In the end, of course, Herbie fleeces Smitty by turning his own "rules" against him. This device turns up in other Abbott and Costello gambling routines.

"I found it very difficult to direct them at first," Lubin recalled. "They were naive as far as filmmaking was concerned. They played to the people on the set instead of the camera. They were used to having a live audience and missed getting laughs. But they learned quickly and we had a lot of fun on that picture."

Lubin had witnessed the boys in action for the first time and realized that he had to stay alert. "After the first day I realized that things were going to happen that I didn't know about," Lubin said. "They were always coming up with things. A lot of the things which were added were spontaneous, and I think you had to be very open minded." The way they performed a routine in rehearsal was no guarantee that it would be performed that way in front of the camera, and no two takes were exactly the same.

"Bud was probably the finest straight man in the business," Lubin said. "Lou had a tendency to run off into something else, and Bud would bring him right back into the scene or the script. That's why they were such a very, very good team. Most comedians are jealous of each other. Bud wasn't. Bud knew that he was a good straight man and he didn't get any laughs and the only way that he was good was in holding Lou in abeyance."

Standard movie-making practice was to cover a scene from three different angles—first in a wide shot, then in close-ups for each of the principal characters. The dialogue and action in each angle had to match closely so that the sequence, when edited together, was seamless. For most actors, repeating a scene several times for the various camera angles was routine. But not for Abbott and Costello. Dann Cahn, whose father, Phil, edited the team's first five pictures, recalled, "My dad used to complain that they never did anything the same way twice. The script girl couldn't control them. That made it hard for my dad to cut scenes together—it was hard to match Lou's position or dialogue from shot to shot. And that made the editing look bad."

In addition to continuity, Lubin had another worry whenever Bud and Lou strayed from the script. "The only thing that was difficult when they added things was, it took a little more time out of your day's work and you had to watch that very carefully," Lubin explained. "Each day was budgeted for so many hours, particularly with the crew. Now, Lou and Bud were on a straight salary for the whole picture, no matter how long it took. But the crew is usually on an eight to ten hour schedule, and they would have to be paid overtime. The studio production manager, Martin Murphy, who supervised all the films in production, would confer with my assistant director and ask, 'How many pages [of the script] did you do?' They didn't ask how *good* did you do, but how many *pages* did you shoot. Then they'd come in and say, 'Look, Lubin, there's a half-hour left and you can only do two more pages. You're behind. What are you going to do about it?' It would drive you mad. Universal was very budget conscious."

Lubin did not have the luxury on either *Buck Privates* or *Hold That Ghost* of shooting Abbott and Costello's scenes simultaneously with more than one camera; it was too expensive. Whenever a shot cuts to a different angle, it's a completely different take. As the budgets of the Abbott and Costello films increased, Lubin was able to add a second camera to cover certain scenes. "Lou never did a scene the same way twice, so I shot all their scenes with two or three

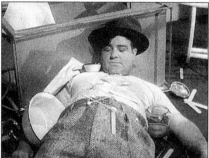

Both medical exam sequences were shot on the same day. Top row: Herbie thinks he's safely over the Army's weight limit, but Smitty turns on a radiator and the extra ounces melt away. Bottom row: Later, at camp, Smitty is inoculated, and Herbie faints.

cameras simultaneously so as not to lose any of his reactions," Lubin explained. "This actually saved time and money, because they were always well-prepared when they walked on a set."

Lubin also covered both medical exam scenes: Herbie's weigh-in (Sc. 25-32), and Smitty's later inoculation (Sc. 82). The Breen censors expressed concern over the draftees' bodies being overexposed in these scenes (hence the t-shirts). They also cautioned that Herbie's wisecrack when Smitty gives him the hot seat, "Brother, you got a very poor sense of direction," must, according to Breen, "be read carefully and without vulgar suggestiveness, if it is to be approved." Although he gives a rotund appearance in his baggy clothes, Costello in a t-shirt doesn't look as if he weighs anywhere near 241 pounds. Breen further urged that Lubin suggest rather than show an actual inoculation. The doctor's arm conveniently blocks our view.

A few days after he started filming *Buck Privates,* Costello reportedly received notification from the Paterson draft board. It informed him that he had been classified 3-A—deferred from military service because it would cause hardship upon his family. (He was later re-classified 1-A in 1943, just weeks after his infant son, Lou Jr., drowned in the family pool.)

Sunday, December 15, was a day off. The following day, choreographer Nick Castle arrived from 20th Century-Fox and began staging the Andrews Sisters' song numbers. (The girls always danced when they sang, unlike most trios before them.) Castle (1910-1968) started as a dancer in vaudeville, and then became a choreographer at Fox in the mid-1930s. One of his early pictures was *Rebecca of Sunnybrook Farm* (1938), for which he trained and directed Shirley Temple. As one of Hollywood's leading dance directors, Castle worked at virtually every studio, with stars like Judy Garland, Bing Crosby, Bob Hope, Martin and Lewis, and the Ritz Brothers.

Patty Andrews recalled, "While Abbott and Costello were filming, we were in a rehearsal hall putting together our production numbers for the next day's shooting. The rehearsal would stop when they called you to the set for a scene you were in. They shot the picture in what, three weeks? And everybody else over at MGM was shooting pictures for two *years!* You never got a full script. In the morning when they did your make-up, somebody would hand you two sheets of paper and that would be your dialogue for the day."

The first full week of production began on the big Grand Central Station set, easily the most opulent in the film. But don't get any ideas that Universal was being extravagant. "Nothing was built for *Buck Privates,*" Lubin said. "We used sets that were already standing. The big staircase in the Grand Central Station scene was built for a musical Charlie Rogers had made." (Possibly *Top of the Town,* in 1937.) The company spent the next few days here, shooting Scenes 38 to 60.

The main sequence on this set is the Andrews Sisters' first number, "You're a Lucky Fellow, Mr. Smith." Lubin explained that he prepared to shoot musical numbers the night before. "Usually, I'd go home at night and look at the script and figure out where I'd cut to break up a musical number into manageable pieces. I had that all mapped out the night before, because in the daytime, if you didn't finish so many pages—bang!—they'd come in and say, 'What the hell's going on?'"

There are two major edits just before the girls begin singing. In the film, Slicker points off camera to the trio and Herbie says, "Oh, the Andrews Sisters!" He starts to take a step but the shot cuts away to the song. This cut omitted Scenes 49 and 50. In Scene 49, the Andrews Sisters are bent over, backsides to camera, filling their hostess kits. Herbie cracks, "*Now* I recognize 'em." Breen's censors warned, "This gag about the posteriors of the Andrews Sisters is definitely unacceptable on the grounds of vulgarity, and must be changed." In Scene 50, which is depicted at upper right, and part of which appears in the film's trailer, the sisters recognize the boys and rush over to greet them. The two teams reminisce, and the pros-

A cut scene between the boys and the Andrews Sisters (see script, Scene 50), before the girls start singing.

pect of a romance between Herbie and Patty is introduced. These flirtations appear throughout the screenplay, but were trimmed from the film. Patty and Lou had a more prominent movie romance in *In The Navy* (1941).

A second cut in this sequence deletes Patty's recitation of an introductory verse to "You're A Lucky Fellow, Mr. Smith." This preamble directly addresses

The recruits enter Universal's big Grand Central Station set, which was a remnant of an earlier film.

Maxene, Patty and LaVerne extol the virtues of the American way in "You're a Lucky Fellow, Mr. Smith."

the capricious nature of the draft lottery and the complaints of the 5% "unlucky" enough to be drafted. (More than 16 million men were required to register, but the lottery initially selected only about 800,000 of them to train for one year.) The song kicks in as a rousing march, with lyrics that extol the virtues of the American way:

You're a lucky fellow, Mr. Smith
To be able to live as you do
And to have that swell Miss Liberty gal
Carrying a torch for you

and

You've got your American Way,
And, buddy, that ain't hay
If some poor suckers could choose
They'd love to be in your shoes

Don Raye's lyrics also reflect the sentiments of President Franklin D. Roosevelt's radio address of May 26, 1940, which rallied the country behind his unprecedented national defense effort:

For more than three centuries, we Americans have been building on this continent a free society; a society in which the promise of the human spirit may find fulfillment. Commingled here are the blood and genius of all the peoples of the world who have sought this promise.

We have built well. We are continuing our efforts to bring the blessings of a free

society, of a free and productive economic system, to every family in the land. This is the promise of America.

It is this that we must continue to build— this that we must continue to defend.

It is the task of our generation, yours and mine. But we build and defend not for our generation alone. We defend the foundations laid down by our fathers. We build a life for generations yet unborn. We defend and we build a way of life, not for America alone, but for all mankind. Ours is a high duty, a noble task.

Dorothy Raye explained, "Don was always scanning the newspapers and jotting down little things he thought were good ideas for a song, or that he could use in a lyric."

After finishing this portion of the song, Lubin backtracked to shoot the arrival of the recruits; Parker's scenes with the chorus girls and his mother; and the interaction between the recruits and the camp hostesses.

In the sequence where the recruits follow the marching band down the big staircase, Smitty and Herbie are at the back of the pack. Herbie carries their luggage while three extras bring up the rear. Lubin decided that the extras were distracted from Bud and Lou. The director sent one of his assistants to cut out the last three men. This assistant, however, approached Abbott, Costello and one of the extras and said, "You three, get out of this shot." Bud and Lou were a bit baffled but obeyed orders. The scene started again and kept rolling until Bud and Lou were

Miss Durling (Dora Clement, left) and the camp hostesses. Front: Jane Frazee; Middle row: the Andrews Sisters, Jeanne Kelly, Elaine Morey. Back row: Nina Orla (obscured), Dorothy Darrell, and Kay Leslie.

supposed to appear. Lubin yelled, "Cut! Where the hell are Abbott and Costello?"

This was the first day on the picture for Jane Frazee. The script (Sc. 38) describes the camp hostesses as either plain-looking or middle-aged except for Judy. But the studio decided to use the opportunity to showcase a few contract starlets—and make the idea of going off to camp more appealing. In cut dialog (Sc. 42), Bob asks Judy who came up with the idea for the hostess corps. Judy replies, "A few million parents who wanted their sons to lead a normal life while they're away for a year." One wonders how the real recruits' wives or girlfriends felt about it.

The starlets appear in different pairings in other

Herbie tells Judy he's a sucker for lollipops.

Universal films of the early 1940s. Brunette Dorothy Darrell, who wed producer Joe Pasternak later in the year, was paired with nineteen-year-old blonde Elaine Morey in *Hello Sucker, Mob Town,* and *Cracked Nuts.* Both appear as USO Hostesses in A&C's *Keep 'Em Flying* later in 1941. Morey, who also turned up in *Pardon My Sarong* (1942) as Amo, later appeared in a handful of films under the name Janet Warren.

Kay Leslie, born Melba Lucille De Closs, was a Salinas, Calif., beauty contest winner, and "one of the Thirteen Baby Stars of 1940," whatever that means. She and Nina Orla, a nightclub dancer with Xavier Cugat's orchestra, were both in Lubin's *Where Did You Get That Girl?* Kay (1916-1991) was also in *The Invisible Woman* (1941). Nina (1920-1987) had a bit part in *One Night in the Tropics,* and appeared in a musical short headlined by Jane Frazee that was produced right after *Buck Privates.*

Jeanne Kelly (1916-1963) had the female lead in the Universal serial *Riders of Death Valley,* which finished shooting as *Buck Privates* started. Born in Houston but educated in Costa Rica, Kelly began her career as a nightclub singer. She broke into movies playing in the Spanish versions of some Hollywood films. Later in 1941 she married director and screenwriter Richard Brooks (1912-1992) and was known thereafter as Jean Brooks. Her later credits include four films in the Falcon series, *The Falcon in Danger*

(1943), *The Falcon and the Co-Eds* (1943), *The Falcon in Hollywood* (1944) and *The Falcon's Alibi* (1946); and three for director-producer Val Lewton, *The Leopard Man* (1943), *The Seventh Victim* (1943) and *Youth Runs Wild* (1944). Sadly, she eventually disappeared from Hollywood and died of complications from alcoholism.

Maria Montez (1920-1951) was considered for a hostess role and her name even appears in some release advertising, but she is not in the picture. Lubin later directed Montez in *White Savage* (1943), (which was Richard Brooks' first screen writing credit), and *Ali Baba and the Forty Thieves* (1944).

Mid-week, the company moved to the interior train coach sets and resumed filming "You're a Lucky Fellow, Mr. Smith." Several of the recruits trade lyrics with the Andrews Sisters. The first to chime in is composer Hughie Prince. The last is lyricist Don Raye, whose line is an odd non sequitur relating good health to the Constitution. It is ironic, however, that this lyric, referring to the Constitution, follows the unfortunate stereotype of the "Uncle Sammy's fair-haired boy" lyric sung by the train's black porter, Bud Harris, and his accompanying dance shuffle. After the United States entered the war, Hollywood and the government monitored screen portrayals of black Americans more carefully, lest the United States be accused of the same prejudices as the Axis powers. These stereotypes undermined efforts to portray America as an ideal democracy and hurt black morale. A later directive from the Office of War Information specifically asked Hollywood to avoid placing blacks in menial or comedic roles on screen. Although it was made well before the OWI edict, *Buck Privates* offended on two counts. It is noteworthy, however, that in the script these lines were to be

"You're a Lucky Fellow, Mr. Smith" continues on the train, where Hughie Prince (top), Bud Harris (center) and Don Raye (bottom) chime in. Harris' line is an unfortunate stereotype.

spoken by black *soldier*. But at this time the army was still segregated, and a black soldier would not be found among white ones.

Snatches of "You're a Lucky Fellow, Mr. Smith" turn up in other Universal films, including the Abbott and Costello pictures *In The Navy* and *Who Done It?* (1942); the Ritz Brothers' *Hi'ya, Chum* (1943); and the eponymous *You're a Lucky Fellow, Mr. Smith,* a 1943 programmer. But the song was never a hit. Only one other artist covered the tune: Frank Sinatra on his 1964 Reprise album, *I Hear America Singing.* Sinatra, in his inimitable style, took liberty with one line: "You're a lucky fellow Mr. Smith, To be able to *swing* like you do..."

After completing the song, Lubin moved on to other scenes on the train, with the exception of the Dice routine, which he filmed the previous week. These included Parker forcing a kiss on Judy, and Bob warning him off. It also included a sequence between Herbie and Parker that was subsequently cut from the film (Sc. 65-66). Herbie places his bags on the overhead rack, but they fall on Parker. Then Herbie sits down next to Parker, crowding him. Finally, Herbie's cheap cigar annoys the playboy, and Parker escapes to the vestibule between the cars in time for his encounter with Judy. When Herbie passes through the cars on his way to the dice game, he puffs his cigar in Parker's face again, repeating the gag.

By the end of the week, cast and crew had moved to Stage 16 (now Stage 18), where veteran art director Ralph M. DeLacy (1886-1978) had built a spartan but versatile recreation hall set. One of the first sequences shot here included Jane Frazee's song, "I Wish You Were Here." The script called for Judy to sing to Henry (Hughie Prince), not Bob, as he writes to his girl.

Breen's censors flagged two lines of dialogue after

In a cut sequence, Herbie takes a seat next to Parker, but his small talk and cheap cigar annoy the playboy.

Judy sings "I Wish You Were Here" to inspire Bob. The Andrews Sisters recorded it for the film, too.

Judy's song. In Scene 105, Patty Andrews asks Bob, "Lonesome, sailor—I mean, soldier?" Breen objected because this was "a 'pick-up' gag used by streetwalkers, and we request this be deleted, or changed." Then in Scene 107, in Miss Durling's office, Parker requests that Judy show him around the camp. The script calls for Judy, with sarcastic double-entendre, to ask, "You don't know your way around?" Breen cautioned, "There must be nothing suggestive in the reading of Judy's line."

During these early scenes in the rec hall, Patty and Herbie have their first exchange in the film. She serves him his fifth double malted and asks sarcastically, "Five double malteds! Why don't you order one more and make it an even half-dozen?" Herbie reasons, "I don't want to make a pig of myself." Bob asks Herbie to tell Parker that the Captain wants to see him. Herbie agrees, and then announces, "Whoever touches the heads on those double malts dies like a dog! Unquote!" This dialogue between Patty and Herbie was added on the set, and does not appear in Scene 111 of the shooting script.

Lubin also shot the illogically logical "Loan Me

$50" routine (Sc. 116). A verbal scene like this was a challenge for the director. "Most of their routines were static," Lubin explained. "In other words, they both stayed in one place and faced each other. As a director I tried to keep them moving, or the camera moving."

The routine is quite close to the script, but a couple of funny exchanges were added on the set:

> SMITTY: Now don't change the subject.
> HERBIE: I'm not changin' the subject—you're tryin' to change my finances.
> SMITTY: I can't help it if you can't handle your finances. I do all right with my money.
> HERBIE: And you're doin' all right with mine too!

Also added was the "Pick a Number" tag. Smitty appears to give Herbie a fair shot at winning his money back by letting him pick a number between one and ten and offering to guess what it is. Herbie chooses a number, and then Smitty proceeds to figure it out by asking a series of rapid-fire questions:

Smitty wants to borrow $50, but Herbie only has $40. So Smitty reasons, "Give me the forty, and you owe me ten."

39

Left: Herbie retreats after seeing his new opponent, Kayo (pro wrestler "Sailor" Al Billings, who was a former US Navy Champion. In the 1950s Billings worked as a ref, but was banned when he testified that pro wrestling was fixed.) Below: To Herbie's frustration, Collins counts out Kayo by fractions. This was Pendleton's first day on the film.

SMITTY: Is the number odd or even?

HERBIE: Even.

SMITTY: Is the number between one and three?

HERBIE: No.

SMITTY: Between three and five?

HERBIE: *(Happily)* No. *(Aside:)* I think I got him!

SMITTY: Between five and seven?

HERBIE: Yeah.

SMITTY: Number six!

HERBIE: Right!

Smitty snatches the bankroll, and Herbie does a delayed take.

On Sunday, December 22, their day off, Abbott and Costello and the Andrews Sisters performed at a star-studded benefit for Mount Sinai Hospital at the Coconut Grove nightclub. The second full week of production began on Monday, December 23, and would include the boxing sequence, followed by the film's most memorable song, "Boogie Woogie Bugle Boy" (Scs. 201-236). Nat Pendleton apparently joined the cast that day, starting as the referee in the boxing sequence.

The boxing scene is a low comedy masterpiece expertly staged by Bud, Lou, and John Grant. Abbott and Costello once performed the scene at the Eltinge Theater on 42nd Street before they formally teamed up; Bud was the referee, while Lou and his partner at the time, Joe Lyons, were the boxers. Lubin explained, "Not being a boxer, I let them do what they wanted

to do. They rehearsed the broad things like the boxing. But as we went on, Lou was always adding things—he and John Grant. John was on the set a great deal."

Costello certainly had experience to draw upon. As a teenager, he boxed briefly under the name Lou King; his career ended when his father happened to attend one of his bouts. A few years later, Lou was a ringside extra in Laurel and Hardy's classic prizefight comedy *Battle of Century* (1929).

The Breen office asked that Lubin "suggest rather than show" Herbie's hotfoot, and cautioned against "undue brutality in the boxing match."

On the set, the boxing scenes were expanded to include the classic referee instructions ("You can't do *this, this* or *this!*"), and amusing fast and slow counts by referee Collins. When Kayo is knocked down, Collins counts him out slowly by fractions. When Herbie hits the canvas, however, the sergeant tries to count him out by twos. Herbie springs to his feet and demands, "What happened to 1, 3, 5, 7, and 9?!" Collins replies, "I don't like those numbers, they're odd." Herbie yells, "*Put 'em in, I like 'em!*" A clever sight gag was also added: Kayo's punch is so fierce, Herbie's trunks spin around his body. One funny scripted line wasn't used: Smitty, from the safety of the corner, shouts, "Why don't you *stop* some of those punches?" Herbie, while being pummeled, yells over his shoulder, "*You don't see any of 'em gettin' by, do you?!*"

Once the boxing sequence was completed, the ring was dismantled and the set was prepared for the "Boogie Woogie Bugle Boy" number, which apparently was originally conceived for Costello. This may have been because Universal executives doubted that the Andrews Sisters' could sing boogie-woogie.

Frank Penny, one of Bud's cronies from burlesque, introduces the Andrews Sisters. The camera swish pans to find the girls seated on stools at the soda fountain—an inside joke recreating a pivotal moment in the sisters' careers. Back in 1937, Dave Kapp, an executive at Decca Records, heard the Andrews Sisters sing on a radio broadcast from the Edison Hotel in New York. The next day, Kapp dispatched an associate to the Edison to find the girls. At the hotel's soda fountain, the man asked Vic Schoen if he knew the trio because someone wanted to sign them. The

Kayo is so anxious to finish off Herbie that he makes a beeline for Herbie's corner, runs into the stool, and knocks himself and Collins out.

sisters, seated within earshot at the counter, whirled around on their stools and cried, "We're the girls!" The man was Lou Levy, who became their manager and, in July 1941, married Maxene.

Boogie-woogie music was actually enjoying its second wave of popularity in 1940. It first appeared in the early 1870s around Marshall, Texas, in the lumber and turpentine camps where black Americans toiled. (In 2010, the Marshall City Commission passed an official declaration naming Marshall as the "birthplace" of boogie-woogie music.) Alan Lomax, in *The Land Where the Blues Began*, wrote: "Anonymous black musicians, longing to grab a train and ride away from their troubles, incorporated the rhythms of the steam locomotive and the moan of their whistles into the new dance music they were playing in jukes and dance halls." The style was often referred to as a "fast western" or "fast blues" to distinguish it from the "slow blues" of New Orleans and St. Louis. The sound migrated to Chicago's South Side where the father of boogie-woogie piano, Jimmy Yancey (1898-1951), refined it in the years before the first World War. Yancey's protégés included Charles "Cow Cow" Davenport and Clarence "Pine Top" Smith, who is said to have coined the phrase "boogie-woogie." Two of Pine Top's protégés, Meade "Lux" Lewis (1905-1964) and Albert Ammons, took boogie-woogie out of the honky tonks and onto the concert stage. Lewis recorded his signature piece, "Honky-Tonk Train Blues," in 1927, when boogie-woogie first reached a broad audience. Then in 1938, Lewis, Ammons, and Pete Johnson played a landmark boogie-woogie concert at Carnegie Hall, initiating a second, wider craze that lasted through the early 1940s. Happily, Jimmy Yancey made it to Carnegie Hall in 1948 with his wife, singer Estella "Mama Yancey" Harris. In 1986,

Yancey was inducted into the rock and roll hall of fame in acknowledgment of boogie-woogie's influence on early rock and roll.

One of the first big bands to experiment with boogie-woogie was the Will Bradley/Ray McKinley Orchestra. One night in 1940 the band was playing an eight-to-the-bar boogie beat instrumental at the Famous Door in New York City. When the moment came for a drum break, drummer Ray McKinley sang out, 'Oh, beat me, daddy, eight to the bar!' Don Raye and Hughie Prince were in the audience, and asked McKinley if they could write a song using that line. They offered to share a writing credit with him, but since Raye and Prince were with Leeds Music and McKinley was with Robbins, Ray put his wife's name on the song instead of his. It turned out to be the band's biggest hit. (The Andrews Sisters recorded it on August 28, 1940.) From then on, every big band had a "boogie-woogie" number, each trying to top "Beat Me, Daddy." There were "Rock-a-Bye Boogie," "Down the Road a Piece," "Scrub Me, Mama (With a Boogie Beat)," "Fry Me, Cookie, With a Can of Lard," and many more.

"Boogie Woogie Bugle Boy" closely follows the template of "Beat Me, Daddy, Eight to the Bar." "Beat Me Daddy" is about virtuoso piano player (legendary Peck Kelley of Dallas, Texas); "Bugle Boy" is about a virtuoso trumpet player (possibly Harry L. Gish, Jr., who Raye and Prince knew). There's a break in "Beat Me" where the singers mimic the sound of a piano: "A-plink, a-plank, a-plink plank, plink plank." In "Bugle Boy," it's a trumpet: "A-toot, a-toot, a-toot did-le ah-dah toot," and so on. (Raye went to the well a third time for "Oceana Roll," a song about a virtuoso syncopated

The Andrews Sisters perform World War II's most famous novelty tune, "Boogie Woogie Bugle Boy."

piano player for Abbott and Costello's next service comedy, *In The Navy.* It was cut from the film.)

Maxene recalled, "When Don and Hughie wrote 'Boogie Woogie Bugle Boy' for us, we had to learn the dance routines at night! We were busy shooting during the daytime, and we were not allowed to learn dancing on Universal's time. We begged the executives to bring in Nick Castle to choreograph that song for the film. Universal didn't want a choreographer. Nick was wonderful. A genius. A very hip guy. So, in spite of the studio, we all made *Buck Privates* big."

All concerned felt vindicated when "Boogie Woogie Bugle Boy" was nominated for an Academy Award for Best Song, and Charles Previn's score was nominated for Best Score. (The Oscar went to "The Last Time I Saw Paris," by Jerome Kern and Oscar Hammerstein, from *Lady, Be Good.* Best Score went to Walt Disney's *Dumbo.*) In September, Universal released a Walter Lantz cartoon of "Boogie Woogie Bugle Boy" (featuring black caricatures) that was also nominated for an Academy Award.

The Andrews Sisters' Decca recording of "Bugle Boy" peaked at number six in 1941. Three decades later, Bette Midler scored with the song. Her version, from her album *The Divine Miss M,* reached number eight in May 1973. Songwriter Don Raye enjoyed the remake. "He liked the Bette Midler version a great deal," his widow, Dorothy, said. "Of course, he liked the Andrews Sisters version better. But he thought Bette did a great job." The Andrews Sisters loved Bette's recording. Patty said, "Fantastic. I loved it. I couldn't get over how great she did it. Because when I was home and that record would start on the radio, I thought it was us!" Bette's rendition sparked renewed interest in the Andrews Sisters and helped ensure their Broadway show, *Over Here!*, the following year.

In August 1999, "Boogie Woogie Bugle Boy" was performed at the Hollywood Bowl in a salute to Universal musicals. It was the only song not played live by the Hollywood Bowl Orchestra: the Andrews Sisters' performance in *Buck Privates* was screened.

"Boogie Woogie Bugle Boy" was inducted into the Grammy Hall of Fame in 2000.

After filming the number, the cast and crew broke early on Christmas Eve and was off on Christmas Day. When everyone returned to the studio on December 26, the recreation hall set was re-dressed for the finale (Scs. 325-340). Over the next few days, "Bounce Me, Brother, With a Solid Four" and the reprise of "You're A Lucky Fellow, Mr. Smith" were shot. Also covered were the closing tags with Smitty, Herbie and Collins; and Judy, Parker and Martin.

"Bounce Me, Brother" was shot on December 26 in a marathon that ran far into the night. Don Raye leads the camp band and does a few clever dance steps to open the number. The Breen office urged Lubin to "avoid the more extreme moves of the 'jitterbug dance'"—likely the waist straddles and skirt-flipping aerials. The World Champion Boogie-Woogie Dancers are led by two of the greatest swing dancers of all time, Dean Collins (1917-1984) and his frequent partner Jewel McGowan. They were known as the "Fred and Ginger of Lindy Hop." (The Andrews' Sisters manager, Lou Levy, also won Lindy Hop contests at Roseland in New York in the mid-1930s.)

Collins (*né* Saul Cohen) once explained, "Jitterbug dancing is Swing, the Lindy Hop, and the Big Apple—they're just different names for the same dance." The Lindy, which evolved from the Charleston, first appeared in New Orleans around 1926, and reached Harlem soon after. George "Shorty" Snowden coined the term "Lindy" after Charles Lindbergh's famous solo flight across the Atlantic in 1927. Cab Calloway coined the term "jitterbug" in reference to Lindy dancers. Collins learned the steps by watching dancers at the Savoy Ballroom in Harlem. "It took New York by *storm*," Collins recalled, "because it was the first dance where you had to be an artist to do it. You really had to know how to *dance*."

Collins arrived in California in 1936 and introduced the "jitterbug," as the dance was now called, to Hollywood's ballrooms and nightclubs. After he won numerous dance contests, Collins made the transi-

Above: Patty and Don Raye.
Below: Dean Collins and Jewel McGowan tear it up.
Bottom: Jewel's signature swivel move.

Briggs (Leonard Elliott) performs an unknown specialty bit that was cut from the film.

tion to dancing in films and, eventually, choreographing. "He was a fantastic teacher," his widow, Mary, recalled. "He could break down the dance. He was just a master at it." He even taught the jitterbug to Arthur and Katherine Murray. Collins always maintained, however, that professional dancers trained in ballet or tap couldn't dance swing. "'Swing' is a street dance, and almost never, *never,* can professional dancers who have not grown up with swing do it authentically. That's because the rhythm itself is entirely different from ballet or tap. In the motion pictures I did [including *Buck Privates*], the kids that I used were 'street' kids—Gene "Shadow" Cole, Gil Hernandez, Connie Wydell. None of them were pro dancers. I put them in because I knew what they could do. Today, you couldn't pay me enough money to train professional ballet or tap people to dance swing. It just can't be done."

Collins danced in or choreographed more than one hundred films between 1939 and 1971. He and Jewel were partners for eleven years and danced together in three dozen films. "She was the greatest dancer I have ever known in my life," Collins said, "and that includes every single dancer I have ever seen in motion pictures. She danced so effortlessly. She was brilliant."

Collins remained a zealous advocate of swing dancing and a feisty purist. "'Lindy,' 'swing,' 'jitterbug'—whatever you want to call it—should really be considered the national dance of America, because it is the longest-lived tempo dance in history. It hasn't changed since 1926." He once cited the swing dancing in later films like *New York, New York* (1977) as "just horrendous. Because they tried to take legitimate ballet dancers and train them. I have third-tier students who are better."

Swing dancing has made a big comeback in recent years in the United States and Europe. Aficionados carefully study and dissect Dean and Jewel's moves in *Buck Privates* and other films.

Collins had fond memories of working on *Buck Privates*. He not only choreographed his own performance, but the Andrews Sisters' steps in "Bounce Me, Brother." "He absolutely loved it," Mary said. "He knew the Andrews Sisters very well, and Patty especially was a very good friend of his. He loved working with all of them—he said it was just great." Dean and Jewel also appear in *Ride 'Em Cowboy* (1942), and *Hellzapoppin'* (1941), which were both produced by Alex Gottlieb.

"Bounce Me, Brother" also turns up in *One Exciting Week* (Republic, 1946) and *Willie and Joe Back at the Front* (Universal, 1952).

During this sequence, the script called for a specialty dance by Patty and Herbie (Sc. 328-9). This may never have been shot. Herbie dances with one of the hostesses (Nina Orla) instead.

The end gag, reprising the Dice game with Sergeant Collins, does not appear in the script.

During the week between Christmas and New Year's Eve, other celebrations were in order. John Grant's 49th birthday was on December 27, and Lee Bowman turned 26 on December 28.

"You're a Lucky Fellow, Mr. Smith" is reprised in the film's finale (Sc. 338-9), complete with an overlapping map of the United States and a montage of the country mobilizing for defense. As we've seen, Harold Shumate's very first script, dated November 4, specified this treatment. The new lyrics continued to play back elements of Roosevelt's May 26 broadcast. But while the verses in the Grand Central Station sequence were addressed to the new recruits and extoled the American way, the lyrics in the finale expressed the need for teamwork to meet the coming crisis, and are directed to all Americans:

The reprise of "You're a Lucky Fellow, Mr. Smith" includes images of the country mobilizing for defense.

You're a lucky fellow, Mr. Smith
Look around you and get a good view
In the shops and stores and down in the mines
Everybody works for you.
There are farmers plowing in the soil,
And the factories are running full speed,
Just to back you up one hundred percent
And we'll follow where you lead!
Wheels are turning and they're hard at work
The wealthy man, little man, banker and clerk
They're punching for you, so you do your part
All the power they need is the beat of your heart!
We're a hundred thirty million strong
And we're sticking with you right along
This is really your lucky day
So, buddy, what'cha say?
Just throw your hats to the sky
Up where the Stars and Stripes fly
And keep your country rolling in high
You're a lucky fellow, Mr. Smith!

These lyrics certainly resonate with President Roosevelt's words:

The development of our defense program makes it essential that each and every one of us, men and women, feel that we have some contribution to make toward the security of our nation.

At this time, when the world—and the world includes our own American Hemisphere—when the world is threatened by forces of destruction, it is my resolve and yours to build up our armed defenses.

We shall build them to whatever heights the future may require.

We shall rebuild them swiftly, as the methods of warfare swiftly change.

On December 29, the day after this reprise of "You're a Lucky Fellow, Mr. Smith" was filmed, FDR delivered one of his most famous fireside chats. He called upon all Americans to step up production of war materiel to aid Great Britain, which had been under attack by the Luftwaffe for several months:

We must be the great Arsenal of Democracy. For us this is an emergency as serious as war itself. We must apply ourselves to our task with the same resolution, the same sense of urgency, the same spirit of patriotism and sacrifice as we would show were we at war. We have furnished the British great material support and we will furnish far more in the future...

I believe that the Axis powers are not going to win this war. I base that belief on the latest and best of information. We have no excuse for defeatism. We have every good reason for hope—hope for peace, yes, and hope for the defense of our civilization and for the building of a better civilization in the future.

I have the profound conviction that the American people are now determined to put forth a mightier effort than they have ever yet made to increase our production of all the implements of defense, to meet the threat to our democratic faith.

As President of the United States I call for that national effort. I call for it in the name of this nation which we love and honor and which we are privileged and proud to serve. I call upon our people with absolute confidence that our common cause will greatly succeed.

Left: The boys are startled to learn that Patrolman Collins is now Sergeant Collins. Above: Collins orders Herbie to get rid of the neckties. Herbie tosses the suitcase out of the tent—and into Collins' head. Note the helping hand inside the tent flap.

By the end of the week, Lubin had wrapped the rec hall set and moved on to the scenes inside the K Company tent. These included the first appearance of Sergeant Collins (Scs. 90-95). There are a few lines that do not appear in the screenplay: Herbie, while fumbling to make up his bunk, cracks, "Twenty-one bucks a month to be a chambermaid!" When Collins makes his entrance, Herbie and Smitty immediately pack up to leave. "Where are you going?" Collins demands. Herbie sputters, "Collect my Social Security." Collins growls, "You can't collect your Social Security until you're 65." Herbie whines, "Seeing you, I aged 35 years."

In this scene Herbie drops the first of several wisecracks denigrating Collins' masculinity. He asks, "Sergeant, will you tuck me in bed?" Later, in the pack-rolling scene, Smitty flips Herbie over his shoulder, and Herbie lands sitting on Collins' chest. "Oh, hello," Herbie pipes up. "What are you doing tonight?" In the "Play the Radio" sequence (Sc. 182-192) he blows Collins a kiss. (The script calls for Herbie to kiss Collins on the cheek, but the Breen office objected, claiming it would prove offensive to many people.) In the KP scene, Collins barks at Herbie, "Don't let me hear any carousing!" Herbie's reply (not in the script) is, "Yes ma'am." Collins snaps back, "*What?!*" Herbie answers, "Yes, sir." "That's better," Collins says. "Well," Herbie reasons, "ya gotta be one or the other."

In the script, this first encounter with the ser-

geant ended with Collins tripping over Herbie's suitcase. But a gag was added where Herbie pitches the suitcase out of the tent and nails Collins in the back of the head. It compliments and sets up a later gag where Herbie tosses a basin of water out of the tent and into Collins' face.

The last Andrews Sisters song to be filmed was "I'll Be With You in Apple Blossom Time" (Scs. 142-146), by Albert Von Tilzer and Neville Fleeson. (Von Tilzer also wrote "Take Me Out to The Ballgame," which Bud Abbott sings in *The Naughty Nineties*.) The ballad, which later became the sisters' theme song, barely made it onto vinyl or into the film. The girls recorded it six weeks earlier on November 14, but not without a fight. Decca vice president Dave Kapp interrupted the recording session and protested, "Don't record it. The last thing America needs is a female Ink Spots!" Lou Levy and the Andrews Sisters swayed Kapp and they finished the record. Weeks later, executive producer Milton Feld tried to keep the song out of *Buck Privates*. It didn't help the sisters' case that the music publisher wanted the penurious studio to pay a $200 usage fee. Arthur Lubin also lobbied for the song. "Milton just couldn't see how it would fit into an Army picture," Lubin explained, "but I convinced him of the boy-girl significance. Even so, Universal was hesitant to spend any kind of money on the Abbott and Costello films." Feld may have felt that "I Wish You Were Here" expressed the same sentiments as "Apple Blossom

Singing "Apple Blossom Time" at 2 a.m.

Time," albeit less memorably. The Andrews Sisters held their ground and paid the publisher's fee themselves.

"'Apple Blossom Time' was so timely for that type of picture during the Second World War," Patty explained. (In fact, the song was originally introduced in 1920.) Universal grudgingly agreed to film the number at the end of a full day's schedule. "We did that at two o'clock in the morning," Patty said. "We had a wonderful cameraman, Milt Krasner. He was a top, top cameraman." Since there were no apple blossoms in California in December, set decorators rigged tissue paper blossoms on the tree branches.

More than thirty years later, in 1974, Patty and Maxene headlined the Broadway musical *Over Here!*

The show featured all new songs inspired by the Andrews' Sisters World War II catalogue, plus a show stopping medley of their real hits. The girls wanted "Apple Blossom Time" in the medley, but again the publisher's fee became an issue. "We had to take it out," Patty explained at the time, "and it just kills me because [the audience] calls for it." Whenever the sisters would explain their dilemma to the theater audience, the crowd would sing the song to them.

Up to now, a record rainfall had interfered with exterior filming all over Hollywood. The bad weather caused *Buck Privates* to run four days over schedule. But during the last week of December the rains relented, and the "Drill" routine—the film's inspiration—went before the camera. "The camp was set up on the back lot," Lubin recalled. "We couldn't afford to leave the studio. There was nothing at Universal in those days but a hillside."

Buck Privates wouldn't have been made if Abbott and Costello didn't have an army drill routine, and they might not have had a drill routine if it wasn't for Charlie Chaplin. In 1918, Chaplin released his hit World War I service comedy, *Shoulder Arms*. (By then, however, that war was virtually over.) The film contains what is probably the first comic army drill to appear on screen, and Lou reportedly saw *Shoulder Arms* twenty-five times. Bud, meanwhile, did a drill routine in a Mutual burlesque show in 1928, years before he met Costello. After teaming up, the boys developed a drill routine for their stage act. They

The film's centerpiece, Abbott and Costello's great "Drill" routine. Joe LaCava, a friend from Paterson, is next to Lou. Next to Joe is Frankie Van, who ran the studio gym. Note the unidentified actor on the end is laughing.

performed the routine in 1937 in *Hollywood Bandwagon* and in 1938 at Loew's State in New York. Although Chaplin's drill may have helped inspire Abbott and Costello's, the two are not very similar, and feature different bits. What's more, since Abbott drills Costello, another dynamic—the team's verbal sparring—comes into play.

Coincidentally, on December 27, Columbia released the Three Stooges short *Boobs in Arms*, which reads like a capsule *Buck Privates*: The Stooges are sidewalk greeting card salesmen who infuriate a man; hide in what they think is a bread line but is a

queue for an enlistment center; accidentally enlist; then discover that the civilian they antagonized earlier is now their sergeant. To top it off, the Stooges do a very brief drill gag. (*Note to A&C fans:* Bobby Barber is one of the men marching with the Stooges.) This wouldn't be the only instance where the Stooges and Abbott and Costello did similar material around the same time. Both teams filmed "Slowly I Turned" in 1944. The Stooges did it in *Gents Without Cents*, while Bud and Lou did it in *Lost in a Harem*. That's one of the hazards of drawing from the same well of standard comedy bits. The misfit drill became a

Herbie fails to turn with the other men and catches a rifle in the back of the head. This gets him out of sync with the squad. Whenever they did the routine, Costello always insisted that the rifle hits be genuine.

vaudeville staple, and an obligatory scene in nearly every service comedy film. Even Joe Besser had his own drill routine. And let's not forget Bill Murray's unique switch on the old drill routine in *Stripes* (1980).

As discussed earlier, the screenplay (Scs. 126-129) called for Pendleton to drill Abbott and Costello, which was absurd since Bud and Lou had been performing the bit for three years.

The routine is longer and more varied in the film. As he prepares to drill the awkward squad, Smitty asks Dick (Don Raye) to "hold my gun," a glaring *faux pas* to anyone who has ever been in the service. It's a rifle, not a gun. Perhaps this is excusable since Smitty and Herbie haven't been in camp very long. Then there are several quick lines to listen for that are not in the script. Abbott barks, "Get your *chins* up!" When Bud says, "Order, arms," Costello cracks, "I'll have a cap pistol." At one point Lou asks, "What time is it?"—which has nothing to do with the routine. Instantly, Abbott snaps back, "None of your business!" and Costello says, "Okay."

When Lou mumbles something under his breath, Bud barks, "What are you doing?!"

"I was talkin' to myself," Costello explains.

"Well don't talk so loud!"

"I gotta hear what I gotta say!" Costello says.

Lou also jeers, "Whatsa matter, big man now, Captain?," and "Pick on somebody else."

All of the lines were left in

Herbie stays out of step until Smitty takes matters into his own hands.

because producer Alex Gottlieb realized that the routine was the funniest thing in the film and used every piece of footage he could to extend it. Arthur Lubin remembered doing several takes because whenever the rifle struck Lou, he would break up. Keen-eyed observers can spot the burly soldier on the end stifle a laugh more than once during the sequence. Lubin covered the routine from a few different camera angles, but since he had only one camera, Bud and Lou had to repeat the scene several times. Dann Cahn recalled, "My father had tons of film, *tons* of film on that. When they ran the dailies they thought, 'Oh my God, what have we got here?' It looked like a lot of nothing. But you know what came out of it. That was all done in the cutting room."

Alex Gottlieb explained, "I said to the cutter, Phil Cahn, 'I want you to dig out every take—print up *everything*. You know, we shot that 'Drill' routine a dozen times, and Lou did it differently each time. I said, 'I want you to recut that routine and make it *at least* twice as long. Everybody said that the 'Drill' routine is the best-cut, greatest routine they've ever seen. When I took Lou into the projection room and ran it, he laughed his head off. He said, 'We never did it like that before.' I said, 'You're damn right you didn't,' and I told him what we did. He said, 'You can do *that*? You can take it and stretch it out?' I said, 'You're just lucky you made so many mistakes!' That 'Drill' routine made him a star."

The footage is used almost in its entirety in the opening of the sequel, *Buck Privates Come Home* (1947). A clip also turns up in Neil Simon's *Biloxi Blues* (1988). Bud and Lou reprised the routine in an episode of their TV series, twice on the live *Colgate Comedy Hour*, and in in Las Vegas in their final gig as a team in 1956.

The "Drill" appears earlier in the shooting script, following their "Loan Me $50" routine and preceding the pack-rolling bit. But that would have placed three

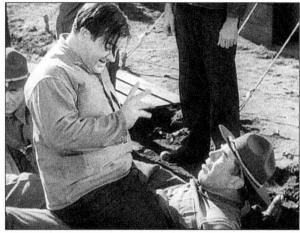

The pack-rolling scene. Smitty tosses Herbie (actually Lou's brother Pat) over his shoulder, and onto Collins.

comedy routines in a row, something Milton Feld always tried to avoid. He strove to space the comedy and music evenly throughout this and every Abbott and Costello picture. In the editing room, the "Drill" was moved after "Apple Blossom Time" and before "You're 40, She's 10."

Taking advantage of the weather, Lubin remained on the exterior camp street and, with dozens of extras in uniform, probably shot the first fall-in of the rookie soldiers (Sc. 86); Captain Williams' speech (Sc. 87-88); and the fall-in for the start of the war games sequence (Sc. 242).

Lubin then shot the "pack-rolling" sequence (Scs. 130-136). As Herbie struggles with his pack, Collins wonders, "How can you be so stupid?" Herbie's scripted reply was, "Well, it ain't easy." In the film, his response is much funnier: "Oh, that just comes to me natural." This sequence also included Pat Costello's first stunt as Lou's double. Pat recalled, "After *One Night in the Tropics*, Frankie Van, who ran the gym on the Universal lot, said to me, 'Why don't you double for Lou?' Ronald Reagan had told me the same thing back in New York, when Bud and Lou were on the Kate Smith program. Well, I told Lou, 'Listen, if Universal ever signs you and Bud to a long-term contract, why don't you let me double for you?'

"Frankie Van was a boxer at one time, a good featherweight or lightweight. He did extra work, stunts, and bits. [Van appears in the "Drill" and "Boxing" routines.] At this point on *Buck Privates* I was Lou's stand-in. As his stand-in, I had to wear make-up and wardrobe like Lou. Somewhere near the end of the day they had a stunt man ready to do this scene where Lou gets tossed over Bud's shoulder

and into Nat Pendleton's lap. Frankie said to me, 'Why don't you tell them you want to do it?' I thought my best bet was to tell Lou. So, I went up to Lou and I said, 'Hey, this is an easy stunt. Why don't I pick it up, it's twenty-five bucks.' Lou said, 'Do you think you can do it without getting hurt, Pat?' I said, 'Geez, I think so.' Lou called the assistant director over and said, 'Let my brother do this stunt.' The a.d. said, 'But he's not a stunt man; he could break his bones,' and all this stuff. But anyway, I did the stunt. That was the first. We worked a quarter hour overtime, so that was another six or seven bucks added on, which was $31 for the day, besides the $10 I got for being a stand-in. So I said to Lou, 'Hey, this is a helluva lot better than standing in.' So he said, 'Well, if you feel like you can do them, okay, but if you don't feel like you can do them, don't.' I never did anything that I thought I couldn't do, or that I thought I would get hurt. I was chicken. Well, the rest is history, because I did go on to do all of Lou's stunts and doubling for him [on the first ten Abbott and Costello films]."

It is curious that Costello was doubled but Bud, who actually does the tossing, was not.

After Collins recovers from Herbie's landing, he receives a note ordering Parker to report to the Captain. In what may be a completely unexpected ad-lib, Herbie snoops over Collins' shoulder and asks, "What's cookin', Sarge?" Pendleton, no doubt used to Costello's ad-libs by this point in the production, snaps back, "Get out of here!"

When they lost daylight, the production unit moved indoors for scenes in the K Company tent, and shot until 8:15 p.m. These scenes included the post-rifle match confrontation between Parker and

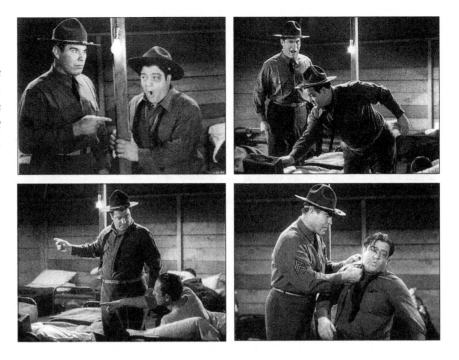

Collins orders Herbie to turn off the radio, but Smitty goads his pal into playing it again and again.

the rest of the company (Sc. 170 and on). It does not appear that Henry, played by Hughie Prince, can back up his threat to Parker, "Yeah, and we're just the guys that can flip you!" The role was originally written for a burly actor. Two stunt men perform the ensuing fight between Parker and Martin.

After the New Year's break, the cast and crew returned to work on Thursday, January 2. Lubin shot more exteriors on the camp street and interiors in the company tent. Maxene Andrews, meanwhile, spent the day before her twenty-fifth birthday with her sisters recording "Boogie Woogie Bugle Boy," "Bounce

Me, Brother, With a Solid Four," and "You're a Lucky Fellow, Mr. Smith" at Decca's Hollywood studios. "Boogie Woogie Bugle Boy" was released in January, with "Bounce Me" as the B-side. "You're a Lucky Fellow, Mr. Smith" was released in February as the B-side to "Yes, My Darling Daughter." "Apple Blossom Time" was released in March as the B-side to "I Yi Yi Yi Yi Like You Very Much." According to *Daily Variety*, "Boogie Woogie Bugle Boy" and "Apple Blossom Time" each sold 100,000 copies in four weeks. "Apple Blossom Time" eventually peaked at No. 5 on the charts.

The male cast members spent a day shooting the war games sequence at nearby Providencia Ranch (now Forest Lawn Memorial Park).

Herbie and Smitty peddle neckties until Patrolman Collins appears. The boys flee, and Collins stumbles over their display table. In a cut scene, Herbie returns to help Collins to his feet, then continues the chase.

Following Martin and Parker's brawl, Herbie turns on a radio. The instrumental break from "Bounce Me, Brother, With a Solid Four" (which appears later in the film) blares forth. Collins storms in and demands, "Who's playing that radio?!" "Nobody," cracks Herbie, "it's playin' by itself." Collins orders him to turn off the radio and keep it off. After Collins leaves, Smitty goads Herbie into playing it again. Collins returns to manhandle Herbie for disobeying orders. The boys repeat this simple yet hilarious business, which is a variation of the burlesque routine "Go Ahead and Sing," without wearing it out. (Another variation turns up in *In Society* [1944].) During filming they added Smitty's empty assurance, "Go on, play the radio. He comes in here again, *I'll* tell *him* off. Leave it to me." That also sets up Herbie's end line. As Collins violently shakes him, Herbie turns to Smitty, who pretends to be asleep, and pleads, "*When are ya gonna tell him!?*"

The following morning the cast and crew began the day about a mile east of Universal City at the Providencia Ranch for some of the war games scenes. (Today it is the site of Forest Lawn.) Cinematographer Jerry Ash replaced Milton Krasner, who was switched to *This Woman Is Mine.* By late afternoon the company returned to the studio and shot various interiors until 7:15 p.m.

On Saturday, January 4, in cloudy weather, Lubin used booster lights to shoot scenes on the back lot's New York streets. These probably included the opening sequences of the film: Parker and Martin's hasty arrival at the recruiting theater, and Smitty and Herbie's "Necktie Pitch" (Scs. 8-12). The routine is slightly different in the script, and included one bit that was cut from the film: after Collins stumbled over the boys' necktie stand, Herbie dashed back into

The delightful novelty tune "When Private Brown Becomes a Captain," aided by once and future Stooge Shemp Howard. Harmonica virtuoso Frank Cook supplies the music.

52

The boys mistake a squad car for a cab, then run down the street to hide in the movies. Outside the theater, Herbie nearly comes to blows with another enlistee (Joe LaCava again). Later, Collins keeps them from deserting.

the scene to help the dazed cop to his feet.

Lubin then moved the production indoors for more interiors, finishing up with Herbie's novelty song, "When Private Brown Becomes a Captain." The idea for this tune dates back to Shumate's second draft, which suggested something like Irving Berlin's "Oh, How I Hate to Get Up in the Morning." It seems inconceivable today, but "Boogie Woogie Bugle Boy" was originally developed for Costello before it was reworked for the Andrews Sisters. The chorus from that early version was salvaged and used to build "When Private Brown Becomes a Captain."

In cut dialogue (Sc. 193), Herbie recites a litany of gripes even before the song begins. The script calls for both Herbie and Smitty to serve on KP, but Costello plays off Shemp Howard instead. Lubin didn't finish shooting this sequence, which clearly required rehearsal, until 11:15 p.m. Due to his epilepsy, Bud rarely worked past 6 p.m. on the team's films, which may help explain his absence. Abbott does appears in a special trailer that was shot on this set earlier in the day; see page 177.

The next day, Sunday, was a day off. At Monday's meeting of Universal's executive committee, an accounting of *Buck Privates* revealed that Lubin still had nearly thirty pages of the script to cover, comprising over nineteen scenes. Most of that included

the war games sequence. The picture had been in production eighteen of the original twenty days scheduled, and was now about $5,000 over budget. Since the war games scenes were all exteriors, a stretch of good weather was required to finish the picture, but contingency plans were made to use rear screen projection in place of outdoor locations.

Meanwhile, over on the back lot, Lubin continued covering the opening sequences on the New York Street and movie theater exterior. After escaping from Patrolman Collins, the boys duck into what they think is a cab but is actually a police car. This blunder foreshadows the next, when Smitty and Herbie think they're registering for a prize drawing but actually enlist. Outside the theater, Herbie cuts in front of another draftee, and they nearly come to blows. Their exchange is not in the script. The enlistee is Joe LaCava, who was part of the "Drill" routine. LaCava (1905-1994) was a childhood friend of Costello's from Paterson. According to one account, when Costello went to Hollywood in 1927 to break into the movies, LaCava went with him. LaCava turns up in many of the team's films and TV shows and also served as Bud's stunt double in the 1950s.

After Herbie and Smitty enlist, they bolt out of the lobby and run into Collins, who is waiting outside the theater. There are two movie posters visible:

Above: "You're 40, She's 10." After the routine, Smitty orders Herbie to toss the water out of the tent. Herbie obeys—and nails Collins again (below).

Herbie: "Oh, I'm a baaaad boy!"

I'm Nobody's Sweetheart Now (1940), directed by Arthur Lubin, and *Hired Wife* (1940), produced by Jane Frazee's future husband, Glenn Tryon.

Later in the day, Lubin's unit moved indoors and worked on various interior sets until 10:15 p.m. It is not likely that many of these scenes included Abbott and Costello because the boys were at Decca's studios recording two "special test" disks. These were probably "When Private Brown Becomes a Captain" and "I'm a Bad Boy," a novelty tune based on Costello's tag line. Unfortunately, neither song was ever released.

On a rainy January 7, while the Andrews Sisters spent the day at Decca recording "I Yi Yi Yi Yi Yi Like You Very Much," and "Yes My Darling Daughter," Bud and Lou were at Universal shooting one of their best verbal routines, "You're 40, She's 10." In the script, this routine follows "Apple Blossom Time," but in the film it follows the "Drill" routine. The back-to-back placement of these two routines—one physical, one verbal—allows us to appreciate the boys' versatility.

"You're 40, She's 10" (scene 150-A) is another quintessential confrontation with logic. It's a showcase for the lecturing straight man, and Bud sells it perfectly. Once again, dialogue was added in performance that is not in the script. To "prove how dumb" Herbie really is, Smitty poses a hypothetical question: "Suppose you're 40 and you're in love with a little girl who's ten years old."

Costello can't help ad-libbing, "*Who's forty?!* If I was forty years old I wouldn't be bathing my feet here in the water—I wouldn't be in the army!"

Abbott tries to move past this and get back into the routine, but Costello has more to say.

"After all, I took my uncle's advice. My uncle told me, he said, 'Herbie, you go in the army.'"

"*What* uncle?" Bud asks, apparently surprised.

"Uncle Sam," Lou continues. "He's my uncle, your uncle—he's everybody's uncle in the army."

"Yes, yes, I understand," Abbott interrupts, trying end it there, but Costello isn't finished yet.

"He's the only relative I got. I *like* my Uncle Sam!" he adds.

Bud breaks in, "I know, we all do, but look—answer this question," and he gets Lou back into the routine.

Patty Andrews observed, "The remarkable person was Bud Abbott. At the time, I was not aware of these things because I was more concerned with our numbers and the things we were going to do in the

Left: Announcer Mike Frankovich explains the war games to a radio—and movie—audience.
Center and right: Parker saves Bob twice from falling off the cliff. The first instance was cut from the film.

picture. But, seeing their pictures now, you realize that Bud Abbott was the greatest straight man that ever lived. I mean, to be able to keep it all together with Lou, when you never knew what Lou was going to do. Bud was fantastic."

A&C's "Hole in the Wall" routine was scripted to follow but didn't make the cut. These routines clearly descend from the classic "Handful of Nickels" bit of Arthur Moss and Edward Frye, popular black vaudevillians whose patter usually began with "I'll prove how dumb you are," followed by a series of unanswerable questions. "You're 40, She's 10," however, is even older; it dates back to at least 1867.

The scene ends with a reprise of an earlier gag, when Herbie tossed a suitcase and hit Collins in the head. This time Herbie tosses a basin of water into Collins' face. According to Randy Skretvedt in *Laurel & Hardy: The Magic Behind The Movies*, the screenplay of *Great Guns* (1941) called for Stan to nearly repeat this water basin gag until Ollie stops him:

"Don't you remember? They did that in *Buck Privates*," Ollie says in the script. Bud and Lou socialized with Stan and following Costello's death in 1959, Abbott considered teaming with Laurel. Ollie died in 1957.

After shooting this routine, a few incidental interior set-ups remained, including the two scenes between Parker and his father in the Colonel's office (Sc. 138 and Sc. 334). Both of these were filmed on January 8. But the bulk of the war games still had to be filmed, and the weather was uncooperative. It rained for the next four days, from Tuesday through Friday, forcing Lubin to fake exteriors on the studio's process stage. A cliff was built for Herbie's "acorn" gag (Sc. 263-A) and Parker's rescue of Bob (Sc. 299).

Lubin also covered scenes of the radio announcer, Mike Frankovich. The adopted son of comedian Joe E. Brown, Frankovich (1910-1992) quarterbacked the UCLA football team and played pro baseball for the Hollywood All Stars before becoming a radio producer, announcer, and sportscaster. Later in 1941 he

Process shot of Herbie stuck in a tree. Smitty asks, "How did you get up in that tree?" Herbie cracks, "I sat on it when it was an acorn!"

55

Left: Parker gloats after winning the war games.

married actress Binnie Barnes (*The Time of Their Lives*). After the war, Frankovich became an independent producer in Europe. He was hired by Columbia Pictures in England and rose to chairman of its British branch. He oversaw production of *The Bridge on the River Kwai* (1957), *The Guns of Navarone* (1961), and *Lawrence of Arabia* (1962). In 1964 he returned to Hollywood as vice president in charge of production, and was responsible for films like *A Man for All Seasons* (1966), *Guess Who's Coming to Dinner* (1967), and *In Cold Blood* (1967). In 1968 he returned to independent producing. Among his later films are *Cactus Flower* (1969), *Bob & Carol & Ted & Alice* (1969), and *The Shootist* (1976). Frankovich received the Jean Hersholt Humanitarian Award at the 1984 Academy Awards.

A radio announcer was a convenient way to explain the war games to an uninitiated audience. Although his monologue consists of long tracts in the script (Sc. 255, etc.), it is more succinct in the film. Two cuts, however, merit attention. An interview with General Emerson in Scene 256, and a later summary by Frankovich in Scene 304, emphasize that a rookie army was being tested against veteran troops—a parallel not lost on audiences who knew the reputation of the experienced Nazi war machine that had stormed most of Europe.

The script called for the war games to go on through the night and into the following day. But night shooting was expensive, and Lubin was already behind schedule. He rushed to finish up his remaining scenes with the principal cast members on Friday, January 10, shooting until 9:10 p.m.

The following day, with a break in the weather, second-unit director Ray Taylor took several stunt men and doubles (including Pat Costello) to Lake Elinor for some wide exterior shots, including the demolition of the blockhouse.

At the executive committee meeting on Monday, January 13, Martin Murphy reported that with the exception of some stock footage of rookie soldiers at Fort Ord, *Buck Privates* was complete. Officials at the base made an entire regiment available to the filmmakers, but the weather in Monterey remained poor. Finally, on Wednesday and Thursday, real recruits were filmed pitching tents and training. The footage was flown back to Universal on Thursday night and incorporated into the film.

Meanwhile, on Tuesday, January 14, music cues written by Frank Skinner were recorded on the studio's scoring stage. Skinner (1898-1968) had experience as an orchestrator and arranger of dance band music before joining Universal in 1935. His contemporaneous scores for *House of the Seven Gables* (1940) and *Back Street* (1941) were nominated for Academy Awards. He later wrote the score for *Abbott and Costello Meet Frankenstein* (1948).

Buck Privates was in production twenty-four days, four more than scheduled, and cost approximately $245,000, or about $12,000 over budget.

The Final Shooting Script

Following is a clean, unmarked copy of the original shooting script for *Buck Privates*. It is interesting to compare where Bud and Lou expanded their routines during actual shooting. Even though their routines are scripted here, it was the genius of their improvisations that gave the film spontaneity—and often gave their director and editor a challenge.

[Signatures: Bud Abbott, Lou Costello, Maxene, Patty, LaVerne, Andrews Sisters]

"B U C K   P R I V A T E S"

by
Arthur T. Horman

[Signatures: Lee Bowman, Alan Curtis, Arthur Lubin, Jane Frazee, Nat Pendleton]

10
x9
DECEMBER x4, 1940

CAST OF CHARACTERS

SLICKER SMITH..........a fly-by-night street merchant, who hands out a fast line of talk and sells dollar neckties, worth at least two cents, for a dime. (Bud Abbott)

HERBIE BROWN..........Smitty's shill and standby. (Lou Costello)

ANDREWS SISTERS.......three entertainers, who are hostesses in an army camp.

RANDOLPH PARKER, III...a scion of the rich, a handsome, attractive and not a bad guy, if he'd just forget that money and background isn't everything.

BOB MARTIN............a darn nice guy, who chauffeurs for Randolph until the draft puts them on an equal level.

JUDY GRAY.............pert and attractive, who learned how to handle herself doing settlement house work - now a hostess in the army.

MICHAEL COLLINS.......a rough, tough police officer whose one aim in life is to discipline Smitty and Herbie -- especially when he becomes their Sergeant in camp.

DICK BURNETTE.........a clever musician, who left his orchestra and baton behind when the draft caught up with him.

MISS DURLING..........who heads the Hostess Corps. She is kindly and understanding, but a disciplinarian with all.

CAPTAIN WILLIAMS......the commanding officer of Company "K" -- the superior of Bob, Randolph, Herbie, Smitty and Dick.

MR. RANDOLPH PARKER, II.Randolph's father - who has learned that being a man is much more important than being a millionnaire.

MRS. RANDOLPH PARKER, II..a blue-blood aristocrat, who thinks Randolph certainly doesn't belong with the common herd.

COLONEL HOUSTON.......Chief officer in the training camp.

Other characters:
Henry.................one of the boys in camp.
Briggs................another boy in camp.
Miss Jones............a hostess
Miss Clark............a hostess
Sergeant Callahan.....also of Company "K"
Edmunds...............Randolph's valet.

Other and sundry army officers and bit players.

"BUCK PRIVATES"
by
Arthur T. Horman
- - - -

CREDIT TITLES to be SUPERIMPOSED OVER STOCK SHOTS (as
available) dramatizing the recent draft. These SHOTS
TO INCLUDE:

        Men filling out registration cards;
        Drawing of draft numbers;
        Lists posted in windows;
        Blank being filled out;
        Etc., etc.

                                        DISSOLVE TO:

1   EXT. MOTION PICTURE MARQUEE - DAY - MED. SHOT

The lettering on the marquee reads:

            U.S. ARMY RECRUITING OFFICE AND
            HEADQUARTERS 2ND DISTRICT DRAFT BOARD

CAMERA ANGLES DOWN from marquee to reveal a line of men
going up to the box office, which bears a sign reading
"INFORMATION". A uniformed officer sits inside the
ticket office. Several uniformed corporals stand in the
lobby. SOUND of traffic noise comes over. CAMERA DRAWS
BACK to reveal an expensive custom-built car as it approaches the curb.

2   EXT. CURB - MED. CLOSE SHOT - THE CAR

Seated in the rear is RANDOLPH PARKER, III, an expensively
dressed young chap. Driving the car is a uniformed chauffeur - BOB MARTIN. The car comes to a sudden jolting stop
before the theatre. Randolph is thrown violently forward.

                    RANDOLPH
                (to Bob, angrily)
        That's no way to drive!

                    BOB
                (not meaning it)
        So sorry, sir.

3   MED. SHOT - CAR

As Bob gets out smartly and opens the rear door. Randolph
steps out of car.

                                        CONTINUED

> RANDOLPH
> (to Bob)
> Come along, Martin..

> BOB
> Yes, sir.

4   INT. THEATRE FOYER - FULL SHOT

At either side of foyer are desks. The desks to the left
have a large sign over them reading: "SELECTIVE SERVICE
MEN REPORT HERE". A similar sign over the other desks,
to the right, reads: "ENLIST HERE". Standing facing
MASTER SERGEANT BURKE, who sits at one of the selective
service desks, is DICK BURNETTE - a good-looking youngster. In the b.g. Randolph and Bob enter..

> BURKE
> Richard Burnette?

> DICK
> That's right.

> BURKE
> Present occupation?

> DICK
> Orchestra leader --

> BURKE
> (with a grin)
> So you'll swing a gun instead
> of a baton. Sit over there.

He indicates a dozen straight-backed chairs lined up
against the wall, some of them occupied by draftees.
Dick moves over to sit down.

> BURKE
> Next --

One of the seated men moves to the desk, but Randolph
gets there first, a letter in his hand.

> RANDOLPH
> (looking at letter)
> I say -- where's Captain Johnson?

> BURKE
> He's busy right now. Have a seat.

> RANDOLPH
> Would you mind telling him that
> Randolph Parker, III, is here?

CONTINUED

                    BURKE
          Randolph Parker...
                    (glances at list)
          Oh, yes. If you'll just wait for
          a few minutes with the other men...

                    MAJOR'S VOICE
                    (o.s.)
          Everything seems to be running
          smoothly, Captain Johnson.

Randolph looks off and goes quickly out of SCENE. Bob
steps up to the desk.

                    BOB
          I'm Robert Martin --
                    (with a grin)
          Number 158.

                    BURKE
                    (grinning)
          A nice number.

                    BOB
          Imagine me being first prize in
          a raffle.

5   MED. SHOT - NEAR DOOR TO THEATRE MANAGER'S OFFICE

A uniformed major is just leaving. Captain Johnson
stands in the doorway.

                    CAPTAIN JOHNSON
          We're getting a fine group of men,
          sir -- more teeth and less flat
          feet.

The Major smiles. The two officers exchange salutes.
The Major starts off and Captain Johnson is about to re-
enter the room when Randolph comes up to him.

                    RANDOLPH
          Captain Johnson -- ?

                    CAPTAIN JOHNSON
          Yes...

                    RANDOLPH
          I'm Randolph Parker, III. Dad's in
          Washington now - heading a defense
          board of some kind -- I suppose you've
          heard from him?

                                        CONTINUED

5   CONTINUED

                              CAPTAIN JOHNSON
                           (hesitantly)
          No...

                              RANDOLPH
                           (glibly)
          Well, I'm sure you will. Dad's bound
          to want me working with him - so about
          this order to report for training...

                              CAPTAIN JOHNSON
          Why, of course, Mr. Parker -- I under-
          stand. If you'll step in here, we'll
          be delighted to take care of you.
                           (indicates doorway)

                              RANDOLPH
          Thanks....

6   INT. THEATRE MANAGER'S OFFICE - MED. CLOSE SHOT - AT DOOR

         As Randolph enters, followed by Johnson. CAMERA ANGLE
         is confined so that we do not suspect the use to which
         this room is put. Randolph is looking back over his
         shoulder, talking to Captain Johnson, and does not get
         a good look at the room until point indicated.

                              RANDOLPH
          You're sure this won't take long?

                              CAPTAIN JOHNSON
          Oh no - will you hang your hat
          there, please?

                              RANDOLPH
          Why - yes.

                              CAPTAIN JOHNSON
          And your coat, too ---

                              RANDOLPH
          My coat.......?!

                              CAPTAIN JOHNSON
                           (still very politely)
          And the rest of your clothes, please.

                              RANDOLPH
                           (puzzled)
          The rest of my -- ?

                                                   CONTINUED

6   CONTINUED

He turns so that he really sees the room for the first
time. CAMERA DRAWS BACK and we see that this is the
Physical Examination Room. Several draftees, stripped
to their waist, are being examined physically.

DISSOLVE TO:

7   EXT. STREET - IN FRONT OF THEATRE - MED. CLOSE SHOT -
RANDOLPH'S CAR

Standing with COLLINS, a uniformed policeman, is a
recruiting Corporal.

CORPORAL
Give the boy a break .. he's report-
ing for service.

COLLINS
Who isn't? I'm going back in the
army myself next week.

CAMERA DOLLIES with Collins as he walks around to get
license number of car. He looks out of SCENE and reacts,
suddenly alert. A gleam comes into his eye. He puts the
ticket book away and starts off decisively.

8   EXT. STREET - (ACROSS AND UP FROM THEATRE) DAY

On a row of distinctly striped neckties hanging from a
typical pitchman's table in a doorway. CAMERA TRUCKS
BACK showing a small crowd of men gathered around the
table. OVER SCENE comes Smitty's voice.

SMITTY'S VOICE
Step right up, neighbors .. a little
closer -- we don't want to block the
sidewalk ... Take a look at these
ties -- feel the material .. here's
a tie that's satin -- it can even be
slept in .. won't wrinkle -- stretch
or tear...

9   MED. SHOT - GROUP

in the f.g. we see SLICKER SMITH, surrounded by the crowd,
in the b.g., HERBIE BROWN is pushing his way forward. He
is the shill in this act and is coming forward to do his
part.

CONTINUED

9   CONTINUED

                    SMITTY
                 (continuing)
          Here's a tie that would sell in
          any good haberdashery for at least
          a dollar and a half. But am I
          asking a dollar and a half? No!
          Am I asking a dollar? No! Fifty
          cents? No! I'm going to let you
          have these ties for ten cents apiece --

10   MED. CLOSE SHOT - CENTERING SMITTY AND HERBIE

The crowd surrounds them. Herbie, anxious to do his part,
starts several times to open his mouth to speak but gets
nowhere, due to Smitty's constant flow of words.

                    SMITTY
                 (continuing)
          -- Where can you get a bargain
          like this? Where can you get a
          tie like this?
                 (noticing Herbie at-
                  tempt to break in)
          Just a minute, young man -- let
          me get in a word or two.

                    HERBIE
          Go ahead, -- I'll listen to you
          for a while.

                    SMITTY
          Thank you! -- Now, neighbors, I
          can't make money at the price I'm
          selling these ties -- I simply want
          to get my merchandise on the market--

He steps around behind the display of ties, ready to do
business. Herbie eagerly pushes forward. Collins -
the cop - approaches in b.g. and stands watching the
scene.

                    SMITTY
                 (noticing Herbie and
                  looking at him as
                  though he had never
                  seen him before)
          Stranger, how much money have you?

11   MED. SHOT - SMITTY AND HERBIE

as they go into their routine. Crowd in b.g.

                         HERBIE
              I have in the vicinity of twenty-
              eight dollars.

                         SMITTY
              Then you have twenty-eight dollars?

                         HERBIE
              In the vicinity - in the neighbor-
              hood. I got three bucks.

                         SMITTY
              Then you have three dollars?

                         HERBIE
              Roughly speaking. When you smooth
              it out I got a buck.

He takes a dollar bill from his pocket, holding it forth,
As they have been speaking, Collins pushed his way forward
until he is almost at Herbie's elbow.

                         HERBIE
                    (picking up tie)
              How can you sell these ties so
              cheap?

                         SMITTY
              We got no rent to pay -- we got no
              overhead and we ain't got no peddler's
              license.

Herbie turns and sees the cop.

                         HERBIE
                    (gulping as he
                     demonstrates)
              Yes, sir - that's a strong tie
              all right - triple reinforced --
              strong as a lion --

He ties the end of the tie to a customer's wrist.

                              CONTINUED

CONTINUED

HERBIE
(continuing spiel)
It positively won't rip, shrink
or fade...
(louder)
Fade...!
(still louder)
FADE, SMITTY - FADE!

Smitty looks up from straightening the ties and sees
Collins, just as Herbie ties the other end of the tie
to Collins' wrist.

HERBIE
Now just try and tear that tie.

He rushes o.s. with Smitty. Collins starts after them but
is dragged back by the man to whom he is tied. Collins
turns back, angrily, and with a heave of his two hands
breaks the tie. He starts after the boys again and falls
over the tie suitcase.

12   MED. CLOSE SHOT - SMITTY AND HERBIE

as they run down street. Herbie looks back -- sees what
has happened and CAMERA PANS with him as he returns to
Collins.

13   MED. CLOSE SHOT - COLLINS

as Herbie comes INTO SCENE and helps Collins get up.

COLLINS
(brushing himself
off as he rises)
What do you think of the little guy
- playing a trick like that on me?

HERBIE
(righteously)
I never saw such a thing.

Suddenly both Herbie and Collins look at each other - realize their relationship - and do a take. Herbie runs away
quickly. Collins starts after him and again falls over the
suitcase.

14   MED. SHOT - SMITTY AND HERBIE

Running down the street through crowd, cop after them.

15   MED. CLOSE SHOT - STREET

Smitty and Herbie come racing down and spot a white and
green car parked at the curb. Its rear door is open.

SMITTY
Come on, Herbie, hop into this cab.

CONTINUED

15   CONTINUED

They jump into cab.

                              HERBIE
                        (without looking
                          at driver)
                    Step on it, driver -- we're trying
                    to get away from a cop.

CAMERA DRAWS BACK as driver turns. We see that two cops
are in the front seat. Smitty and Herbie react and quickly
pile out of the car. They dash off just as Collins races
up in pursuit.

16   MED. CLOSE SHOT - LINE OF MEN

In front of the theatre previously established. Smitty and
Herbie come running around corner.

                              SMITTY
                    Quick, Herbie - get in that line.
                    We'll hide in the movie.

They quickly get into the line, squeezing in ahead of a
few men.

                              HERBIE
                    Yeah -- and when we get in, we'll
                    stay a long time.

                              SMITTY
                    Neighbor, you ain't foolin'.

17   CLOSE SHOT - AT CORNER

Collins, the cop, comes around the corner. He looks fran-
tically for the boys, then spots them in line o.s. and
smiles grimly.

18   MED. SHOT - LINE - FEATURING SMITTY AND HERBIE

                              HERBIE
                    Well, we got rid of that dumb
                    cop again.

The line of men advances and Smitty and Herbie come to the
ticket office.

19   MED. CLOSE SHOT - AT TICKET BOOTH

                              SMITTY
                        (to Herbie)
                    Get us a couple tickets.

                              HERBIE
                        (as he comes to window)
                    Okay.
                        (to Line Sergeant)
                    How much to get in?
                                                    CONTINUED

19   CONTINUED

                          LINE SERGEANT
            Nothing. We're going to give you
            twenty-one dollars..

                          HERBIE
            Bank night, huh?

                          SMITTY
            Come on, Herbie - or we won't get
            a seat.

        They start into theatre. Line Sergeant behind the window
        shakes his head approvingly.

20   MED. FULL SHOT - LOBBY

        As Smitty and Herbie push their way through the other men
        toward the door to the theatre where a Corporal, in uniform,
        is standing.

                          1ST CORPORAL
            ,on't push, boys -- take your time.

21   CLOSE SHOT - AT DOOR

                          HERBIE
                         (to soldier)
            Hey, mister, what picture's playing?

                          1ST CORPORAL
            You're in the army now.

                          HERBIE
            Good - I never saw that picture.

        The attendant at the door opens it and Smitty and Herbie
        are swept into the theatre by the push of the men behind
        them.

22   INT. THEATRE LOBBY - MED. FULL SHOT

        There are men signing their names before each desk. Smitty
        and Herbie enter in b.g. A Technical Sergeant comes up to
        them.

                          TECHNICAL SERGEANT
                         (to Herbie)
            Draftee?

                          HERBIE
            No - not a bit.

                                              CONTINUED

22   CONTINUED

                              TECHNICAL SERGEANT
                           (indicating enlist-
                              ment desk)
                  Right over there.

                                  SMITTY
                  Hurry up -- register before they
                  start the drawing.

Smitty and Herbie go over to the table indicated.

23   MED. CLOSE SHOT - AT TABLE

                              2ND CORPORAL
                  Step right up, boys.
                           (offers pen and paper)

                                  HERBIE
                           (to Smitty)
                  Ain't the ushers polite here?

He takes the offered pen, signs his name - then hands it to
Smitty, who does likewise.

                              2ND CORPORAL
                  Congratulations, men -- you're
                  in the army now.

                              SMITTY & HERBIE
                  Thanks....
                           (they do a take)
                  Army?!!

Smitty and Herbie start to run off, followed by 2nd
Corporal.

                              2ND CORPORAL
                  Hey - wait a minute!

24   REVERSE ANGLE

Standing in the lobby doorway, as big as life, is Collins,
the cop. Smitty and Herbie go into a walk, then stop.

                                  COLLINS
                           (politely)
                  Going some place, boys?

                                  HERBIE
                           (looking back at
                              soldier - then
                              at Collins)
                  Yeah - we're going some place.
                  We're going in the army - and
                  you can't touch us.

                                              CONTINUED

24   CONTINUED
                              COLLINS
                  So - you're going in the army?
                          (he grins)
                  Well, boys, I'll be seeing you.

He breaks into a hearty laugh.

                              SMITTY
                          (picks up laugh)

                              HERBIE
                          (picks up laugh -
                           then stops suddenly)
                  WHAT AM I LAUGHING FOR?

                                            DISSOLVE TO:

25   INT. THEATRE MANAGER'S OFFICE - SAME AS SCENE 6) -
          MED. SHOT

Smitty and Herbie are sitting on the far end of a long bench
with other men, all of them in their underwear, waiting to
get weighed. There is a radiator under the part of the
bench where Smitty and Herbie are sitting. At the moment
a big bruiser is on the scale with an officer adjusting
weights.

                          MEDICAL LIEUTENANT
                          (reading scales)
                  Two hundred and **thirty nine** -
                          (to man)
                  You just made it. If you'd been
                  over two hundred and forty we'd
                  had to turn you down.

26   TWO SHOT - SMITTY AND HERBIE

                              HERBIE
                          (beaming)
                  Did you hear that, Abbott? Over
                  two hundred and forty they won't
                  take you. Am I lucky?
                          (pats stomach)
                  Two hundred and forty one....

                              SMITTY
                  You lucky dog.

Smitty looks down and his eyes light on something.

27   CLOSE SHOT - RADIATOR

As Smitty's **hand** comes INTO SCENE, and turns on the heat.

                                            DISSOLVE TO:

28   TWO SHOT - SMITTY AND HERBIE

          Herbie is moving uneasily as perspiration pours down his
          face. Smitty is also perspiring a bit.

                              SMITTY
                    Sit still, will you? You act like
                    you're getting a hot foot.

                              HERBIE
                            (squirming)
                    A hot foot? Brother, you got a
                    very poor sense of direction.

          CAMERA MOVES IN to CLOSE SHOT of Herbie.

                                        DISSOLVE TO:

29   CLOSE SHOT - HERBIE

          He is perspiring like a cloudburst.

                              HERBIE
                            (wiping face)
                    Boy, this is arson!

                              MEDICAL LIEUTENANT'S VOICE
                    Next --

          CAMERA DRAWS BACK TO INCLUDE Smitty, who nudges Herbie.

                              SMITTY
                    That's you, Herbie.

          CAMERA PANS with Herbie as he starts toward scales.

                              HERBIE
                    So long, Smitty - have a good time
                    in the army.
                            (pats stomach)
                    Two hundred forty one --

30   MED. CLOSE SHOT - AT SCALES

          as Herbie steps on.

                              MEDICAL LIEUTENANT
                            (reading scales)
                    Congratulations, my boy -- you
                    made it by two ounces.

          Herbie does a take and looks at the scales and over at
          Smitty o.s.

31   CLOSE SHOT - SMITTY

He is turning off the radiator.

32   CLOSE SHOT - HERBIE

as he burns.

DISSOLVE TO:

33   INT. THEATRE FOYER - CLOSE SHOT - CAPTAIN JOHNSON

CAPTAIN JOHNSON
-- and that I will obey the
President of the United States --

VOICES OF MEN
-- andthat I will obey the
President of the United States --

CAMERA DRAWS BACK TO REVEAL roomful of draftees, including
Smitty and Herbie, Dick, Bob and Randolph. Their right
hands are raised.

CAPTAIN JOHNSON
-- and the orders of the officers
appointed over me, according to the
rules and articles of war --

MEN
-- and the orders of the officers
appointed over me, according to
the rules and articles of war.

34   MED. SHOT - THE GROUP

CAPTAIN JOHNSON
You men will report at the High Street
Armory next Tuesday afternoon at five
o'clock. We will entrain from the
railway station at seven. Until then,
dismissed.

As the men break up, Randolph turns to Bob.

RANDOLPH
Will you get my hat, Martin? I
left it in the other room.

BOB
(respectfully)
May I speak to you a moment first?

CONTINUED

34   CONTINUED

                         RANDOLPH
              Yes - what is it?

Bob moves to one side, Randolph steps over with him.

35   TWO SHOT - RANDOLPH AND BOB

                           BOB
              I've worked for you for two years --

                         RANDOLPH
              That's right.

                           BOB
                       (sentimentally)
              It's been quite an experience.
              I've carried you upstairs and put
              you to bed any number of times --

                         RANDOLPH
              Why bring that up?

                           BOB
                   (smiling reminiscently)
              I've gotten you out of fights with
              headwaiters and gambling house
              bouncers --

                         RANDOLPH
                       (impatiently)
              Yes, yes --

                           BOB
                       (still sweetly)
              Waited hours for you to come out of
              night clubs and cabarets -- Remember
              that winter night I froze both my
              ears waiting?... And that accident
              you had, when I took the rap and
              went to jail for you?
                       (he chuckles)

                         RANDOLPH
              That's ancient history.

                           BOB
              Yeah - but we're both in the army
              now, and I think it's about time
              to tender my resignation.

                         RANDOLPH
              All right - tender it.

                                        CONTINUED

35   CONTINUED
                              BOB
                   Yes, sir - here it is!

He brings up a swift uppercut which catches Randolph flush
on the jaw, flooring him. Bob exits from the room.

36   MED. CLOSE SHOT - RANDOLPH

He comes to his feet, sore. SOUND of closing door COMES
OVER. He stands glaring at the door.

37   MED. CLOSE SHOT - SMITTY AND HERBIE

Taking in SCENE with open-eyed amazement.

                            SMITTY
                   What do you think of that?

                            HERBIE
                   It gives me an idea.

He socks Smitty suddenly, flooring him.

                            HERBIE
                   Turn on the heat and get me in
                   the army, will you!

                                        FADE OUT.

FADE IN:

38   INT. RAILWAY STATION - NIGHT - FULL SHOT

The station is crowded with friends, relatives and sweethearts, as well as the usual railway station attaches. Down
the steps leading into the concourse marches a military
band, preceded by the colors and color guard. (This com-
prises the American flag, a fictional regimental flag, and
two color guards.)

Throughout this SCENE the band plays "YOU'RE IN THE ARMY NOW"
Following the band, marching in hardly military formation, are
recruits and draftees. They are still in civilian clothes,
carry suitcases and other personal property. Additional
friends, relatives and sweethearts walk beside them, as well
as the necessary army officials.

At one side of the station are grouped approximately a dozen
camp hostesses in their trim uniforms. These include MISS
DURLING, a middle-aged, kindly disciplinarian, wearing the
uniform of an army hostess, who is in charge of the

                                        CONTINUED

38   CONTINUED

        Camp Greeley Hostess Corps; MISS CLARK, a middle-aged woman,
        MISS JONES, a plain-looking hostess, and JUDY GRAY. They
        are busy filling their kits with cigarettes, candy and chew-
        ing gum assorted along the table.

            b.g. over railway gates is a large sign reading:
            MP GREELEY SPECIAL.

39   MED. CLOSE SHOT

        CAMERA TRUCKS with the recruits as they march through sta-
        tion, CENTERING on Smitty and Herbie directly behind Bob.
        Herbie is carrying a number of suitcases and he is having
        a little trouble with his feet, trying to keep in step.
        CAMERA MOVES to CENTER Randolph -- several files behind
        Bob. Hurrying alongside Randolph is EDMUNDS, a sad-visaged
        valet. He is loaded down with extra coats and several bags.

                        SERGEANT'S VOICE
                Detail -- halt!

        The men stop, Herbie bumping into the men in front of him.

40   MED. CLOSE GROUP SHOT

        CENTERING Captain Johnson, SERGEANT, and MISS DURLING as
        they come to a stop near the head of the column.

                        CAPTAIN JOHNSON
                        (to Staff Sergeant)
                Let the men fall out until train
                time -- to say their goodbyes...

                        SECOND STAFF SERGEANT
                        (saluting)
                Yes, sir.

        He exits FROM SCENE.

41   MED. SHOT - DRAFTEES - FEATURING SMITTY AND HERBIE,
        BOB, PARKER AND EDMUNDS

        as the Second Staff Sergeant gives the order.

                        SECOND STAFF SERGEANT
                You men can fall out, but don't go
                out of this area... Say your good-
                byes and when I say "fall in", be
                here. Dismissed!

        As the men break up:

                                                CONTINUED

41   CONTINUED

                    HERBIE
        What kind of talk is that? Fall in --
        fall out! I'd like to run out!

                    SMITTY
        You can't - you're in for a year, just
        like the draftees.

                    BOB
                (turning to them)
        Weren't you two drafted?

                    HERBIE
        Naw - I'm an involuntary volunteer.

42   MED. CLOSE SHOT - CAPTAIN JOHNSON AND MISS DURLING

                    CAPTAIN JOHNSON
                (to Miss Durling)
        Your hostess corps can go into
        action now, Miss Durling.

                    MISS DURLING
        Yes, sir.

CAMERA DOLLIES with her as she moves over to a group of
uniformed hostesses who are filling their kits with supply
of cigarettes, chewing gum, chocolate bars, etc. Included
in this group are JUDY GRAY, the ANDREWS SISTERS, and two
plain-looking hostesses, MISS JONES and MISS CLARK.

                    MISS DURLING
        Start to work as soon as your kits
        are filled, girls.

CAMERA PICKS UP Judy, DOLLIES with her as she starts circulating among the soldiers.

                    JUDY
        Cigarette, soldier?... Care for
        some chewing gum?... Compliments of
        the army... Cigarette, soldier? Etc.

The fourth soldier she comes to is Bob, who is standing
with his back to her.

                    JUDY
        Cigarette, soldier?

                    BOB
                (turning)
        Why, I ---
                (recognizes her)
        Judy Gray! What are you doing
        here?

                                        CONTINUED

42   CONTINUED

                    JUDY
    I joined the army.

                    BOB
    Go on!

                    JUDY
    Certainly -- I'm a camp hostess now.
    It's something new -- we're going to
    try to give the boys a feeling that
    the camp is their home -- you know,
    add the feminine touch.

                    BOB
    Who thought that one up?

                    JUDY
    A few million parents who wanted
    their sons to lead a normal life
    while they're away for a year.

                    BOB
    Well, it'll certainly make being
    drafted a lot more popular.

                    JUDY
    I think it's pretty popular now.
                (with smile)
    See you later, Bob.

She moves on through the group of draftees, offering
cigarettes, chewing gum, etc. CAMERA PANS with her, then
CONTINUES PANNING to CENTER Randolph. He is surrounded by
three chorus girls, who are showering him with attention.
CAMERA MOVES IN for CLOSER SHOT on THE GROUP.

                    CHORUS GIRLS
                (ad lib)
    Things won't be the same without
    you, Randy.

    I'm dying to see you in a uniform!

    Are they going to make you a captain
    or a general?

    Can't you get out of it, Randy?
    After all, you have twelve polo
    ponies dependent on you!

                    EDMUNDS
                (clears throat)
    Excuse me, sir, but your mother is
    in sight.

                    RANDOLPH
    That's all I need---
                (to the girls)
    Scram, you beautiful things!

                                        CONTINUED

42   CONTINUED - 2

The girls gang him, kiss him goodbye, then duck off into
the crowd. This leaves him with a face full of lipstick.

                    EDMUNDS
           She's coming this way-- you'd
           better wipe your face, sir.

Randolph turns his back, starts wiping his face with his
handkerchief. Edmunds looks out of scene.

                    EDMUNDS
           Hurry, sir-- Hurry!

43   MED. CLOSE SHOT-TO INCLUDE MRS. PARKER

working her way toward her son. She is an immaculately
groomed woman, of the poised, cultured type. Captain
Johnson is escorting her. They come to Edmunds and
Randolph, just as Randolph turns.

                    MRS. PARKER
           Randolph, my boy!

She embraces him, carefully, so as not to muss herself,
then steps back.

                    MRS. PARKER
           I phoned your father-- he'll have you
           out of the army in no time at all.

                    RANDOLPH
           Thanks, mother. Did he say how long?

                    MRS. PARKER
           Oh-- a week at the most. I suppose
           you'll just have to make the best
           of the ordeal.

                    CAPTAIN JOHNSON
           If you'll pardon my saying so, Mrs.
           Parker, it won't be an ordeal. As a
           matter of fact, a year in the army
           can do a great deal for any boy.

Randolph starts staring toward someone out of SCENE.

                    MRS. PARKER
                 (to Captain Johnson)
           Oh -- I can understand how it may
           benefit some men -- those who have
           no advantages in their homes --
           but after all, he is a Parker.

                    CAPTAIN JOHNSON
           I know, but...

                                        CONTINUED

43   CONTINUED

                    MRS. PARKER
                 (continuing as if
                  he'd never spoken)
            His education and background should
            certainly entitle him to more than
            these other young men. After all,
            how can they make a Yale man a
            private?

She gives an eloquent lift of her eyebrows. Captain
Johnson suppresses a smile. She turns to her son again--
realizes that he is staring out of scene, smiling. Curious, she turns, follows his gaze.

44   MED. SHOT - RANDOLPH'S ANGLE TO JUDY

circulating among the soldiers.

45   MED. CLOSE SHOT - JUDY

As she happens to glance in Randolph's direction, does a
slight take.

46   MED. SHOT - RANDOLPH FROM JUDY'S ANGLE

He is smiling broadly in her direction.

47   ). CLOSE SHOT - JUDY

a bit puzzled, not knowing whether she is acquainted with
this chap or not. Deciding that she is not, she moves on
about her work, CAMERA DOLLYING with her. As she comes up
to Smitty and Herbie -

                    HERBIE
            How's business? Could you use a
            good advance man?

                    JUDY
                 (with a smile)
            This is all free -- compliments
            of the army!

She hands Herbie a bar of candy and goes on.

48   MED. CLOSE SHOT - SMITTY AND HERBIE

As Judy goes out of SCENE, Herbie staring after her.

                    SMITTY
                 (suspiciously)
            There must be a catch.

He turns and notices Herbie.

                                        CONTINUED

48   CONTINUED

SMITTY
Will you stop looking at her?

HERBIE
Aw - I was only looking at her to
see if she was looking at me to
see if I was looking at her.

SMITTY
Well, stop it and look over there!
          (indicates)
Remember when we were in vaudeville?
That kid sister team on the same bill
with us -- the Andrews Sisters?

HERBIE
          (looking out of scene)
Oh, yeah --

The boys start toward girls o.s.

49   MED. CLOSE SHOT - THREE ANDREWS SISTERS

Their backs to CAMERA - they are bent over filling their
kits.

HERBIE'S VOICE
Now I recognize 'em!

Smitty and Herbie come into SCENE, put their heads together and harmonize:

SMITTY & HERBIE
Three little sisters are we---
And we sing a song to thee----
A song to thee.....

The three girls turn around.

50   MED. SHOT - ANDREWS SISTERS AND HERBIE & SMITTY

PATTY
Smitty and Herbie!

HERBIE & SMITTY
Hi'ya, kids!

The Andrews Sisters ad lib greetings.

SMITTY
Last time we saw you girls I dangled
the three of you on one knee.

CONTINUED

50   CONTINUED

               HERBIE
How the old joint has changed.
Remember when you all sat on my lap?

               PATTY
I can't remember you ever _having_ a
lap!

               SMITTY
What are you doing here?

               PATTY
Going to entertain you boys in camp.

               HERBIE
Say -- I'm gonna like the army all
right --
          (to Laverne)
You wanta mother me?

               SMITTY
Wait a minute, Herbie - there's
three of them and two of us.

               HERBIE
That's okay -- one for me, one for
you, and one for me.

               PATTY
Gotta go to work now, boys. See
you in camp?

The girls start out - Herbie stops Patty.

               HERBIE
          (whispers)
Look - you wouldn't kiss me goodbye,
would you?

               PATTY
No, I wouldn't.

               HERBIE
I didn't think you would.

Patty runs after her sisters.

O.S. a bugler SOUNDS a FANFARE in boogie woogie style.

                              CONTINUED

50   CONTINUED - 2

MUSICAL NUMBER (#1)   "YOU'RE A LUCKY FELLOW, MR. SMITH"

(NOTE: If any additional entertainment is used in
this sequence, it will occur prior to this spot in
the script.)

51)   In the OPENING of this Patty hops up on the information
52)   desk and recites the verse to the assembled men and
53)   relatives. Throughout this verse and throughout the
54)   SCENE we show the reactions of men to the verse and to
55)   the stirring lyrics of the song.
56)
57)   VERSE
58)   Now, see here, Mister Smith,
59)   Or whatever your name may be,
60)   You seem like a pretty nice guy
                   So I'd like you to listen to me.

                   I don't want to butt into your business,
                   But I've heard you complain a lot
                   About all the bad luck you have
                   And the good luck that others have got.

                   I'd say you're just a little mistaken
                   You've got plenty of luck, my friend,
                   I think you should open your eyes
                   And discover this country again!

From verse we go into the SONG with the Andrews Sisters
singing--

                    CHORUS
          You're a lucky fellow, Mister Smith
          To be able to live as you do,
          And to have that swell Miss Liberty Gal
          Carryin' the torch for you.
          You're a lucky fellow, Mister Smith
          Do you know just how highly you rate?
          You should thank your lucky stars
          And I mean you should thank all forty eight!
          Man! you've really got a family tree
          with Washington, Jefferson, Lincoln and Lee
          You're lucky to have ancestors like that;
          Don't you know you were born with a feather
                              in your hat!
          You're a very, very wealthy gent,
          I don't care if you haven't a cent
          You've got your American way,
          And brother, that ain't hay!
          If some poor suckers could choose
          They'd love to be in your shoes!
          That proves that your good
          For-tune's no myth
          You're a lucky fellow, Mister Smith!

                                 CONTINUED

51
to
60

CONTINUED

On the final chord of the vocal chorus, the army band blares
out an instrumental chorus in march tempo, over which are
heard commands of the officers and non-coms for the men to
fall in line, and we see them in tempo to the music singing the refrain - marching through the gate to the train.
INCLUDED in these SHOTS should be Mrs. Parker, Bob saluting
to Judy as he goes by -- Randolph giving Judy an apprais-
ing look -- Herbie, burdened with luggage, still out of
step and having trouble with his feet.

> SMITTY
> Those bags are too much for you.
> Got a redcap.

> HERBIE
> Why should I get a redcap? What's
> the matter with the hat I got on?

DISSOLVE TO

61   CLOSE SHOT - TRAIN WHEELS

turning in the rhythm of the MUSIC of our song.

62   MED. FULL SHOT - ENGINE

going full speed.

63   CLOSE SHOT - TRAIN WHISTLE

DISSOLVE TO

64   INT. TRAIN COACH - NIGHT - TRUCKING SHOT

The coach is crowded with draftees. The Andrews Sisters
move down the aisle, singing special choruses of MR. SMITH,
with response from the boys. As they reach the end of the
car they sing their 16 bar solo, closing the doors as they
exit on the finish of the songs.

ANDREWS SISTERS:-You're a lucky fellow, Mr. Smith!

1ST SOLDIER:-   You can say that again. Yes, ma'am!

PATTY:-   Can you use some smokes?

1ST SOLDIER:-   Don't mind if I do.

ANDREWS SISTERS:-Charge it to your Uncle Sam!
                You're a lucky fellow, Mr. Smith!
                You should really be shouting with joy....

COLORED SOLDIER:-Yes'm that's just what ah'm doin' 'cause ahh
                Uncle Sammy's "fair-haired-boy!"

CONTINUED

64   CONTINUED

ANDREWS SISTERS:-Boys! You're rollin' in a lot of wealth.

LAVERNE:-   Your speech is free!

MAXINE:-   Yes sir-ee!

PATTY:-   And you've got your health!

2ND SOLDIER:-   Sure, we've got our health. And tell me why
                                                              not!
                       Take a look at the great constitution
                                                     we've got!

PATTY:-(TALKS)   Say! This fellow we've been talking to
                       Might be our president before he's through.

PATTY:-(SINGS)   And I mean that all on the square.
                       Well, say now, I declare....

ANDREWS SISTERS:-You're blushing red, white and blue --
                       But, Buddy, that's all right too
                       Because those colors look swell on you!
                       You're a lucky fellow, Mr. Smith!

(NOTE: Throughout the following scenes, ending with Scene
79, the melody will be underscored in rhythm with the wheels
of the train, and intermingled with the sound effect of the
train. This will be increased in volume and lowered to
punctuate the end of each short sequence on the train.

At the conclusion of the crap game, Scene 74, it will start
to increase in volume, ending on a high crescendo at the
conclusion of Scene 79.)

65   MED. SHOT

CENTERING Randolph, seated at forward end of coach. Dick
and HENRY, a husky young draftee, sit opposite Randolph.
All the draftees in SHOT are applauding the music. Randolph
is obviously bored. Herbie comes INTO SCENE, carrying his
suitcases and smoking a vile cigar.

                         HERBIE
                    (to Dick and Henry)
              Hi'ya, boys.

A lurch of the train sends his suitcases toppling onto
Randolph.

                         HERBIE
              Thanks for catching 'em.

                         RANDOLPH
                    (not meaning it)
              A pleasure.

                                                       CONTINUED

65   CONTINUED

                           HERBIE
              Better get 'em up on the rack, I guess.

He climbs on the seat by Randolph, starts placing suitcases
in overhead rack. One of them slips, falls on Randolph.

                           HERBIE
              The stubborn typo.

66   CLOSE GROUP SHOT - THE FOUR

as Herbie finishes putting suitcases in rack, plops himself
into the seat next to Randolph. This crowds Randolph
considerably.

                           HERBIE
                     (as he sits down)
              Pardon my hips.
                     (relaxing)
              Well, we're on our way to camp.
              Tally-ho!
                     (to Randolph, who is
                     looking out the window)
              Brown's the name.
                     (after a pause)
              How about it, chum -- you got a
              handle?

Randolph turns, looks at him.

                           HERBIE
              A monicker -- a tag -- You know -
              what's your mamma call you?

                           RANDOLPH
              Randolph Parker, the Third.

                           HERBIE
                     (extending hand)
              Herbie Brown - first, last and always.
                     (laughs immoderately)
              Have a cigar?

                           RANDOLPH
              I'm getting more than I want of
              one right now. Excuse me.

He climbs over the feet, gets to aisle of car, CAMERA PULL-
ING BACK SLIGHTLY as he gets into aisle, several draftees,
passing by, bump into him, knocking him back onto Herbie's
lap. The draftees, not even hesitating, ad lib "Excuse Me's"
over their shoulders. Randolph scrambles off Herbie's lap,
CAMERA PANNING SLIGHTLY to HOLD him in SHOT as he struggles
with the door at end of coach.

67   INT. CAR PLATFORM - <u>NIGHT</u> - MED. CLOSE SHOT

as Randolph comes onto platform. He straightens his mussed
clothing, adjusts his hat, takes a cigarette from an elegant
case. He is fumbling for his lighter when Judy comes onto
platform from the car ahead. She sees Randolph searching for
match, steps to him.

                    JUDY
          Need a light, soldier?

                    RANDOLPH
          Yes -- thanks.

68   CLOSE TWO SHOT

as Judy strikes and holds a match to Randolph's cigarette.
The jolting of the train causes them both to sway. He
takes her hand to steady the match. As he gets light, she
blows the match out. She realizes he is still holding her
hand, tries to free it.

                    RANDOLPH
          Don't go away.

                    JUDY
          I have to - I'm on duty.

                    RANDOLPH
          A hostess' duty is to keep the soldiers
          happy. Well, I won't be happy until
          we're better acquainted.

                    JUDY
          We've a full year to become
          acquainted.

                    RANDOLPH
          But <u>I'll</u> be out of the army in a week -

The train gives a violent lurch, flinging her against him.
He seizes the opportunity, kisses her. Immediately she pulls
free. She slaps him sharply in the face - turns and enters
the car from which Randolph came.

69   INT. COACH - MED. CLOSE SHOT - AT DOOR

as Judy comes in, a look of anger still on her face. She
pushes her hair back. Bob steps in to her.

                    BOB
          What's the matter, Judy?

                    JUDY
          Just a fresh recruit trying out
          the Manual of Arms.

Bob looks out glass in door, reacts and starts off.
                                        CONTINUED

69   CONTINUED

                              JUDY
                         (catching his arm)
                    Bob, don't -- it wasn't anything,
                    really.

He pulls away, opens the door and disappears onto the
platform. Judy, a bit upset, remains at the door, trying to
look out and see what is happening. Patty Andrews comes
INTO SCENE.

                              PATTY
                    Judy - we're running low on chewing
                    gum. Have you any you can spare?

                              JUDY
                    Why - yes.

She starts taking chewing gum from her kit bag, hands it to
Patty.

70   INT. CAR PLATFORM - MED. CLOSE TWO SHOT - RANDOLPH AND BOB

                              BOB
                    I'm just telling you - stay
                    away from her.

                              RANDOLPH
                    I'll pick my own company.

                              BOB
                    Maybe on Park Avenue, but not in
                    the army. Keep away from Judy.

                              RANDOLPH
                    Oh - private stock, uh?

Bob moves to swing at Randolph when car door opens and four
or five recruits, including Herbie, come through - getting
between the two men.

                              HERBIE
                    You seen my pal?

                              BOB
                    Next car.

Randolph and Bob wait for this group to pass, but the recruits are followed by Maxine Andrews and Miss Durling, who
remain on the platform. Miss Durling breaths deeply.

                              MAXINE
                         (to Miss Durling)
                    I always preferred cinders to cigar
                    smoke.

                                              CONTINUED

70   CONTINUED

MISS DURLING
Do you boys mind if we share the
platform with you?

BOB
Not at all.

Randolph and Bob stand a moment in silence, except for the
RUMBLING of the train. Realizing that the women block
their intended battle:

BOB
(to Randolph)
Shall we finish our dance later?

RANDOLPH
It's a date.

They move off.

71   INT. WASHROOM - NIGHT - CLOSE SHOT - SMITTY & DRAFTEES

squatting on floor.

SMITTY
Am I covered?

DRAFTEES
With everything we've got.

In B.G. Herbie parts curtain and watches dice game.

SMITTY
Hup, dice! Ride 'em, reap 'em and
bring 'em home.
(rolls dice and looks down)
And I got it -- Any more, boys?
Any more?

He gathers up the money on the floor. The other boys get up.

BOYS
(ad-libs)
You cleaned me --
That's my lesson for tonight --
Talk about hot dice ---

SMITTY
(hurt)
What - no players? Come on, boys,
here's a chance to get even.

Herbie moves in closer to Smitty.

HERBIE
What are you playing?

CONTINUED

71   CONTINUED

                        SMITTY
        Dice.

                        HERBIE
        Dice?

                        SMITTY
        Yes, didn't you ever shoot dice?

                        HERBIE
        Nope. Will you teach me how to play it?
                (getting down on floor)

72   TWO SHOT - SMITTY AND HERBIE

                        SMITTY
        It'll be a pleasure. You see, these
        dice have numbers on them from one
        to six. NOW, if you throw a six and
        one, that's seven, if you throw five
        and two, that's seven and if you throw
        four and three, that's seven -- YOU WIN.

                        HERBIE
        Oh, you can win in this game?

                        SMITTY
        Certainly - BUT.

                        HERBIE
        I figured there'd be a BUT in it.

                        SMITTY
        If you throw one and one, one and two,
        or two sixes, you lose. How much do
        you want to play for?

                        HERBIE
                (puts a bill on floor)
        Shoot ten bucks.

                        SMITTY
        WHAT?

                        HERBIE
        Did I say it wrong?

                        SMITTY
        You said it perfect. Are you sure
        you never shot dice before?

                        HERBIE
        No sir.

        Smitty puts down bill. Herbie holds dice in both hands,
        shuts his eyes and lets them drop in front of him.

                        HERBIE
                (opening eyes and looking)
        Five and two. I think I win.

                                        CONTINUED

>   SMITTY
> I know darn well you win. Pick
> up one of those bills.

>   HERBIE
> Let it ride.

>   SMITTY
> Let it ride?

>   HERBIE
> You wanta play some more, don't you?

>   SMITTY
> Certainly.

>   HERBIE
> FADE ME.

>   SMITTY
> Fade you? Where did you learn that?

>   HERBIE
> I heard it at the cigar counter.

>   SMITTY
> You'd better stay away from the
> cigar counter.

Smitty covers money on floor. Herbie shakes dice like
real crapshooter and gives them a good roll.

>   HERBIE
> WHAM!

>   SMITTY
> What's this WHAM business?

>   HERBIE
> Cigar counter.

>   SMITTY
>   (looking at dice)
> Four.

>   HERBIE
> Little Joe!

>   SMITTY
> Little Joe. You never shot dice before
> but you know all the names.

>   HERBIE
> Cigar counter.
>   (shakes dice and rolls)
> Seven - I win again.

>   SMITTY
> No, you lose. Four was your point.
> Now it's my turn. Cover that money.

>   HERBIE
>   (covering money)
> Now I have to use my money.

                                        CONTINUED

Smitty rolls the dice and reads them.

                    SMITTY
        Five.

                    HERBIE
        Little Phoebe!

Smitty looks at him.

                    SMITTY & HERBIE (together)
        Cigar counter!

Smitty rolls dice.

                    SMITTY
        Five's my point.

                    HERBIE
                (looking at dice)
        Two ones - you lose.

                    SMITTY
        Wait a minute. What did I throw the
        first time.

                    HERBIE
        Five.

                    SMITTY
        That's right. And what did I throw
        the second time?

                    HERBIE
        Two.

                    SMITTY
        All right. Now how much is five and
        two?

                    HERBIE
        Seven.

                    SMITTY
        Well, then I throw a seven - I win.

                    HERBIE
        Oh, you add them up?

                    SMITTY
        Of course you add them up. They only
        run up to six on the dice. How are you
        going to throw a seven if you don't add
        them up? Shoot the bankroll.

Herbie covers money - Smitty rolls dice.

                    SMITTY & HERBIE
                (reading the point)
        Six!

                                            CONTINUED

72   CONTINUED -3

                              SMITTY
                    Three ways to make it. I'll make
                    it the hard way.
                              (rolls dice - reads)
                    Six!

He starts to pick up the money, but Herbie stops him.

                              HERBIE
                    Wait a minute! What did you throw
                    the first time?

                              SMITTY
                    Six.

                              HERBIE
                    And what did you throw this time?

                              SMITTY
                    Six.

                              HERBIE
                              (taking money)
                    Well, add 'em up! Six and six,
                    box cars - freight trains. ADD
                    'EM UP!

He gets up and starts off.

73   SHOTS
74
75   of other men reacting to the crap game, to intercut with
          SCENE 72.

76   EXT. COUNTRY - STOCK SHOT - TRAIN

          racing through country. OVER SCENE the MUSIC of "You're
          a Lucky Fellow, Mr. Smith" SWELLS again.

77   CLOSE SHOT - TRAIN WHEELS - (STOCK)

          The wheels go round in rhythm to the MUSIC as it reaches
          a final crescendo.

                                              DISSOLVE TO

78   EXT. CAMP GREELEY - STOCK SHOT

          ESTABLISHING the camp.

79   STOCK SHOTS (AS AVAILABLE)
80
81   SHOWING Camp activities. (This is to get over the wide
          variety of training that our boys will receive in camp
          and not to give the impression that they have already done
          these things.)

                                              DISSOLVE TO

82   INT. MEDICAL EXAMINATION ROOM - MED. SHOT

Smitty, Herbie and several other men lined up for inoculation. As two army doctors are about to inoculate Smitty,
Herbie faints.

                                        DISSOLVE TO

83   INT. SUPPLY ROOM - MED. SHOT

Smitty, Herbie, Randolph and Bob and several other men are
being issued uniforms by supply sergeant. Suppy sergeant
adds last item of uniform to stack of folded clothing in
front of Herbie.

                    SUPPLY SERGEANT
            There you are -- and if they don't
            fit perfectly, bring them back.

                    SMITTY
            I've heard how army uniforms fit!

                    HERBIE
            Yeah -- in 1918 my uncle had an
            overcoat that didn't move until
            he'd taken three steps.

                    SUPPLY SERGEANT
            If these don't fit better than the
            clothes you got on, I'll eat 'em.

                                        DISSOLVE TO

83-A   INT. SUPPLY ROOM - DAY - MED. SHOT - AT FOOT MEASURING
        MACHINE

A line of men are being fitted for shoes. The man preceding Herbie takes his foot out of the machine and goes on.

                    SUPPLY SERGEANT
                    (to soldier o.s.)
            Size eight and a half - D width.
                    (to Herbie)
            Step right on, brother.

                    HERBIE
                    (indicating machine)
            What's this silly looking gadget?

                    SUPPLY SERGEANT
            This machine gives us your correct
            shoe size. Put your foot in there
            and pick up those buckets of sand.

Herbie puts his foot in the machine.

                                        CONTINUED

83-A   CONTINUED

                              HERBIE
                Don't I get no play pen and shovel?
                         (tries to pick up
                         buckets of sand)
                I must be undernourished.

Lifts buckets with all the strain of a weight-lifter.
The officer adjusts the screw.

                              HERBIE
                Set the alarm for nine thirty - my
                foot's asleep.

                         SUPPLY SERGEANT
                         (to soldier o.s.)
                Size ten - E width.

Herbie steps off the machine and looks down at it dis-
dainfully.

                              HERBIE
                What a procedure!
                         (he sighs)
                Go ahead and measure me for my hat.
                         (he stands on his head)

84   INT. SUPPLY ROOM - ANOTHER ANGLE - MEN (SAME AS IN ABOVE
         SCENE)

         They are now stripped to underwear - each carries his
         civilian clothes. They come up to a cubbyhole-window
         bearing a sign over it reading: "CIVILIAN CLOTHES DEPOT."
         Inside is a first-class private.

                              RANDOLPH
                         (as he hands in clothes)
                Keep these clothes handy -

         Herbie, next in line behind Randolph, deposits his clothes.

                              HERBIE
                Clean 'em -- press 'em -- give 'em
                a double dose of mothballs.....then throw
                'em away.

                                             DISSOLVE TO

85   INT. SHOWER ROOM - MED. FULL SHOT - DRAFTEES - CENTERING
         BOB - RANDOLPH - SMITTY AND HERBIE - (this set consists of
         a row of lockers with arrow sign reading: "Showers")

         The men are waiting their turns to shower. Showers can be
         HEARD running.

85   CONTINUED

                              BOB
                         (to Randolph as they
                          both go to showers)
                    You oughta raise the devil about
                    no private shower.

                              HERBIE
                         (to Smitty as they
                          walk toward shower)
                    Hmmm, hmmm, silly procedure - taking
                    a bath in the daytime!

                                                    DISSOLVE TO

86   EXT. "K" COMPANY STREET - DAY - FULL SHOT

A detail (30 men) of new draftees, in uniforms and campaign
hats, comes marching toward CAMERA. They carry their
barracks bags. (NOTE: Nowhere in the picture will our
draftees wear uniform jackets. Their clothes, outside of
fatigue outfits, will be confined to trousers and army
shirt.) SERGEANT CALLAHAN is in command. Standing a bit
to one side is CAPTAIN WILLIAMS. With him are FIRST
LIEUTENANT POOLE, and SECOND LIEUTENANT ALBRIGHT.

                              CALLAHAN
                    Detail -- halt! Right - face!

He turns, salutes Captain Williams. The Captain returns
his salute. Sergeant Callahan steps aside.

                              CAPTAIN WILLIAMS
                    At ease, men -- you may put down
                    your equipment.

As the men place the equipment on the ground in front of
them --

87   MED. SHOT

ANGLING over some of the men to Captain Williams.

                              CAPTAIN WILLIAMS
                    I'm Captain Williams, commanding officer
                    of this company -- This is 1st Lieutenant
                    Poole and 2nd Lieutenant Albright.

88   CLOSE SHOT - CAPTAIN WILLIAMS

                              CAPTAIN WILLIAMS (Continuing)
                    Men, I am as new to you as you are to me --
                    but we both have the same job ahead of us,
                    and I believe we'll find it an interesting
                    one. A great many people are counting on
                    our success -- people from all walks of
                    life who are contributing to this great
                    national defense program just as much as
                    you or I. I refer to the factory workers,
                    the farmers, the citizens whose taxes are
                    paying for this training -- the people of
                    America.

89   MED. SHOT - CENTERING CAPTAIN WILLIAMS

                              CAPTAIN WILLIAMS
                         (in a slightly lighter vein)
                    No one expects you to be seasoned
                    soldiers over night -- but we're going
                    to do everything we can to help you in
                    every possible way, and if we all work
                    together, I'm certain we'll make "K"
                    Company a unit of which any army can be
                    proud.
                         (turns to Callahan)
                    Sergeant Callahan, appoint Acting
                    Corporals and assign the men to their
                    tents.

                              CALLAHAN
                         (saluting)
                    Yes, sir.

          Captain Williams moves back to a position with his Lieuten-
          ants, as Sergeant Callahan counts off the first seven men.

                                                      DISSOLVE TO

90   INT. SQUAD TENT - DAY - MED. SHOT

          As seven men - Randolph, Bob, Dick, Smitty, Herbie, Henry
          and Briggs - enter, carrying their equipment. The sides of
          the tent are furled.

                              HERBIE
                         (indicating walls)
                    Hey look - this tent isn't finished!
                    The joint hasn't even got walls.

          In the b.g. the other men select their cots and drop their
          equipment.

90-A   MED. CLOSE SHOT - RANDOLPH AND BOB

          They have adjoining cots. Randolph makes up his cot, quickly
          and efficiently. The others are clumsily attempting to
          emulate him.

                              BOB
                    I never knew you made up your own
                    bed at home.

                              RANDOLPH
                    There are a lot of things even you
                    don't know about me.

90-B   FULL SHOT

          Smitty and Herbie are arranging their equipment. As they
          do, we hear Sergeant Collins' voice.

                              COLLINS' VOICE (o.s.)
                    Hello, boys --
                              HERBIE (without turning, fearful)
                    Smitty - that voice sounds familiar.
                              SMITTY
                    Too familiar.

          They turn slowly, looking toward entrance.

91   MED. CLOSE SHOT - COLLINS

          Previously seen as a cop, but now in Army uniform and wear-
          ing sergeant's stripes.

91   CONTINUED

                                COLLINS
                    I'm Collins, your sergeant. Who's
                    Acting Corporal of this squad?

                                BOB
                    I am, Sergeant.

The men ad lib greetings, Smitty and Herbie making theirs
very weak. Collins sees them, recognizes them.

                                COLLINS
                    Well, well - this is going to be
                    more fun than I hoped for!

He moves over to them.

92   MED. CLOSE THREE SHOT - COLLINS - SMITTY AND HERBIE

                                COLLINS
                    So you're in my outfit?

                                HERBIE
                    Not any more -- we're resigning.
                    Pick up the stuff, Smitty.--

                                COLLINS
                    Where do you think you're going?

                                HERBIE
                    To join the Marines.

                                COLLINS
                    No you don't! Put that stuff down!

                                HERBIE
                    Yes, officer - I mean, sergeant.

Collins jerks the pitchman's suitcase from Herbie. It
automatically opens, the ties streaming from it and the
legs unfolding.

                                COLLINS
                    Just what do you think you're going
                    to do with this?

                                HERBIE
                    It's a frame-up -- It was planted on
                    me! I never saw it before in my life.

                                COLLINS-
                    Agghhh!
He throws the suitcase to one side, glares at Smitty and
Herbie, who try to smile disarmingly - then walk over to cots.

93   MED. CLOSE SHOT - RANDOLPH AND BOB

As Collins comes to a stop by their bunks - looks at neatness
of cots.

                                COLLINS (to Randolph)
                    Good job - where'd you learn to do it?

                                RANDOLPH
                    Military school.

                                COLLINS
                    Why didn't you tell the Top Sergeant
                    about it? You might have been made
                    Acting Corporal, instead of him.
                                (indicating Bob)

                                RANDOLPH
                    Who wants to be Acting Corporal for a week?

                                    CONTINUED

93   CONTINUED

                              COLLINS
            What?

                              RANDOLPH
            You can have the army, by next Monday
            I'll be through with it.

                              COLLINS
            Oh -- you're the one they're talking
            about -- the boy with the big drag.

Randolph stretches out on his cot.

                              RANDOLPH
            That's me.

                              COLLINS (sharply)
            Well, drag yourself over and show those
            skulls how to make their bunks....

94   MED. SHOT - TO INCLUDE SMITTY AND HERBIE

                              COLLINS
                        (to Smitty & Herbie)
            .... and pay attention to the way
            he does it, understand? If you can't
            stand up like a soldier - maybe you
            can sleep like one.

                              SMITTY & HERBIE
                        (together)
            Yes - Sergeant.

                              COLLINS
            And police up those buttons!
            Store that stuff away! Get rid
            of that necktie case of yours!

As Collins starts away, he falls over Herbie's suitcase.
He angrily picks it up and shoves it at Herbie. Herbie
takes it and walks away with it.

                              COLLINS
                        (to Smitty)
            I don't want any trouble with you,
            understand?

                              SMITTY
            Yes, Sergeant.

                              COLLINS
            Okay.

95   MED. CLOSE SHOT

Herbie looks very hurt as he puts the suitcase down.
Collins turns to exit and again falls over Herbie's
suitcase. He picks himself up and gives Herbie a look
that shrivels him up. The Sergeant finally controlls
himself and walks out as Smitty comes up to Herbie.

                                          CONTINUED

95   CONTINUED

                              HERBIE
                    Smitty, you know what?

                              SMITTY
                    What?

                              HERBIE
                    I don't think he likes me.

                                        DISSOLVE TO:

96   EXT. RECREATION HALL - 'NIGHT' - MED. SHOT

        A flood-lighted sign identifies the building. Lights
        are streaming from the windows - soldiers are entering
        the building. SOUND of laughter and talk come over SCENE.

                                        DISSOLVE TO:

97   INT. RECREATION HALL - NIGHT - GROUP SHOT

        Dick is seated at piano. A few draftees with a guitar, a
        harmonica, and possibly a banjo, stand near him trying out
        a number. Judy, carrying stationery supplies, passes by,
        humming. CAMERA PANS with her as she goes to writing desks.

98   MED. CLOSE SHOT - AT WRITING DESK

        Henry is seated there, biting on his pencil. He looks
        up as Judy comes into SCENE.

                              JUDY
                    Having a little trouble?

                              HENRY
                    Sort of... what do you write a girl
                    when you -- when you...
                              (blushing)
                    -- you know what I mean.

                              JUDY
                    It's simple. You start with "Dear Sweetheart"...

                              HENRY
                              (writing)
                    "Dear Sweetheart" --

        From this we go into -

        MUSICAL NUMBER (#2) "WISH YOU WERE HERE"

99)   PICKUP SHOTS - COVERING Judy's rendition of number,
100)   including Bob's pleased reaction.
101)
102)
103)

104   MED. CLOSE SHOT - JUDY

    As she finishes song, Bob comes into SCENE.

                        BOB
          Hello!

                        JUDY
          Hello!
                (looking him over)
    Well, you're really in the army now.

                        BOB
                (smiling)
    What the well-dressed draftee will
    wear. Seen any more of my ex-boss
    - if you know what I mean?

                        JUDY
                (firmly)
    I know what you mean - and I haven't
    seen him - and I don't intend to.

                        BOB
    You don't know the man like I do.
    He'll be around --
                 (with a grin)
    - but so will I.

    Patty Andrews comes walking into SCENE.

105   MED. SHOT - JUDY - BOB AND PATTY

                        PATTY
             (with admiring look at Bob)
    You sure get all the cute ones, Judy.
    Miss Durling wants to see you.

                        JUDY
    Thanks, Patty.
            (to Bob, as she leaves)
    Take good care of her.

    She goes out of SCENE.

                        PATTY
    Lonesome, sailor --?
              (catches herself)
    I mean, soldier?

106   MED. CLOSE SHOT - AT DOORWAY TO MISS DURLING'S OFFICE

        As Judy comes up to door and KNOCKS.

                              MISS DURLING'S VOICE
                    Come in.

        Judy opens door and exits inside.

107   INT. MISS DURLING'S OFFICE - MED. CLOSE SHOT - AT DOOR

        As Judy enters. Judy reacts at what she sees. CAMERA
        ANGLES to include Miss Durling and Randolph.

                              MISS DURLING
                    Miss Gray - this is Private Randolph
                    Parker.

                              RANDOLPH
                         (putting on act)
                    How do you do, Miss Gray. I've been
                    most anxious to know you.

                              JUDY
                    Oh - how do you do.

                              MISS DURLING
                    Mr. Randolph saw you in the recreation
                    hall tonight, and asked for a formal
                    introduction.

                              RANDOLPH
                         (acting shy)
                    You see, I'm new here, and I don't
                    make friends easily. I thought if
                    Miss Durling could spare you - you
                    might show me around.

                              JUDY
                         (with double entendre)
                    Don't you -- know your way around?

                              RANDOLPH
                    Not in this neighborhood.

                              JUDY
                    Oh --

                              MISS DURLING
                    Now run along, the two of you!
                    Take good care of her, Randolph.

                                              CONTINUED

107   CONTINUED

                              RANDOLPH
                    I'll do my best.

Randolph gives Miss Durling a winning smile, takes Judy
by the arm and starts her from the room. CAMERA HOLDS
on Miss Durling as she beams after them, fondly; then,
remembering her position, she becomes her very efficient
self as she returns to her desk work.

108   INT. RECREATION HALL - MED. CLOSE SHOT - JUDY AND RANDOLPH

As they come out of Miss Durling's office.

                              RANDOLPH
                    I had to see you again. I wanted to
                    tell you...

Judy cuts in on him, her voice cool and impersonal, in
the tone of a professional guide.

                              JUDY
                    This is the main recreation room.
                    Sodas, soft drinks and ice cream
                    may be purchased at the fountain,
                    also all kinds of candies, cigarettes,
                    cigars and chewing tobacco.

109   MED. CLOSE SHOT - BOB - AT WRITING DESK

He looks over - sees Judy and Randolph together - and
takes at the sight.

110   TWO SHOT - JUDY AND RANDOLPH

CAMERA TRUCKS with them as they go through building.

                              JUDY
                           (continuing)
                    In the reading room are the latest
                    copies of all magazines, as well as
                    a carefully selected library. The
                    camp motion picture theatre is in
                    the first building to the west --

                              RANDOLPH
                    Which way is west?

                              JUDY
                           (indicating)
                    That way

                                                    CONTINUED

110   CONTINUED

                              RANDOLPH
                          (acting confused)
                    You go out the door here -- the
                    theatre is over there. I'd be sure
                    to get lost. Would you mind going
                    with me?

                              JUDY
                    As far as the ticket office.

She starts off at a brisk walk, Randolph after her.

111   MED. CLOSE SHOT - BOB

He gets an idea, looks around and spots Herbie.

                              BOB

              Herbie --
                              HERBIE
                          (turning)
                    Yes, Corp...

Herbie comes over to him and Bob whispers in his ear.
Herbie beams knowingly, and starts off.

112   EXT. RECREATION HALL - NIGHT - MED. CLOSE TWO SHOT -
        RANDOLPH AND JUDY

                              JUDY
                          (still impersonal)
                    That's the theatre - you can see
                    the ticket office from here.

                              RANDOLPH
                    Yes ... but I can't see myself
                    going to a movie alone. How about
                    forgetting what happened on the train?

                              JUDY
                          (innocently)
                    What happened on the train?

                              RANDOLPH
                    It was your own fault, you know.

                              JUDY
                          (still playing innocent)
                    My fault?

                              RANDOLPH
                    Certainly .. Ask any man if he'd
                    pass up a chance to kiss you.
                                                    CONTINUED

112   CONTINUED

                    JUDY
          Nonsense!

                    RANDOLPH
          I'll prove it! Hey, soldier! Hey!

                    JUDY
                 (quickly)
          Shhhh!!

At this point Herbie comes into the SCENE.

                    HERBIE
          Private Parker?

Randolph turns.

                    HERBIE
                 (very military)
          Captain Williams' compliments, and
          the Captain would like to see you
          in his tent at once.

He gives an exaggerated salute, goes out of scene - back
towards recreation hall.

                    RANDOLPH
          Of all times! Maybe he's had word
          from dad - I'd better go.

                    JUDY
          Of course.

                    RANDOLPH
          I'll be right back.

                    JUDY
                 (mocking him)
          I can hardly wait.

He goes out of SCENE - away from recreation hall.

113   EXT. RECREATION HALL - MED. SHOT - NEAR ENTRANCE

As Herbie comes up to entrance, Bob steps out.

                    HERBIE
          Okay, Corp - she's all yours.

                    BOB
          Thanks, pal.

CAMERA PANS with Bob as he goes toward Judy.

114   MED. CLOSE TWO SHOT - BOB AND JUDY

As Bob takes Judy's arm, she turns and looks at him in
surprise.

                                         CONTINUED

                            BOB
                          (grinning)
          You may not know it, but I just saved
          you from a fate worse than death.

                            JUDY
                          (puzzled)
          Meaning what?

                            BOB
          The Captain doesn't want to see
          Randolph, but I want to see you.

                            JUDY
          Oh, the old army game - is that it?

                            BOB
          Call it anything you like - it's
          still boy wants girl when other
          boy wants her too.

          He takes her arm possessively and marches Judy in the dir-
          ection previously indicated for the theatre.

115   INT. RECREATION HALL - AT CANDY COUNTER - MED. SHOT

          Smitty is looking longingly at the things for sale. The
          Andrews Sisters are behind the counter.

                            PATTY
          May I help you?

                            SMITTY
          I can't even help myself... I,..
                          (sees Herbie
                           passing in b.g.)
          Hold everything!
                          (very friendly,
                           to Herbie)
          Hello, neighbor -- How you feeling?

                            HERBIE
          Not a penny.

116   MED. SHOT - HERBIE

          As Smitty walks over to him.

                            SMITTY
          Who said anything about money?

                            HERBIE
          You got that certain look in your eye.

                            SMITTY
          You cleaned me in that crap game last
          night, didn't you?

                                                    CONTINUED

116   CONTINUED

                        HERBIE
          You gave me a lesson - that's all
          I know.

                        SMITTY
          Okay - just for that I'll let you
          loan me fifty bucks.

                        HERBIE
          All I got is forty dollars.

                        SMITTY
          All right. Give me the forty and you
          owe me ten dollars.

                        HERBIE
               (handing over money)
          Okay, here's the forty and I owe you ten.
               (does take)
          WHO OWES YOU TEN?

                        SMITTY
          Don't get excited. How much did I
          ask for?

                        HERBIE
          Fifty dollars.

                        SMITTY
          And how much did you give me?

                        HERBIE
          Forty dollars.

                        SMITTY
          So -- you owe me ten dollars.

                        HERBIE
          That's right.
               (does take)
          Yeah, but you owe ME forty dollars.

                        SMITTY
          Okay, here's your forty dollars.
               (returns money)
          Now give me the ten dollars you owe me.

                        HERBIE
          All right, here's the ten dollars -
          BUT, I'm paying it on account.

                        SMITTY
          On account?

                        HERBIE
               (paying money)
          Yeah, on account of I don't know how
          I owe it to you.

117   WIDER SHOT

as Smitty, pouting, starts off.

> SMITTY
> If that's the way you feel, that's the
> last time I'll ever ask you for fifty
> dollars.

Herbie runs after him, taking hold of his arm.

> HERBIE
> Aw, Smitty, I can't lend you fifty
> dollars -- all I got now is thirty.

> SMITTY
> Okay, give me the thirty and you owe
> me twenty.

> HERBIE
> This is getting worse all the time. First
> I owe you ten, now I owe you twenty.

> SMITTY
> Why do you let yourself run into debt?

> HERBIE
> I didn't run into it - you pushed me.

> SMITTY
> Here, give me that money. NOW, I asked
> for fifty dollars, and you gave me
> thirty. Right?

> HERBIE
> Right.

> SMITTY
> Which makes you owe me twenty. Thirty
> and twenty is fifty.

> HERBIE
> Oh no, it ain't - twenty-five and
> twenty-five is fifty. You can't put
> that one over on me.

> SMITTY
> Here, take back your thirty dollars.
> Now give me the twenty you owe me.
> > (accepts bills from Herbie)
> You're a fine guy- won't lend a pal
> fifty dollars.

> HERBIE
> I only got ten dollars.

> SMITTY
> > (takes the ten)
> So you loan me the ten. Now I'll tell
> you what I'll do -- Just because we're
> pals - I'll forget the other forty.

                                      CONTINUED

                              HERBIE
                            (touched)
               Gee, Smitty, that's darned nice of you!
               I don't know anybody else that would do that!

                              SMITTY
               And what's more, I'll buy you a root beer.
               Come on.

Smitty goes out of SCENE.

                              HERBIE
                            (tenderly)
               What a pal -- what a pal!
                            (suddenly realizing)
               Hey! I BEEN ROBBED!!!!

He chases after Smitty.

                                            FADE OUT.

          FADE IN:

118   MONTAGE SEQUENCE (STOCK AS AVAILABLE)

        SHOWING various types of training given recruits during first
        thirty days. These may include: squad maneuvers - skirmish
        tactics - erection of pup tents - bayonet drill - rifle
        range practice - marching - etc. (This should not include
        mechanized equipment, which will be used in MONTAGE covering
        sham battle.)

        OVER this MONTAGE we SUPERIMPOSE a series of OVERLAPPED
        TRANSPARENCIES of our principals marching:

            (1) CLOSE TWO SHOT - RANDOLPH AND DICK

                              DICK
               How come you're still in the army, pal?

                              RANDOLPH
               Don't worry - I'll be out of here in
               a few days.

                              DICK
                            (disbelieving)
               Go on! You been giving us that for a month!

            (2) CLOSE TWO SHOT - COLLINS AND HERBIE

        Herbie a little behind and off to one side of Collins.

                              COLLINS
               I'll make a soldier out of you yet!
               Pick 'em up and lay 'em down!

                              HERBIE
               I'll lay 'em down, but I don't know if
               I got the strength to pick 'em up!

            (3) CLOSE THREE SHOT - BOB - HENRY AND BRIGGS

                              HENRY
               I've put on five pounds since the
               army's been feeding me.

                                            CONTINUED

118   CONTINUED

                              BOB
                    You sure go for that all-you-can-eat
                    stuff.

                              BRIGGS
                            (grinning)
                    Who doesn't?

(4) CLOSE TWO SHOT - HERBIE AND SMITTY

                              SMITTY
                    This pack of mine gets ten pounds
                    heavier every five minutes.

                              HERBIE
                    You aren't in condition like me --
                    Mine feels lighter all the time.

They move PAST CAMERA - make a right turn - and we see that
Herbie's pack has come undone and its contents are pouring
from it.

                                        DISSOLVE TO:

119
thru   OMITTED
125

126   EXT. "K" COMPANY STREET - MED. SHOT - (DAY)

        as the Awkward Squad (including Smitty and Herbie) marches
        down street under the command of Collins. CAMERA TRUCKS
        WITH THEM.

                              COLLINS
                    Come on, get in step! One, two,
                    three, four. One, two, three four.
                    Detail - halt!

        The Awkward Squad comes to a jolting stop.

                              COLLINS
                    Right - Dress! Ready - Front!
                    At ease! Attention!

        Herbie, in an attempt to click heels, knocks his feet out
        from under himself and falls. Smitty picks him up. Collins
        walks over - inspecting the squad and comes to a stop before
        Herbie.

127   GROUP SHOT - FAVORING COLLINS AND HERBIE

                              COLLINS
                    Attention!

        Herbie stands sloppily.

                                        CONTINUED

127   CONTINUED

> COLLINS
> (to Herbie)
> Throw out your chest!

> HERBIE
> What for? I'm not through with it yet.

> SMITTY
> Do what the Sergeant tells you. Throw
> out your chest!

Herbie draws back, makes an exaggerated move and throws out
his stomach.

> COLLINS
> (disgusted)
> Never mind. -- Present arms!

Herbie throws his gun at Collins, who throws it back to
Herbie. This is repeated until Herbie throws the gun on
the ground.

> HERBIE
> I quit! This ain't gettin' me
> no place.

Collins, restraining his temper, picks up Herbie's gun and
hands it to him.

> COLLINS
> Attention!

The men line up.

128   FULL SHOT

> COLLINS
> Right face!

The men wheel right - Smitty's gun hits Herbie on head.

> COLLINS
> Left face!

This command brings Smitty and other men in line with
Herbie and facing Collins.

> COLLINS
> (getting Herbie
> into line)
> When I give you a command, execute it.
> (raises voice -
> to others)
> Right face - Right face!

CONTINUED

128   CONTINUED

The other men turn right, but Herbie is still feeling his
head and does not turn. Collins is walking toward head of
line and does not notice that Herbie has not turned.

                    COLLINS
          Forward -- march!

129   MED. SHOT

The other men walk one way - Herbie marches forward.
Collins turns and sees the situation.

                    COLLINS
          Detail - Halt!

He studies the set-up.

                    COLLINS
          Right face - forward march!

Smitty and the men march one way - Herbie the other. As
they are almost even, Collins gives the order.

                    COLLINS
          Detail - Halt!

He looks at the situation with disgust.

                    COLLINS
          Right face. Forward march!

The other men march forward. Herbie marches other way.

                    HERBIE
                 (as they pass)
          Hi'ya, fellows.

                    COLLINS
                 (angrily)
          Detail - Halt! Right face!

The men comply.

                    COLLINS
          Right face!

Sees that other men are facing away from him and Herbie is
facing toward him.

                    COLLINS
          Forward march!

                                        CONTINUED

129   CONTINUED

The men march and as they are about to pass each other, the
Sergeant speaks:

                              COLLINS
                    Detail - Halt!

Men comply and he studies situation.

                              COLLINS
                    Right face. Forward march!

Herbie marches right into Smitty.

                              COLLINS
                         (quickly)
                    Detail - Halt!

Men stop.

                              COLLINS
                    Left face!

The men turn, which leaves the men and Smitty with their
backs to him and Herbie facing him again. Collins scratches
his head and has a bright idea.

                              COLLINS
                    Right face!

As Herbie starts to turn, the Sergeant grabs him and keeps
him from moving.

                              COLLINS
                    Right face -
                         (men comply)
                    Right face -
                         (men comply)
                    Right face -
                         (men comply)

Collins sighs with relief as he realizes the men are all in
their proper positions.

                              HERBIE
                         (to Collins)
                    Boy, we sure have a time with
                    these dumb guys!

Collins gives him a look of complete exasperation.

                                        DISSOLVE TO:

130   EXT. "K" COMPANY STREET - MED. SHOT

A group of company "K" men, including Smitty, Herbie,
Randolph, Bob, Dick, Henry and Briggs, are gathered around
watching Sergeant Collins demonstrate the proper way to
roll an army pack. CAMERA MOVES in to CENTER the
Sergeant as he speaks.

                    COLLINS
          Some of you boys have been getting
          away with murder the way you roll
          your packs. Now I'm going to show
          you the right way for the last time.
          You start with the shelter half -
          fold it like this....

He folds the pack quickly and efficiently.

                    COLLINS (to Herbie and Smitty)
          Did you see how I rolled this pack?

                    HERBIE
          Oh - very neatly.

                    COLLINS
                  (ominously)
          Okay. Come over here and do it.

The rest of the men watch, amused, as Smitty and Herbie
go over to Collins, who unrolls the pack and dumps the
stuff on the ground.

                    HERBIE
          This is a fine thing for the army
          to give anybody.

                    SMITTY
          What do you mean?

                    HERBIE
          By the time a guy got this together,
          he'd be too tired to fight.

                    COLLINS
          Come on - roll it up.

                    HERBIE
                  (fumbling with
                   equipment)
          Well - I'm trying.

                    COLLINS
                  (shaking his head)
          How can you be so stupid?

                    HERBIE
          Well - it ain't easy.

131   GROUP SHOT - CENTERING RANDOLPH

        SOUND of automobile horn comes OVER. The men, in-
        cluding Randolph, glance out of SCENE.

        CAMERA SWINGS to FOLLOW an expensive custom-built
        automobile that is chauffeur driven. In the back seat
        is RANDOLPH PARKER, II, a distinguished looking gentleman
        of about fifty.

132   MED. CLOSE SHOT - GROUP - CENTERING RANDOLPH

                        RANDOLPH
                     (involuntarily)
        Dad!

                        HENRY
        That your father?

                        RANDOLPH
        In the flesh. Goodbye, boys -- it's
        been nice knowing you.

        Randolph starts out of SCENE.

                        COLLINS' VOICE
        Where you going, Parker?

133   WIDER SHOT - THE GROUP

                        RANDOLPH
                   (turning back to group)
        I just saw my father drive by and I....

                        COLLINS
        Wait until this instruction period's over.

        Randolph hesitates, shrugs, moves back to the group.

                                        DISSOLVE TO:

134   GROUP SHOT - FEATURING SMITTY AND HERBIE

        They have finally whipped the army pack together. It is
        a mess.

                        COLLINS
        All right - on his back.

                        HERBIE
        Oh - now I got to play piggy back?

                        COLLINS
                     (disgusted)
        No - not you - the pack.

                                        CONTINUED

134   CONTINUED

Herbie starts to put the pack on Smitty's back but gets the
shoulder straps so confused that while Smitty's arms are in
it, Herbie's are, too. Smitty, impatient at Herbie's fumbling,
yells:

SMITTY
Will you let go?

He bends forward to pull himself away. In so doing, he
tosses Herbie over his head, directly into Collins' arms.
Collins gives him a look of disgust and drops him.

135   WIDER SHOT - AT EDGE OF GROUP

A motorcycle dispatch bearer comes up, swings off his
machine. He goes to Sergeant Collins and presents him with
a message. Collins glances at it, then looks up.

COLLINS
Private Parker!

Randolph walks over to him.

RANDOLPH
Yes, Sergeant...

COLLINS
Report to General Emerson immediately.

RANDOLPH
Yes, Sergeant.....

He gives Bob and the other squad members a know-it-all
smile and follows the dispatch bearer to his machine.

136   MED. CLOSE SHOT - AT MOTORCYCLE

As Randolph climbs into sidecar and dispatch bearer starts
the machine. Randolph gives a mocking wave of his hand to
the men o.s.

WIPE TO:

137   INT. MAJOR GENERAL EMERSON'S OFFICE - FULL SHOT

Mr. Parker, Captain Williams and General Emerson are
present. The General is seated behind his desk, the Captain
nearby and Mr. Parker is standing before him. He appears
to have lost his temper as he speaks quite heatedly.

CONTINUED

137   CONTINUED

> MR. PARKER
> General Emerson, I agree with every-
> thing you've said, but this boy is
> my son.

> GENERAL EMERSON
> (calmly)
> I understand, Mr. Parker, but our
> policy in all these matters is.....

> MR. PARKER
> (interrupting)
> I know what your policy is -- I
> helped make it in Washington.

General Emerson looks at Captain Williams - they sigh -
shrug their shoulders.

> GENERAL EMERSON
> All right, Mr. Parker -- we'll try
> to see it your way.

There is a KNOCK at the door.

> GENERAL EMERSON
> Come in.

138   MED. CLOSE SHOT - AT DOOR

It opens and Randolph steps in. He salutes.

> RANDOLPH
> Private Parker reporting, sir.

> GENERAL EMERSON'S VOICE
> At ease.

Randolph relaxes and CAMERA PANS with him as he goes over
to the other men.

> RANDOLPH
> Hello, dad!

> MR. PARKER
> Hello, son!

He moves to Randolph and they shake hands affectionately.

139   MED. CLOSE SHOT - MR. PARKER AND RANDOLPH

> MR. PARKER
> (looking over Randolph)
> You're looking better than your
> letters intimated.

CONTINUED

139   CONTINUED

                RANDOLPH
     Oh, I feel fine - but I thought
     you'd forgotten me.

                MR. PARKER
           (with a wry smile)
     Your mother didn't give me a
     chance. I came down here as soon
     as I could.

                RANDOLPH
           (lower tone)
     Have you -- fixed it up?

                MR. PARKER
           (in same tone)
     I had a little difficulty -- but
     it's all taken care of.

                RANDOLPH
           (relieved)
     That's fine. Why don't you have
     the General show you around the
     camp while I get out of this uniform
     and into my civvies.

140   MED. SHOT - THE GROUP

                MR. PARKER
     I can't.

                RANDOLPH
           (puzzled)
     Why not?

                MR. PARKER
     Because I've got to return to
     Washington at once -- and because
     you're not getting out of that
     uniform.

Randolph looks around, bewildered.

                RANDOLPH
     But dad, you just said --

                MR. PARKER
           (interrupting)
     That I'd just fixed everything up?
           (with grim smile)
     Well, I <u>have</u>.

                                  CONTINUED

140   CONTINUED

> GENERAL EMERSON
> (to Randolph)
> It seems that your father has a
> little more respect for army life
> and army institutions than you have.

> CAPTAIN WILLIAMS
> We were quite ready to cooperate
> with Washington authorities, but....

> MR. PARKER
> (interrupting)
> But I talked them out of it. This
> camp may be a little short on sport
> roadsters and chorus girls but it's
> excellently equipped to make a man
> out of a playboy. You're going to
> stay here the full year and like it!

141   CLOSE SHOT - RANDOLPH

His mouth practically drops open as he gets the full import
of his father's words.

> FADE OUT.

FADE IN:

MUSICAL NUMBER (#3) - "APPLE BLOSSOM TIME"

142   EXT. ROAD NEAR CAMP - (NIGHT) - MED. CLOSE SHOT

CAMERA TRUCKS with approximately a group of soldiers as they
stroll along, singing "Apple Blossom Time." As they round
the bend of the road, the three Andrews Sisters are seated
on the fence, enjoying the moonlight.

143   MED. CLOSE SHOT - ANDREWS SISTERS

As they join in the song, with the MALE CHORUS furnishing
the accompaniment.

144)
145)   SHOTS TO INTERCUT WITH ABOVE
146)

147   EXT. HILLTOP - MED. CLOSE SHOT - RANDOLPH AND JUDY

They are seated, also enjoying the lovely night. OVER this
entire SCENE the HUMMING of the male chorus continues.

> RANDOLPH
> Did I remember to say thanks for
> keeping this date?

CONTINUED

147   CONTINUED

                              JUDY
                    Mere curiosity.

                              RANDOLPH
                                   (puzzled)
                    Curiosity?

                              JUDY
                    Yes .. why a certain soldier decided
                    to stay in the army. That's gossip
                    item number one in camp today.

Randolph gives her a quizzical glance.

                              RANDOLPH
                    Maybe he wanted to be near you.

                              JUDY
                    Of course, it couldn't be because he
                    decided the army might do him some
                    good?

                              RANDOLPH
                    What good?

148   CLOSE TWO SHOT - JUDY AND RANDOLPH (FAVORING JUDY)

                              JUDY
                    My dad had some pretty fair ideas
                    about that. He was a captain in the
                    Fighting 69th.

                              RANDOLPH
                    Maybe he'll tell me some day.

                              JUDY
                                   (soberly)
                    He died at Chateau Thierry --
                    rescuing a wounded private in no
                    man's land.

                              RANDOLPH
                                   (honestly)
                    I'm sorry.

                              JUDY
                    I remember mother telling me how he
                    believed army life changed boys
                    into men. He always said it was
                    the great leveler -- it doesn't care
                    how much a man has in the bank --
                    or how little .. all the army cares
                    about is how much of a man -- a man
                    can be.
                                             CONTINUED

148   CONTINUED

                    BOB'S VOICE
          You're wasting your breath on him,
          Judy.

They look up and CAMERA PULLS BACK as Bob enters
SCENE.

                    BOB
                    (to Randolph)
          Captain Williams' compliments -- and
          the Captain wishes to see you in his
          tent at once.

                    RANDOLPH
          My respects to the Captain, and I'm
          not dumb enough to fall for that old
          gag again. On your way, fellow.

                    BOB
          This is as far as I go.

He sits next to Judy.

                    RANDOLPH
                    (belligerently)
          I said, on your way!

                    BOB
          And I said - this is as far as I go.

                    RANDOLPH
                    (sighing)
          All right, we'll just act like you're
          not here.
                    (turns to Judy)
          Now about Sunday - how do you think
          we should start the day?

                    BOB
          Forget it - Judy's promised to spend
          her day off with me.

                    RANDOLPH
          Why don't we let Judy decide?

Before Judy can answer, Collins' voice interrupts.

                    COLLINS' VOICE (o.s.)
          Private Martin, did you tell Private
          Parker the Captain wanted to see him?

149   MED. SHOT

Bob, Judy and Randolph look up to discover Sergeant
Collins standing close to them.
                                   CONTINUED

149   CONTINUED
                              BOB
                    I did, Sergeant.

                         COLLINS
                        (to Randolph)
                    Do you need an engraved invitation,
                    or are you going to keep the Captain
                    waiting all night?

                         RANDOLPH
                        (flustered)
                    I thought he was kidding - I thought....

                         COLLINS
                    Stop thinking -- and get going!

                         RANDOLPH
                    Yes, Sergeant --

He throws a look at Bob, then hurries out of Scene. Bob
grins broadly, looking after Randolph as he hurries away.

                         COLLINS
                    And you, Martin!

                              BOB
                    Yes, Sergeant?
                         COLLINS
                    That cot of yours is a disgrace.
                    Everything out of place - blankets
                    soiled - rifle barrel dirty --

                              BOB
                    What! I'm sure I left it in order.

                         COLLINS (sarcastically)
                    I know - somebody else mussed it up.

                              BOB
                    Someone must have - I.....

                         COLLINS
                        (interrupting)
                    But you'll straighten it out!
                    On your way!

Bob glares rebelliously at the Sergeant and goes out of
SCENE.

150   MED. CLOSE SHOT - JUDY AND COLLINS

                         JUDY
                        (looking after Bob)
                    Don't tell me he needs a valet to
                    keep his things in order.

                         COLLINS
                    No - he does a good job of it
                    himself. It took me ten minutes
                    to scramble his stuff.
                        (sits beside Judy)
                    Say - isn't Sunday your day off?

Judy reacts - as we

                                        FADE OUT

150-A   INT. SQUAD TENT - MED. CLOSE SHOT - NIGHT

     Smitty is sitting on the bed, cleaning gun. Herbie is
     sitting on opposite bed, with gun beside him. He is hold-
     ing a shoe and soaking his feet in a pan of water.

                   HERBIE
           (throwing shoe to Smitty)
What shoes! My feet are killing me.

                   SMITTY
           (pulling pair of dice from
             toe of Herbie's shoe)
No wonder - look at what was in them.

                   HERBIE
How do you like that - and I thought
I had fallen arches all the time.
           (picks up his gun
             and looks at butt)
This is nice wood, ain't it?

                   SMITTY
Yeah. What is it - maple, walnut
or cherry?
                   HERBIE
It's --
           (does take)
How do I know what flavor it is? I
don't go round bitin' wood to see
what it tastes like. What do I
look like - a woodpecker?

                   SMITTY
You don't have to get sore about it.

                   HERBIE
I'm not getting sore - but every time
I talk to you I get into an argument.

                   SMITTY
Then why don't you talk to yourself?

                   HERBIE
I get too many stupid answers.

                   SMITTY
Oh why don't you go somewhere and get
wise to yourself?

                   HERBIE
I suppose you can tell me where to go?

                   SMITTY
Certainly I can. Suppose you walk into
a railroad depot and you buy a ticket.
Where are you going?

                   HERBIE
I'm not going anywhere.

                                 CONTINUED

                         SMITTY
          Then what are you buying a ticket for?

                         HERBIE
          I'm not buying a ticket.

                         SMITTY
          Then what are you doing in the depot?

                         HERBIE
          I don't know. You put me there.

                         SMITTY
          Now wait a minute. Let's get this
          right. You're in a depot. Now what
          are you doing there?

                         HERBIE
                   (very angry)
          I don't know.
                         SMITTY
          Well, what does anyone go to a depot for?

                         HERBIE
          Two or three things!

                         SMITTY
          Well, what are you doing there?

                         HERBIE
          I'm going away.

                         SMITTY
          Where are you going?

                         HERBIE
          Away.
                         SMITTY
          Away where?
                         HERBIE
                   (very angry)
          Oh - I'll go to Baltimore. I don't
          want to go, but I'll go.

                         SMITTY
          Why go to Baltimore? What's the
          matter with Philadelphia?

                         HERBIE
           Look - I picked Baltimore because I
          got friends there.

                         SMITTY
          Well, suppose you had friends in
          Philadelphia?

                         HERBIE
          Then I'd go to Philadelphia.

                                               CONTINUED

                    SMITTY
And what happens to your friends
in Baltimore?

                    HERBIE
I'm not talking to them any more.

                    SMITTY
Suppose Sergeant Collins was in
Philadelphia?

                    HERBIE
Then I'd go to Chicago.

                    SMITTY
This whole thing don't make sense.

                    HERBIE
Then why don't you ask me something
sensible?

                    SMITTY
All right. Say you're forty years
old and you're in love with a little
girl ten years old.

                    HERBIE
This is going to be a pip. Now I'm
going around with a ten-year-old girl.
I got a good idea where I'm going to
wind up.

                    SMITTY
All right, wait until I finish. You're
forty, she's ten. You're four times as
old as that girl. Now you couldn't
marry her, could you?

                    HERBIE
Not unless I came from the mountains.

                    SMITTY
Never mind that. You're forty and she's
ten. You're four times as old as that
girl. So you wait five years. Now the
little girl is fifteen, you're forty-five.
You're only three times as old as the
little girl. Now you wait fifteen years
more. The little girl is thirty and
you're sixty. Now you're only twice as
old as the little girl.

                    HERBIE
She's catching up - isn't she?

                                CONTINUED

150-A   CONTINUED - 3

                    SMITTY
        Yes. But here's the question. How
        long do you have to wait until you
        and the little girl are the same age?

                    HERBIE
        That's ridiculous. If I keep waiting
        for that girl, she'll pass me up. She'll
        wind up older than I am. Then she'll
        have to wait for me.

                    SMITTY
        Why should she wait for you?

                    HERBIE
        Well, I was good enough to wait for her.
        After all, if the girl loves me she should
        be willing to wait for me. I love the
        girl, I'll marry her.

                    SMITTY
        Do you know the girl?

                    HERBIE
        No.

                    SMITTY
        Then why should you marry a girl you
        don't even know? I'm surprised at you.
        I thought you took love seriously, but
        NO, you're one of those fellows who
        wears his heart on his sleeve. You're
        willing to marry the first girl that
        comes along.

                    HERBIE
        I'm a bad boy.

        He starts to push the pail of water under the bed.

                    SMITTY
        Ahhhh - throw out that pail of water
        and go to bed!

        Herbie sighs, picks up the pail of water and heaves it
        out toward the open tent flap.

150-B   MED. CLOSE SHOT AT TENT FLAP

        Collins comes walking through into the tent just as the
        stream of water comes sailing from Herbie's bucket. He
        splutters and burns as the water gets him full in the
        face. Herbie takes and dives under the bed.

                                        FADE OUT:

FADE IN

151   EXT. RIFLE RANGE - <u>DAY</u> - CLOSE TWO SHOT - RANDOLPH & BOB

firing from prone position. Randolph is firing rapidly
and easily, Bob slowly and painstakingly. Randolph finishes, rises, CAMERA PANNING him to Sergeant Collins, who is
checking scores for these two targets.

                         COLLINS
              Nice shooting, Randolph.
                    (hands him score card)
              Keep this and frame it.

                         RANDOLPH
              What for? -- It isn't half as hard
              as a round of skeet.

He moves off as Bob steps up to the Sergeant.

                         BOB
              Isn't it a shame he's as good as he
              thinks he is?

                         COLLINS
              He's plenty good with a gun all
              right.
                    (hands Bob his score
                    card)
              You're not so bad yourself.

CAMERA PANS COLLINS as he starts out of SCENE.

152   MED. CLOSE TRUCKING SHOT

LEADING Collins as he comes to two scoring desks. Thumb-
tacked to the desks are cardboard squares, lettered "K"
and "L." At one desk is Callahan, at the adjoining desk is
top SERGEANT MARKS of "L" Company.

                         CALLAHAN
              How are the men doing?

                         COLLINS
              Best in the regiment.

                         MARKS
              Oh, yeah? -- I've got some Tennessee
              boys in my company that can shoot the
              spots out of the five of spades at
              three hundred yards.

                         COLLINS
              Baby stuff! My boys can stand five
              hundred yards from a deck of cards and
              shuffle 'em!

                                              CONTINUED

152   CONTINUED

                              MARKS
                    Maybe you'd like to cook up a
                    five-man match?

                              COLLINS
                    Any day you want!

                              VOICE
                         (o.s. - calling)
                    Sergeant Marks!

                              MARKS
                    Coming!
                         (to Collins)
                    How about Sunday afternoon?

                              COLLINS
                    It's a date.

                              MARKS
                    See you later.

He exits.

                              CALLAHAN
                    Do you think we can take them?

                              COLLINS
                    Look at the scores -- with Parker
                    shooting number one, we'll top them
                    by fifty points.

                                        DISSOLVE TO

153   INT. TENT - MED. FULL SHOT - DAY

Briggs and Henry are busy cleaning their guns. Dick is
writing some music on a score sheet. Bob is sewing up a
hole in his sock. Smitty enters the tent.

                              SMITTY
                    Well, boys, our fortunes are made --
                    every dime in the company is on that
                    rifle match tomorrow -- over five
                    hundred bucks.

                              BRIGGS
                    Including my dollar and a half?

                              SMITTY
                    Including the works. We're all in
                    except Randolph.

                                        CONTINUED

153   CONTINUED

                              DICK
                    What's the matter? Won't he bet
                    on himself?

                              SMITTY
                    He doesn't know about the betting --
                    Collins said not to tell him.

                              DICK
                    Why not?

                              SMITTY
                    In the first place, he's got
                    too much money, and in the
                    second place, there isn't enough
                    "L" Company money to cover his
                    idea of a small bet.

                              BOB
                    What odds did you get?

                              SMITTY
                    I just collected the dough --
                    Herbie's placing it. Those "L"
                    Company guys will feel so sorry
                    for him and his baby face that
                    they'll maybe give him five to
                    four or seven to five.

                              HERBIE'S VOICE
                    What do you mean? -- Five to four
                    or seven to five?

154   MED. CLOSE SHOT - THE TENT FLAP

        as Herbie comes in.

                              HERBIE
                    I gave those push-overs the
                    business - I got us a _real_
                    set-up.

155   MED. SHOT

        as the others surround Herbie.

                              SMITTY
                    You did, huh?

                              HERBIE
                    I'll say I did. I got ten
                    to one.

                                                      CONTINUED

155   CONTINUED

AD LIBS

Ten to one!
What did you do -- hypnotize them?
Will they be sorry!
Herbie, you're a genius!
Etc.

SMITTY

That's terrific! I was afraid
we'd have to settle for even
money.

HERBIE

It just took a little handling.
I told those "L" Company fellows
how good our team was and they
insisted on ten to one.

SMITTY

Insisted, huh?

HERBIE

Yes, sir -- forced it on me!
Why, we'll be plutocrats! Ten
to one!

SMITTY
(with sudden
suspicion)
Ten to one, uh, who put up
the ten?

HERBIE
(brightly)
I did. Ten bucks of our to one
of theirs -- ten to one.

The boys react as Smitty gives Herbie a push in the face
that sends him sprawling.

156   CLOSE SHOT - HERBIE

As he does a back flip and lands against wall of tent.

HERBIE
(plaintively)
Now what did I do?

DISSOLVE TO

157   EXT. "K" COMPANY STREET - (DAY) - CLOSE SHOT -
       BULLETIN BOARD

       Various notices are thumb-tacked on this board. CAMERA MOVES
       in CENTERING notice, reading.

                    THE FIVE MEN WITH THE HIGHEST SCORES WILL
                    COMPOSE THE "K" COMPANY TEAM IN THE MATCH
                    WITH "L" COMPANY

                    THE MATCH WILL START AT ONE O'CLOCK
                    SUNDAY AFTERNOON

       CAMERA PANS OVER to typewritten list, headed:

                    INDIVIDUAL RIFLE SCORES

       The list starts off:

                    1.   Private Randolph Parker
                    2.   Sergeant Michael Collins
                    3.   Private Edward Briggs
                    4.   Private Jesse Tow
                    5.   Private Henry Sloan

                         Alternate:
                    6.   Act. Corp. Robert Martin

       A hand comes INTO SCENE and travels down to the sixth name.
       We IRIS DOWN to CENTER the finger and the sixth name - Bob's.

158   CLOSE SHOT - RANDOLPH

       standing by bulletin board, his finger on the list. An idea
       comes to him and he smiles, thoughtfully. CAMERA ANGLES
       BACK to INCLUDE Sergeant Collins, Henry and Briggs as they
       walk into SCENE and look at bulletin board.

                         COLLINS
                    How's your trigger-finger?

                         RANDOLPH
                       (flexing his fingers)
                    I haven't made up my mind yet.

                         COLLINS
                    We're all banking on you to win for us.

                         RANDOLPH
                       (drily)
                    Thanks.

       He goes OUT OF SCENE as the men look after him, puzzled and
       disturbed.

                                              DISSOLVE TO:

159   OMITTED
160   OMITTED

161   OMITTED

162   EXT. RECREATION HALL - (DAY) - MED. CLOSE SHOT - JUDY

        as she comes from recreation hall, looks around for Bob.

                         RANDOLPH'S VOICE
                          (Southern style)
                Good afternoon, ma'am. You-all
                goin' my way?

        CAMERA PULLS BACK to INCLUDE Randolph who has been standing
        to one side of the door. His right wrist is bandaged.

                         JUDY
                Oh - hello.

                                        CONTINUED

162   CONTINUED

She continues to look around.

                        RANDOLPH
            If you're waiting for Bob - he
            won't be around to keep his date.

                        JUDY
            I know - the Captain wanted to see him.

                        RANDOLPH
            No - he's shooting with the company
            rifle team. Hear 'em?

163   CLOSE TWO SHOT - RANDOLPH AND JUDY

They both listen. Faintly, from a distance, comes the
SOUND of intermittent rifle fire.

                        JUDY
            I thought you were the star of
            the team.

                        RANDOLPH
            I was -- until this morning, and
            then the strangest thing happened --
                    (indicating arm)
            -- to my wrist.

Judy looks at him suspiciously.

                        RANDOLPH
                    (blandly)
            I could hardly move it. When I told
            Captain Williams -- he replaced me
            with the sixth man on the score sheet.

                        JUDY
                    (keenly)
            And Bob was the sixth man, of course?

                        RANDOLPH
            Of course.

                        JUDY
            How does your wrist feel now?

He gives her a wise grin, as he unrolls the bandage from his
wrist and tosses it aside.

                        RANDOLPH
            What do you think?

                        JUDY
                    (her temper rising)
            And you walked out on your rifle team -
            just to chisel a date with me? Is
            that it?
                                            CONTINUED

                              RANDOLPH
            You're a lot more interesting than
            any target around this camp.
                         (possessively)
            I've borrowed a station wagon from
            Service Company --it's parked just
            around the corner --

164   CLOSE TWO SHOT - FAVORING JUDY

                                JUDY
            You think of everything, don't you?

                              RANDOLPH
            Well - I try...

                                JUDY
            - everything but loyalty to the boys
            who counted on you.

                              RANDOLPH
                         (lightly)
            Oh - come on! What's a riflematch?

        Judy looks at him and shakes her head.

                                JUDY
            You ought to write a book -- "How to
            Lose Friends and Infuriate People"....

                              RANDOLPH
                         (still lightly)
            I did it all for you.

                                JUDY
            I'm not flattered! The men you sold
            out -- your company -- bet every cent
            they had on the team, on you!

                              RANDOLPH
            I didn't know that -- but I'll square
            whatever they lost.

                                JUDY
                         (sarcastically)
            With what? Money?

                              RANDOLPH
            Of course.

                                JUDY
            Everything's just so much money to
            you, isn't it? Well, let me tell
            you one thing -- there's no price
            tag on loyalty or friendship.

                              RANDOLPH
                         (getting mad)
            I didn't ask for this uniform --
            why should I take it seriously?

                                                  CONTINUED

                              JUDY
                           (with bite)
             Sure -- they're all out of step but
             Randolph -- Randolph Parker the third.
             You've got a fancy name and fancy
             ideas. It's time somebody knocked
             them out of you.

                           RANDOLPH
             Now, Judy --

                              JUDY
                       (as if he hadn't
                        interrupted)
             After what you did today, the only
             friend you'll have in camp is the guy
             that looks at you out of a mirror.
             And if he had any sense, he'd keep as
             far away from you as I'm going to.

165   WIDER SHOT

       as Judy turns on her heel and goes into the recreation hall.

                           RANDOLPH
             Now wait a minute --

       He starts after her, reaching the door just in time to have
       it slammed in his face. He turns away from the door, angry
       at first, then with a look of indecision coming over his
       face. SOUND of rifle match grows louder. Randolph listens
       to it, not as satisfied with himself as he has been. He
       moves away from the building.

166   INT. RECREATION HALL - NEAR DOOR - (OR WINDOW) -
       MED. CLOSE SHOT - JUDY

       looking out toward Randolph who is out of SCENE. Patty
       comes into the SHOT, stands looking in same direction as
       Judy.

                           PATTY
             So you fell for him after all.

                           JUDY
             Fell for him? I just told him off!

                           PATTY
                         (knowingly)
             That's what I mean.

                           JUDY
                         (dissembling)
             Do you think I'd talk like that to
             a man I - liked?

                                        CONTINUED

166   CONTINUED

> PATTY
> You wouldn't waste that much effort
> on a man you <u>didn't</u>!

CAMERA MOVES IN for a CLOSE TWO SHOT. For a moment, Judy
is about to deny Patty's charge, then a look of doubt
comes over her face.

>>>>>> DISSOLVE TO:

167   INT. SQUAD TENT - <u>NIGHT</u> - FULL SHOT

In addition to the members of the squad (excepting
Randolph and Collins) - several other soldiers are
present. Henry is glumly cleaning his rifle. Herbie is
listening to a portable radio, which continues to PLAY
softly throughout SCENE.

> HENRY
> Well, we doggone near beat 'em
> at that.

> SMITTY
> And I'll bet we have doggone
> near thirty cents left in the
> company.

> DICK
> Too bad Randolph hurt his wrist.

> BOB
> (tartly)
> Too bad it couldn't have been his
> head.

168   OMITTED

169   MED. SHOT - THE GROUP

They all turn as Briggs comes running into tent.

> BRIGGS
> (grimly)
> What do you think I just found out?

> BOB
> (drily)
> "L" Company is sorry we lost and
> they won't take our money?

> BRIGGS
> No. I found out nothing was wrong
> with Randolph's wrist. He spent
> half the afternoon playing billiards
> in the recreation hall.

>>>>>> CONTINUED

169   CONTINUED

                              BOYS
                            (ad lib)
                    Well, what do you know!
                    Of all the tricks!
                    So that's the kind of a guy he is!

                              SMITTY
                    And on account of a rat like him,
                    we gotta go broke till payday!

                              HERBIE
                    Ten paydays for me.

          CAMERA PANS SLIGHTLY to PICK UP Randolph, who has entered
          tent in time to hear last line.

                              RANDOLPH
                    Say, boys --

          They look at him, then elaborately look away.

170   GROUP SHOT - CENTERING RANDOLPH

          as he comes over to them.

                              RANDOLPH
                    I'm sorry we lost the rifle
                    match.....

                              HENRY
                    What do you mean -- we?

                              RANDOLPH
                    And I want you to let me make
                    good your losses. Tell me how
                    much you dropped.

          He pulls out a well-filled wallet. There is silence
          for a moment, then:

                                                    CONTINUED

170   CONTINUED

                              SOLDIER
                             (rising)
                    Think I'll take a walk -- there's
                    a strange smell around here.

        He exits, followed by the other visiting soldiers.

171   CLOSE SHOT - RANDOLPH

        As he watches them go - then turns to look at the others.

172   MED. SHOT

        The men in the tent are obviously turned away from Randolph.

                              RANDOLPH
                             (to everyone
                              in tent)
                    I said I was sorry - I apologize.
                    What do you want me to do -- rub
                    my nose in the dirt?

                              HENRY
                    No - wise guy -- we want to do
                    that for you!

        He makes a lunge for Randolph, but Bob jumps in between,
        grabs Henry.

                              BOB
                    Lay off, Henry -- don't sock him.

                              HENRY
                    Why not?

                              BOB
                    Because he's mine!

        He pushes Henry aside, turns and smacks Randolph, knocking
        him backwards over a cot.

173   MED. CLOSE TWO SHOT - RANDOLPH AND HERBIE

        as Randolph picks himself up.

                              HERBIE
                    Give him ten to one for me.

        CAMERA PANS with Randolph as he throws himself on Bob,
        and a terrific fight starts.

174
175
176   PICKUP SHOTS - FIGHT
177
178   With first Bob and then Randolph gaining the advantage.

179   CLOSE SHOT - AT FLAP OF TENT

Herbie peeps out. Then turns to others in tent.

> HERBIE
> Jiggers, the sergeant!

He turns just in time to catch a wild blow on his eye.

180   FULL SHOT - THE TENT

Randolph and Bob stop their brawl.

> RANDOLPH
> We'll finish this later!

> BOB
> You mean, I will!

All the men scramble toward their cots, get in bed and
pull their blankets over them.

> SMITTY
> Herbie - the light!

Herbie races for the lantern. (The electric light on
tent pole)

181   CLOSE SHOT - HERBIE

standing on tiptoe, he turns off the light.

182   MED. CLOSE SHOT - AT ENTRANCE TO TENT

as Sergeant Collins enters.

> COLLINS
> (angrily)
> What kind of a brawl s going on
> in here?
> (looks around, spies
> some one, then speaks
> ominously)
> Come on outta there!

183   MED. SHOT

ANGLING PAST Sergeant Collins to Herbie, who is trying to
hide behind tent pole. Sergeant Collins moves to him.

                         COLLINS
            I might have known it was you!

                         HERBIE
                        (quickly)
            Not me. I wasn't fighting. I had
            nothing to do with it.

184   CLOSE TWO SHOT - HERBIE AND COLLINS

                         COLLINS
            Yeah - that's how you got the eye!

Herbie turns his head and we see he has a terrific shiner.
He puts his hand up to it and winces. He begins to cry.

                         COLLINS
            Pipe down! You're shot full of luck
            that I don't put you on K.P.

Sergeant exits from the tent. Herbie gives a hopeless
shrug, moves over to his cot.

                         HERBIE
            What a life! What an army! And what
            a Sergeant to be in that army!

He sits by the radio, turns it up so that it is playing
a bit loudly.

185   EXT. COMPANY STREET - NIGHT - MED. CLOSE SHOT - COLLINS

Checking the tent ropes. He is about to move on when
SOUND of radio comes over. He straightens up, reacts
and reenters the tent.

186   INT. TENT - MED. SHOT

as Collins enters.

                         COLLINS
            Who's playing that radio?

                         HERBIE
            Nobody - it plays by itself.

                                        CONTINUED

186   CONTINUED

COLLINS
Turn it off. The boys have to be
up at six in the morning.

Herbie gives an "must I <u>always</u> be wrong?" shrug. Collins
exits from the tent.

187   MED. CLOSE TWO SHOT - HERBIE AND SMITTY

SMITTY
Aw - don't listen to him - go on -
play it.

HERBIE
(meekly)
You heard what he said.

SMITTY
Don't pay any attention to that guy -
go on play the radio - play it loud!

Herbie turns on the radio.

188   EXT. "K" COMPANY STREET - <u>NIGHT</u> - MED. CLOSE SHOT -
SERGEANT COLLINS

He is walking away from the tent when the radio MUSIC
starts again. He does a burn and CAMERA PANS with him
as he turns and goes back to tent.

189   INT. SQUAD TENT - MED. CLOSE SHOT - SMITTY AND HERBIE

As Collins comes into SCENE

COLLINS
What did I tell you? Didn't I tell
you the boys were sleeping -- didn't
I tell you they've got to get up in
the morning?
(with final
emphasis)
Now, don't play it!

Herbie goes over and turns off radio. Collins exits.
Herbie starts back to his cot.

SMITTY
Go on - play it.

CONTINUE D

189   CONTINUED

                         HERBIE
            What's the matter with you? You
            heard what the guy said, didn't you?

                         SMITTY
            You're an American citizen, aren't you?

                         HERBIE
            Yes.

                         SMITTY
            This is a free country, isn't it?

                         HERBIE
            Yes.

                         SMITTY
            Go on - play it.

Herbie goes over and turns on radio.

190   EXT. "K" COMPANY STREET - MED. SHOT - SERGEANT COLLINS

The Sergeant is just walking past the tent. He hears
the MUSIC - does a burn - turns quickly and runs into
the tent.

191   INT. SQUAD TENT - MED. SHOT

AS Collins enters quickly and grabs Herbie.

                         COLLINS
            Didn't I tell you not to play that
            thing?
                    (Herbie nods)
            Didn't I tell you the boys were
            sleeping?
                    (Herbie nods)
            Well, what are you going to do about
            it?

Herbie kisses him on the cheek - Collins pushes him away.

                         COLLINS
            Look, Brown, I don't like wise guys
            and the next wise remark out of
            you - somebody's going to punch you
            in the nose.

Collins turns to exit.

                                        CONTINUED

191   CONTINUED

                          SMITTY
            I'd like to see you do it.

                          COLLINS
                     (turning quickly)
            I'll do it all right.
                     (grabs Herbie by
                     shoulder)
            Why don't you be quiet?
                     (indicating Smitty)
            - like your buddy here?
                     (to Herbie)
            Now remember - one more remark
            and I'll punch you in the nose.
                     (turns to exit)

                          SMITTY
            Yes, you will.

       Collins turns and grabs Herbie.

192   MED. CLOSE SHOT - COLLINS AND HERBIE

                          COLLINS
            Yes, I will!

       He gives Herbie a good shaking and as he starts away,
       Herbie grabs him by the shoulders.

                          HERBIE
            Trying to get away, uh?

       Collins looks at Herbie wearily - turns off the radio
       set and moves to go.

                          COLLINS
            I don't know what the army's coming
            to.

                          HERBIE
            Neither do I.

       Collins whirls around and believing Smitty has made the
       last remark, grabs him up.

                          COLLINS
            Sticking your nose into this, uh?
            Okay - you both get K.P. duty
            tomorrow morning.

       As Smitty and Herbie look at each other mournfully, we

                                        DISSOLVE TO:

193   INT. CORNER OF KITCHEN - DAY - GROUP SHOT

Smitty and Herbie, as well as a half dozen other soldiers,
are peeling a high pile of onions. A radio is playing softly.

                        HERBIE
            Where's a piece of writing paper?
            What's the address of the President
            of the United States?

                        SMITTY
            Now what's the matter?

                        HERBIE
            I'm gonna give in my notice. I'm tired
            of this army business. If you want to
            do this, they make you do that. If you
            want to do that, they make you do this.
            If you want to stay up, they make you go
            to bed. If you want to stay in bed, they
            make you get up. If you don't get up,
            they stick a bugle in your ear....
                    (does bugle call)
            - AND MAKE YOU GET UP! -- I'm going
            wacky in khaki!

Herbie looks o.s. - spots somebody, quickly sticks his hand
inside the pile of onions and the MUSIC stops. A moment
later Collins walks through SCENE.

                        COLLINS
                    (toughly)
            Did I hear a radio in here?

                        HERBIE
            Oh no, sergeant.

                        COLLINS
            I better not.

He goes o.s. Herbie turns and parts the pile of onions
with his two hands, disclosing the radio buried among
the onions. He turns it on again.

MUSICAL NUMBER (#4) "WHEN PRIVATE BROWN BECOMES A CAPTAIN"

194   HERBIE
195   That Sergeant always makes me boil
196   I'd like to fry the guy in oil
197   No matter what you do, he's always squawkin'....
198   But, you just wait, and don't forget
        I'll get to be a Captain yet
        And that's the day that I'll do all the talkin'....

                        SOLDIERS
        Three cheers for the Red, White and Captain Brown
        Hep....Hep....Hep....Hooray....

                                        CONTINUED

194
to
198

CONTINUED

HERBIE

When I become a Captain
The title will be strictly unofficial
You won't find me high-falutin'
Forget about salutin'
Just step up and call me by my first initial....

SOLDIERS

Three cheers for the Red, White and Captain B...
Hep....Hep....Hep....Hooray....

HERBIE

When I become a Captain
There'll be no reveille to spoil your slumber
There'll be no more K.P. duties
We'll draft a bunch of cuties
And, instead of doing drills, we'll do the rhumba....

SOLDIERS

Three cheers for the Red, White and Captain Brown
Hep.....Hep....Hep....Hooray....

SOLDIER

Well, say, just what do you think is wrong with this army??

HERBIE

I'm glad you asked me that, my friend, and I can
   tell you in two words .... Puh ------- lenty!!

The way I see it:

There's too much cold, and too much heat...
Too many M.P.'s walkin' the beat,
Too many hikes, too many marches,
Too many feet with fallen arches,
Too much water in the soup
Too many pairs of pants that droop...
         (Herbie catches his breath)
Too many orders, too many drills
Iodine and C.C. pills
Too much mud and too much rain
Too many aches and too much pain
Too many blisters and too many corns
Too many drums and too many horns
         (Herbie catches his breath)
Too much workin' like a slave
Too many spuds that need a shave
Too many rules and too much law,
And, well, it's the darndest mess I ever saw....

CONTINUED

194 CONTINUED
to
198

SOLDIERS

Three cheers for the Red, White and Captain Brown --

Sergeant Collins comes in behind Herbie during above line
and soldiers stop singing.

HERBIE

Hep ... Hep ... Hep ... Hooray ... (stops singing as he
                            sees Collins)

COLLINS

So! You wanta be a Captain?
    (Herbie nods sheepishly)
Well, I just had a talk with the
General about you, and we decided
that we ought to make you an Admiral.

HERBIE

Oh .. an Admiral? Gee, do they
have Admirals in the army?

COLLINS

Why, sure! We're going to put you
in charge of all the vessels!

HERBIE

Oh, boy!!

DISSOLVE TO:

198-A INT. KITCHEN - DAY - CLOSE SHOT - HERBIE
disconsolately drying a mountain-high pile of pots and pans.

HERBIE

Vessels!

FADE OUT

FADE IN

198-B EXT. RECREATION HALL - NIGHT - CLOSE SHOT
ON sign tacked near door. It reads: "BOXING TONIGHT".
CAMERA SWINGS to door as a few soldiers go inside. OVER
SCENE can be heard CHEERS.

198-C INT. RECREATION HALL - NIGHT - FULL SHOT

The dance floor has been converted into a boxing ring,
which is surrounded by soldiers. A hell-for-leather bout
is just finishing. In b.g., on a band stand, are Dick and
the camp orchestra enjoying the fight and occasionally vent-
ing their enthusiasm with a drum ROLL - or saxophone scale.

199 MED. CLOSE SHOT - AT ENTRANCE

AS Randolph comes in. Henry and Briggs turn and give him
a side-long glance.

RANDOLPH
  (very friendly)
Hi'ya, fellows.

CONTINUED

199   CONTINUED

Henry and Briggs look at each other knowingly, then go on.
Randolph shrugs, spots someone o.s. CAMERA PANS with him
as he starts across room.

200   MED. CLOSE SHOT - JUDY

watching fight, as Randolph comes into SCENE.

                    RANDOLPH
                    (honestly)
            Judy, can I see you a minute?

She turns, sees who it is.

                    JUDY
            Excuse me. I think I heard Miss
            Durling calling.

She moves off, leaving Randolph standing alone.

201   MED. CLOSE SHOT - FIGHT RING

The army ATHLETIC INSTRUCTOR is acting as fight announcer.
BILL McGUIRE, a skinny youngster, wearing a bathrobe is
just climbing through the ropes.

                    INSTRUCTOR
            Next bout -- four rounds - Private
            Bill McGuire of "E" Company vs
            Private Eddie Anders of "K" Company.

A CHEER goes up from the crowd. Into the ring comes
Sergeant Collins. He goes to the instructor, whispers
in his ear.

                    INSTRUCTOR
            Correction -- Private Anders is unable
            to fight this evening --
                    VOICES
                    (from crowd)
            He's doing K.P.!
            He's fighting potatoes!

LAUGHTER from the crowd.

                    INSTRUCTOR
            Private Bill McGuire challenges any
            man his weight.

202   GROUP SHOT - "K" COMPANY MEN

seated on the ground. Among them are Smitty, Herbie
and Dick. Sergeant Collins enters SCENE.

                    INSTRUCTOR'S VOICE
                    (challengingly)
            Particularly any man from "K" Company.

203   CLOSE TWO SHOT - SMITTY & HERBIE

Surrounded by other soldiers. Smitty is just lighting a
cigarette.

                                            CONTINUED

203   CONTINUED
                              COLLINS' VOICE
                    Are we gonna let him get away with
                    <u>that</u>?

                              SMITTY
                    We certainly aren't.

He reaches over, places the lighted match in Herbie's shoe.

204   INSERT: MATCH IN HERBIE'S SHOE
The match is burning close to the shoe.

                              COLLINS' VOICE
                    Come on, men - for the honor of
                    Company "K" -- who'll volunteer?

205   GROUP SHOT
ANGLING PAST Sergeant Collins to the men.

                              COLLINS
                    I said - <u>who'll</u> <u>volunteer</u>?

                              HERBIE
                    Ye-o-W!

He leaps to his feet, clutching his foot.

                              COLLINS
                    Now you're showing some company
                    spirit, Herbie.

Collins takes him by the arm and starts off.

                              COLLINS
                         (as they go)
                    I've got some trunks just your size.
                    Military trunks.

                              HERBIE
                    Military?

                              COLLINS
                    Yeah - your stomach goes over the top.

206   MED. CLOSE SHOT
CAMERA TRUCKS with them as Collins practically pulls Herbie
through the crowd.

                              HERBIE
                    Look, Sergeant, I don't want
                    to fight this guy. I ain't even
                    mad at him.

                              COLLINS
                    What's the matter with you? Scared
                    of that little guy?

Collins indicates ring and Herbie looks over.

207   EXT. OUTDOOR ARENA - MED. CLOSE SHOT - BILL McGUIRE

        sitting in the corner of the ring.

208   TWO SHOT - HERBIE AND COLLINS

                          HERBIE
                     (gaining courage)
            Oh - that's the guy I'm gonna
            fight? Okay, keep 'im in the
            ring. He's a pushover -- a set-up.
            I can picture myself now -- the whole
            place is crowded... I step into the
            ring -- I take off my robe -- the
            crowd lets out a terrific roar.....

                          COLLINS
            What happened?

                          HERBIE
            I forgot to put on my trunks.

        Collins gives him a look and pushes him on through the
        crowd.

209   CLOSE SHOT - AT RING

        AS Dick comes over and whispers to announcer, who grins,
        Dick exits from SCENE.

                          ANNOUNCER
                     (raising voice)
            While we're waiting for Private
            Brown, you'll hear from your
            new camp orchestra -- featuring
            the one and only Andrews Sisters!

        CAMERA PANS to band stand where Dick is just resuming his
        place. Before the band stand the Andrews Sisters.

210   CLOSE SHOT - BUGLER

        He slurs into a swing break of "Boogie Woogie Bugle Boy".

        MUSICAL NUMBER (#5)   "BOOGIE WOOGIE BUGLE BOY"

211   MED. CLOSE SHOT - ORCHESTRA

        They pick up on the bugle break and go into musical
        number.

212   MED. SHOT - ANDREWS SISTERS

        AS they start singing.

        He was a famous trumpet man from out Chicago way
        He had a boogie style that no one else could play;
        He was the top man at his craft -
        But then his number came up and he was gone with the draft.
        He's in the army now a-blowin' reveille -
        He's the boogie woogie bugle boy of Company B!
        They made him blow a bugle for his Uncle Sam,
        It really brought him down because he couldn't jam;
        The Captain seemed to understand, because the next day
        The "Cap" went out and drafted a band,
        And now the Comp'ny jumps when he plays reveille --
        He's the Boogie Woogie Boy of Company B!
        A--toot! A--toot! A-toot did-le ah-dah toot,
        He blows it eight to the bar - in boogie rhythm --
        He can't blow a note unless a bass and guitar is playin' with 'im--
        He makes the Comp'ny jump when he plays reveille,
        He's the Boogie Woogie Bugle Boy of Company B!
        He puts the boys to sleep with "Boogie" ev'ry night -
        And wakes them up the same way in the early bright;
        They clap their hands and stamp their feet,
        Because they know how he plays when some one gives him a beat
        He really breaks it up when he plays reveille --
        He's the Boogie Woogie Bugle Boy of Company B.

213   FULL SHOT

        Soldiers enjoying the entertainment.

214   PICKUP SHOTS
215
216   Audience listening to musical number. As Andrews Sisters
217   conclude number, audience applauds and cheers.
218

219   MED. CLOSE SHOT

As Herbie, in trunks, comes down the aisle toward the ring,
followed by Smitty, with a pail of water and other equipment carried by a second. CAMERA TRUCKS with them. As
the boys pass the Andrews Sisters the girls jump up.

220   MED. SHOT

As the three girls practically surround Herbie.

                         PATTY
          Our hero!

                         HERBIE
                    (modestly)
          Stick around, girls - this won't
          take long.

                         MAXINE
          Get in there and win, Champ!

                         HERBIE
                    (hopefully)
          You girls don't want to kiss me for
          luck, do you?

                         LAVERNE
          Sure...
                    (Herbie wipes
                     mouth for kiss)
          ...if you win!

                         HERBIE
          Oh! Lemme at him!

He turns to run for the ring, takes two fast steps and does
a pratt fall over Smitty's bucket.

                         HERBIE
                    (getting up)
          He pulled a rabbit punch on me!
          Come on, Smitty!

Smitty follows him as he hurries to ring.

221   MED. CLOSE SHOT - THE RING - HERBIE'S CORNER

Herbie, followed by Smitty, crawls through the ropes into the
ring and takes his seat.

                    INSTRUCTOR'S VOICE
          Presenting the human buzzsaw of
          Company "K" -- Herbie Brown!

Herbie gets up from stool, takes a bow, his hands over his
head. The CROWD ROARS. As Herbie seats himself, Smitty
comes up close to him.

                                             CONTINUED

221   CONTINUED

                              SMITTY
                This is going to be a cinch. Now
                when you get him in the ring --
                          (illustrates punch)
                One -- three... One -- three...

                              HERBIE
                What happens to "two"?

                              SMITTY
                "Two" you get.

                              HERBIE
                That's what I thought.

                         INSTRUCTOR'S VOICE
                And as referee for this special event,
                Sergeant Collins of Company "K" --

        There is APPLAUSE. The WARNING BELL SOUNDS. Herbie gets
        up, takes hold of the ropes and begins to do knee bends,
        bouncing around with loads of pep.

222   MED. CLOSE SHOT - OTHER CORNER OF RING

        KAYO McGONIGLE crawls into the ring and motions to McGuire,
        who has been sitting there to scram.

                              KAYO
                You're too light for him -- so
                they put me in.

                              McGUIRE
                Say, thanks --

        Kayo takes his seat.

223   FULL SHOT - RING

        Collins is in the center, ready to referee. The BELL SOUNDS.
        Herbie completes his exercises, turns around and starts
        toward the other corner. As he sees Kayo coming toward him
        his knees begin to buckle and by the time he is in the
        center of the ring he falls down.

224   CLOSE SHOT - SMITTY

                              SMITTY
                          (yelling)
                Foul!

225   MED. CLOSE SHOT

        Collins begins to count over Herbie, who gets up at the
        count of three and takes a posing position.

                                              CONTINUED

225   CONTINUED

                         HERBIE
                    (motioning for Kayo
                    to go away)
          What do you want to come over here
          for? Look at all the room you got
          over there. What are you trying to
          do -- muscle into my territory?

                         COLLINS
          Come on, boys -- make a fight out of it.

                         HERBIE
          Okay - you asked for it.

Kayo stands motionless in the center of the ring as Herbie
shadow boxes all around him until he is almost ready to drop
from exhaustion, not laying a glove on Kayo.

                         COLLINS
                    (angrily)
          What are you doing?

                         HERBIE
           I'm tiring him out.

Kayo puts one glove on Herbie's head.

                         HERBIE
          One -- three ... One -- three...

As Herbie counts, where there should be a count of "two",
Kayo smacks Herbie one on the jaw.

                         HERBIE
                    (over shoulder to
                    Smitty o.s.)
          You were right. "Two" I get.

226   MED. CLOSE SHOT - JUDY AND BOB

Randolph comes through the crowd and manages to find a
place beside Judy.

                         BOB
                    (to Judy - with a
                    glance at Randolph)
          Funny how some people never get
          wise to themselves.

                         RANDOLPH
                    (grimly)
          Nothing like the army -- just one
          big happy family.

227   FULL SHOT - RING

As Kayo chases Herbie around ring,

CONTINUED

227   CONTINUED

                         COLLINS
              Come on, fight!

                         HERBIE
              Okay.

Herbie starts sparring with referee.

                         COLLINS
                    (indicating Kayo)
              Over there.

Herbie turns to face Kayo.

228   MED. SHOT - RING

Herbie walks toward Kayo with gloves over his face. He opens
gloves to peek at Kayo and gets   hit on the nose. This
happens three times in a row.

229   CLOSE SHOT - SMITTY - IN CORNER

                         SMITTY
              . Why don't you stop some of those
                punches?

230   MED. CLOSE SHOT - HERBIE AND KAYO

                         HERBIE
                    (over shoulder)
              You don't see any of 'em getting
                by, do you?

231   MED. GROUP SHOT - MEN OF COMPANY "K"

They ad lib CHEERS of encouragement to Herbie.

232   MED. CLOSE SHOT - RING

Kayo backs Herbie to ropes. Herbie gets his arm under rope
unconsciously and as he tries to punch Kayo, the rope catches
his arm. He can't understand why his punch doesn't reach as
far as the boxer. Kayo is doing a terrific job on Herbie
when the GONG RINGS.

                         HERBIE
              Boy, are you lucky! I was just
              gonna give it to you.

233   MED. CLOSE SHOT - HERBIE'S CORNER

Just as Herbie is about to sit down, Smitty grabs him by
the shoulders.

                         SMITTY
              What's the matter with you? Give
              it to him. What are you waiting for?

                                        CONTINUED

233   CONTINUED

Herbie tries to sink back for a little rest. Just as he is
about to reach the seat, Smitty grabs him again.

                    SMITTY
          Trying to make me look bad in there,
          uh? Give him that one-three business
          some more.

                    HERBIE
                 (wearily)
          Yeah -- I'll give it to him.

He tries to sink into the seat and again Smitty catches him.

                    SMITTY
          Now quit stalling and mix it up.

The WARNING BELL RINGS.

                    SMITTY
                 (continuing)
          How do you feel?

                    HERBIE
                 (on verge of collapse)
          Fresh as a daisy -- fit as a fiddle.

He tries to sit down and again Smitty catches him. The BELL
RINGS and Smitty turns.

                    SMITTY
          There you are -- all rested up.

Smitty takes a drink of water from the bottle in his hand,
mops his face with a towel, and starts to get out of the ring
Herbie turns to stagger toward center of ring.

234   CLOSE SHOT - KAYO

He bounces up from his stool and CAMERA PANS with him as he
rushes over toward Herbie.

235   FULL SHOT - RING

Herbie, weaving unsteadily, unconsciously steps aside and
Kayo smacks his head on the ring post. He crashes backwards
catching Collins on the chin and knocking out both himself
and the referee. Herbie walks forward in a daze as the
CROWD CHEERS - and steps through the ropes.

236   MED. CLOSE SHOT - OUTSIDE OF RING

Herbie thinks he is at the steps...He moves his leg to stand
on the the first step and falls forward on his face in a
complete arc...

                                        FADE OUT:

FADE IN:

237   EXT. DRILL GROUNDS - CLOSE SHOT - BUGLER

silhouetted against morning sky, playing "First Call."

238   INT. SQUAD TENT

Bugle CALL OVER. The men wake up, start to climb sleepily into their clothes, except Herbie.

> HERBIE
> Shut off that alarm clock!

Smitty dumps him out of bed.

WIPE TO:

239   EXT. CAPTAIN WILLIAMS' TENT - MED. SHOT

Captain Williams is speaking to Sergeant Callahan. The Sergeant salutes, turns, hurries toward CAMERA, moving on the double. CAMERA HOLDS on the Sergeant until he is at CLOSE range.

> CALLAHAN
> (directly to CAMERA)
> Full packs! Everybody with full
> packs!

He starts off hurriedly.

WIPE TO:

240   INT. SQUAD TENT - MED. SHOT - AT TENT FLAP

as Collins sticks his head in.

> COLLINS
> Fall in in five minutes with full packs!

> BOB
> Roll packs, men! Step on it!

> HERBIE
> Roll packs? It took me half the night
> to get mine apart!

WIPE TO:

241   EXT. DRILL GROUNDS - CLOSE SHOT - BUGLER

playing the bugle command "Fall In."

WIPE TO:

242   EXT. "K" COMPANY STREET - FULL SHOT

as the company falls in with full equipment. A few belated stragglers hurry to their places in line.

> CALLAHAN
> (saluting Captain)
> All present and accounted for.

CONTINUED

242   CONTINUED

                              CAPTAIN WILLIAMS
                    Take your post... Squads right --
                    March!

243   PICK-UP SHOTS (STOCK)
244
245   of the company marching.

246   EXT. COUNTRY ROAD - DAY - TRUCKING SHOT - MED. CLOSE

        ON our squad marching along.

                              HERBIE
                    I'm gonna write my Congressman
                    about this!

                              SMITTY
                    Yeah - what's the idea!

                              BRIGGS
                    A guy I know in supply company heard
                    a guy in headquarters company say
                    that the regimental sergeant major
                    said that there was some kind of a
                    hike coming up.

                              COLLINS
                    Quit talking in the ranks -- dress
                    up those lines!

247   STOCK SHOT - DAY

        Infantry company marching down the road. An airplane
        dives toward the column.

248   EXT. COUNTRY ROAD - DAY - CLOSE SHOT - CAPTAIN WILLIAMS

        as he gives three long blasts on his whistle.

249   STOCK SHOT (CONTINUATION)

        as the men scatter to shelter at the sides of the road,
        the plane swooping low over their heads. SOUND of machine
        gun OVER.

250   EXT. COUNTRY ROAD - CLOSE THREE SHOT - RANDOLPH, BOB,
        HERBIE AND SMITTY

        piled on top of each other in the ditch at the side of
        the road as they disentangle.

                              HERBIE
                    I knew I should of stood in bed!

                              BOB
                    What goes on here?

                              RANDOLPH
                         (squinting upward)
                    Looks like a sham battle to me.

                                             SWISH PAN TO:

251   STOCK SHOTS (AS AVAILABLE) - DAY
252
253   of field artillery, armored squad cars, marching infantry
254   columns, etc.

SWISH PAN TO:

255. INT. FIELD HEADQUARTERS TENT - DAY - MED. SHOT
      FAVORING CIVILIAN RADIO ANNOUNCER

He is speaking into microphone. The tent is well filled
with American army staff officers. The officers, including
Brigadier-General Emerson, are studying a large relief map
upon which have been placed colored flags. To one side are
field switchboards, operated by Signal Corps men. A steady
buzz of conversation comes over from these men as they
receive reports from the battlefront.

                    ANNOUNCER
                (in staccato style)
        Good morning, ladies and gentlemen of the
        radio audience -- this is Arthur Duncan
        speaking to you directly from the central
        observation point for the most extensive
        army games ever attempted by the United
        States in peacetime. Present here to
        observe these maneuvers, in addition to
        commanding officers of the two opposing
        armies, are high-ranking officials of the
        War Department, as well as military
        observers from Central and South America.

        The newly-trained recruits of Camp Greeley
        have been organized as the White Army under
        command of Brigadier-General Emerson. They
        will defend a designated area against the
        invasion of a Blue Army, under command of
        General John E. Henshaw, which is comprised
        of seasoned soldiers from Fort Hanson.

        All the latest developments in mechanized
        air and land equipment are being employed
        in this extensive maneuver. At this very
        moment the experienced Blue Army is moving
        rapidly through a valley leading to a
        theoretical industrial center. The novice
        White Army is advancing steadily forward
        to repulse the attack.

As he has been speaking, CAMERA MOVES UP to FEATURE the
large relief map and flags on it which are moved in
accordance with his description.

                    ANNOUNCER
                (turning to officers)
        General Emerson, would you care to comment
        on this morning's first action?

256   MED. CLOSE GROUP SHOT - AT MICROPHONE

as Brigadier-General Emerson steps up to microphone.

> EMERSON
> I'd be glad to, Mr. Duncan.
> (into microphone)
> The performance of the new soldiers of
> Camp Greeley - after only a few months
> of intensive military training - is
> indeed gratifying. The early forced
> march and subsequent airplane attack
> came as a complete surprise but these
> raw recruits reacted like veterans.
> While the men of the Blue Army are
> better prepared and better equipped, I
> have full confidence in the morale and
> initiative of the boys of Camp Greeley.

> WIPE TO:

257   EXT. WOODLAND - DAY - MED. SHOT

The men of "K" Company grouped in the shelter of the trees
and listening to Captain Williams. The men are affixing
white armbands. CAMERA MOVES IN, CENTERING Captain
Williams as he addresses the men.

> CAPTAIN WILLIAMS
> ...and remember that we're being watched
> by umpires -- staff officers -- who'll
> make reports on the conduct of every
> company. Unofficially, I can tell you
> that the company with the best report
> will be selected as color company of the
> regiment.

258   CLOSE GROUP SHOT - SMITTY, COLLINS AND HERBIE

> SMITTY
> How do the umpires figure out the answer
> if we don't really shoot the other guys?

> COLLINS
> With a bookful of rules.

> CAPTAIN WILLIAMS
> That's right. Suppose ten of our men catch up
> with eight of the Blue Army men. We outnumber
> 'em, so we've captured 'em. They get five
> tanks loose against one of ours - our tank is
> wiped out. One of our airplanes drops a flour
> sack for a bomb. If it lands on a battery of
> field artillery, the battery is destroyed.

> HERBIE
> How do I know if I get destroyed?

> COLLINS
> The umpire puts a sign on you - "This
> mugg is as dead as he looks."

> DISSOLVE TO:

259   EXT. PLATEAU - FULL SHOT

The "K" Company men are stealthily moving along, Herbie at
the far end of the line. Captain Williams is no longer
with his company. Collins motions for the men to stop.

259   CONTINUED   COLLINS
                                    (low)
                    Head in there for cover when I give
                    the signal.

260   MED. CLOSE SHOT - HERBIE

       SHOOTING over the edge of a cliff in the f.g. to Herbie in
       the b.g. Herbie, unaware of the sharp drop, watches the
       o.s. Collins for orders.

261   GROUP SHOT - "K" COMPANY MEN (INCLUDING HERBIE)

       Now we cannot see the edge of the cliff.

                                    COLLINS
                                    (low)
                    All right men... forward!

       Herbie grips his gun bravely and charges forward, going
       over the cliff and out of sight. The other men continue
       on across the plateau.

262   GROUP SHOT - "K" COMPANY MEN

       They turn at Herbie's o.s. cry. CAMERA PANS with them as
       they rush to edge of cliff.

263   MED. SHOT - EDGE OF CLIFF

       as the men come running up and look over fearfully.

263-A MED. CLOSE SHOT - SIDE OF CLIFF

       Perched on a tree, shooting out from the cliff, is Herbie;
       he looks up and sees the other men, who are looking down
       at him.
                                    SMITTY
                    For heaven's sake, how did you get
                    in that tree?

                                    HERBIE
                                    (burned)
                    How did I get up in this tree?
                                    (scornfully)
                    I sat on it when it was an acorn.

       The men lean down to pull him up.
                                                DISSOLVE TO:

264   EXT. HILL COUNTRY - NIGHT - PANNING SHOT

       SWINGING with a signal flare fired from a Very pistol.
       It streaks upward, a mere spark, bursts into brilliant
       light.
                                                QUICK CUT TO:

265   STOCK SHOTS (AS AVAILABLE) - NIGHT
266
267   Field battery firing... light tanks advancing through
268   underbrush... stokes mortar crew in action... machine
269   guns firing... boys advancing as skirmishers.
270
                                                DISSOLVE TO:

271   INT. FIELD HEADQUARTERS TENT - NIGHT - MED. CLOSE SHOT
ON ANNOUNCER AT MICROPHONE

who holds a number of dispatches in his hand.

                    ANNOUNCER
              (in same staccato style)
          Since dawn today, the White Army has fought
          heroically to repulse the invading Blue Army
          which attacked with mechanized columns
          following a terrific bomb barrage. It
          appears that the Blue Army has executed an
          excellent Pincer movement, and that the White
          Army may soon be trapped so that the Blues
          have a clear road to the objectives they
          seek to destroy.

As he has been speaking, CAMERA DRAWS BACK to REVEAL same
officers as established in Scene 255. The men are leaning
over the relief map, studying the progress of the sham
battle. At background's field switchboards, one of the
Signal Men scribbles a few words on a slip of paper and
hands it to an orderly who hurries over to Emerson and in
turn gives him the paper.

272   CLOSE SHOT - RELIEF MAP

as Brigadier-General Emerson's hand moves the flags,
advancing one wing of the Blue Army. The depicted strategy
is that of the Pincer movement, with the Blue Army advancing
in two extended columns.

                    ANNOUNCER'S VOICE
          A report from field headquarters indicates
          that the White Army has been forced to
          retreat to a position that exposes the
          Schuylerton reservoir. This reservoir has
          been designated the chief objective of the
          entire maneuver. If the Blue Army can
          succeed in surrounding the marker for the
          reservoir before the White Army can destroy
          that marker, the Blues will be declared
          victorious.

                                        DISSOLVE TO:

273
274
275   OMITTED
276

277   EXT. GULLY - NIGHT - MED. CLOSE SHOT

Sergeant Callahan, Smitty, Herbie, Dick, Bob, Randolph, Briggs
and six other "K" company men are huddled in a small gully.
The scene is intermittently lighted by star shells OUT OF SCENE
There is a DIN of rifle fire, machinegun fire, etc. CAMERA
MOVES IN, CENTERING CALLAHAN who finishes reading a dispatch
in his hand.

                                        CONTINUED

277   CONTINUED

                              CALLAHAN
                  Men - three miles west is the blockhouse
                  that is the marker for the Schuylerton
                  reservoir.

          As Callahan speaks, he uses a stick to draw a diagram on
          the ground, in explanation of his words.

                              CALLAHAN
                            (continuing)
                  The Blue Army, which has control of all
                  the roads leading to it, will attempt to
                  surround that blockhouse before we can
                  destroy it. If they are successful, they
                  will be declared the winners of these war
                  games. Our platoon has been given the vital
                  job of reaching the blockhouse and blowing
                  it up before it can be surrounded by the
                  Blue Army. We have been ordered to split up
                  into three patrols of four men. Each
                  patrol will attempt to reach the objective
                  from a different approach. One must get
                  through and blow up that blockhouse before
                  it is captured by the Blue Army. First
                  patrol --
                            (picks up paper - looks
                            keenly at men and starts
                            to read off names)
                  Corporal Martin in charge -- Randolph,
                  Smith, Brown --

          As he speaks,

                                                    DISSOLVE TO

278   EXT. GULLY - DAWN - MED. SHOT

          as a line of skirmishers (White Army) appears, passes the
          gully, disappears into the night. In the early morning
          light we see the three patrols, each composed of four men,
          clamber out of the gully and disappear in the direction
          taken by the skirmishers.

                                                    DISSOLVE TO

279
to
283   OMITTED

284   EXT. HILLSIDE - DAY - MED. SHOT

          as Bob and his patrol, consisting of Randolph, Herbie and
          Smitty, reach a narrow ledge. The hillside rises vertically
          for about eight feet.
                                                    CONTINUED

284   CONTINUED

                         HERBIE
              What do we do now? Fly?

                         SMITTY
              Yeah - why go this way?

                         BOB
              It's a shortcut to the dam. If we
              can get over the mountaintop, there's
              less chance of our being captured.

                         HERBIE
                    (disgusted - as he
                    looks up)
              A fine army - no elevator service!

                         RANDOLPH
              Stand here - hold your hands like
              this.

He moves Herbie into position, back against hillside.
As Herbie folds his hands, Randolph uses them for a step;
then, stepping on Herbie's shoulder, he gains the next
spot.

                         RANDOLPH
              Hurry up!

Bob climbs up next, then Smitty.

285   MED. CLOSE TWO SHOT - HERBIE AND SMITTY

Smitty above - Herbie still on ledge.

                         HERBIE
              Who boosts me up?

                         SMITTY
              Grab yourself by the collar.

                         HERBIE
                    (demonstrating)
              Like this?

                         SMITTY
              Yeah - now lift.

Smitty scrambles OUT OF SCENE. Herbie tries the collar
gag, then looks disgusted. He sits down and takes off his
shoes, wearily.

                         HERBIE
              Drop me a postcard an' let me know
              what happens.

286   EXT. CREST OF HILL - MED. CLOSE SHOT - RANDOLPH, BOB &
        SMITTY

                            BOB
                       (looking o.s.)
                  One more hill to go.

                          RANDOLPH
                        (squinting)
                  Yeah - and it looks like the worst.

                            BOB
                       (challengingly)
                  Want to quit?

                          RANDOLPH
                  Lead on, Corporal.

        The three men start out.
                                          DISSOLVE TO:

287   EXT. FOOT OF STEEP HILLSIDE - CLOSE THREE SHOT - BOB,
        RANDOLPH AND SMITTY
                            BOB
                  Start climbing.

                          SMITTY
                  You mean - climb that?

        CAMERA PANS to ANGLE UP the almost vertical mountainside -
        PANS back to the three men.

                            BOB
                  Sure - it's the back door to victory.

                          SMITTY
                  Looks more like the front door to Heaven.

        The men start up the hillside.
                                          DISSOLVE TO:
288   OMITTED
289   OMITTED

290   EXT. HILLSIDE - DAY - LONG SHOT - BOB, RANDOLPH & SMITTY

        climbing the hillside.

291   EXT. HILLSIDE - MED. CLOSE SHOT - BOB, RANDOLPH & SMITTY

        as the boys come to a tough bit of going. Randolph scrambles
        up, gains a comparatively level place. He helps Smitty up
        beside him. As Bob starts to scramble up, Randolph holds
        out his hand, but Bob ignores it. Bob loses his foothold,
        starts to fall backwards - Randolph grabs him, pulls him
        up to safety.

292   CLOSE THREE SHOT- BOB, RANDOLPH AND SMITTY

resting for a moment and breathing heavily.

                         RANDOLPH
                    Next time, take my hand.

                         BOB
                    I don't need any help from you.

                         RANDOLPH
                    Let's get one thing straight,Martin-
                    I don't like you any better than you
                    like me, but we've got a job to do
                    and it's going to take teamwork to
                    get it done.

                         BOB
                    Yeah, teamwork--like in a rifle match.

293   MED. SHOT

As the men get to their feet and start up the hillside.
Bob takes the lead, starts working off toward the right.

                         RANDOLPH
                    We'll do better this way.
                         (points left)

                         BOB
                    What do you mean-- better? It's
                    three times as steep!

                         RANDOLPH
                    But it's solid rock. That way you'll
                    run into scree.

                         SMITTY
                    Into what?

                         RANDOLPH
                    It's a mountain-climbing term. Means
                    loose rock, shale, bad footing.

                         BOB
                         (sharply)
                    This isn't a yodeling party! Come on.

                         RANDOLPH
                    It's not safe, I tell you.

                         BOB
                    I'm commanding this patrol. If you're
                    afraid, stay behind.

He starts off, toward the right. The others follow.

294   PICKUP SHOTS
295
        of the men as they move across shale slide, working their
        way upward.

296   MED. CLOSE THREE SHOT

        with Bob in the lead. His footing gives way and he falls,
        sliding OUT OF SCENE. Randolph makes a grab for him but
        misses. CAMERA HOLDS on Randolph and Smitty as they cling
        to their precarious footing, leaning out as much as they
        dare to see what became of Bob.

297   EXT. MOUNTAINSIDE- MED. CLOSE SHOT- BOB

        Clinging to a precarious hand-hold. It's obvious that he
        cannot hang on long.

298   MED. CLOSE TWO SHOT- RANDOLPH AND SMITTY

        Randolph peers down keenly and then starts climbing toward
        Bob. Smitty looks after him, aghast.

299   MED. SHOT- RANDOLPH

        as he works his way down to a point near Bob.

                        RANDOLPH
                Grab my ankle-- climb up over me.

300   PICKUP SHOTS- BOB AND RANDOLPH
301
302   as Bob climbs up Randolph and the two work their way to
        safe ground.

303   MED. SHOT- BOB AND RANDOLPH IN F.G.

        Smitty on far side of bad ground in b.g.

                        BOB
                   (calling to Smitty)
                Go on back-- don't cross that stuff!

        He turns to Randolph, holds out his hand.

                        BOB
                Thanks, fellow-- you saved my life.

                        RANDOLPH
                You owe me a nickel.

        Randolph goes out of SCENE, leaving Bob looking after him.

                                        DISSOLVE TO:

304   INT. FIELD HEADQUARTERS - <u>DAY</u> - MED. CLOSE SHOT

Present are the men established in Scene 255. Officers are grouped over the map. An Aide approaches Brigadier-General Emerson and hands him a slip of paper.

> ANNOUNCER
> (into microphone,
> after glancing at
> papers in his hands)
> Ladies and gentlemen - this has been a thrilling and exciting day. The heart of every citizen in these United States would be filled with pride to have witnessed the splendid showing that the newly-trained recruits of the White Army have made against the superior and more experienced forces of the Blue Army.
>
> Latest reports from the front indicate, however, that the Blue Army is rapidly approaching the Schuylerton reservoir and it appears certain they will gain control of that vital spot within the next few minutes and be declared the winner of these maneuvers. The White Army will need some last-minute miracle to reach and destroy the reservoir. It looks like the Blues have the White forces on the one-yard line with about fifty seconds to play - if you know what I mean.

304-A   GROUP SHOT AT MAP

FEATURING BRIGADIER-General Emerson and General Henshaw.

> HENSHAW
> (turning to Emerson)
> General Emerson, your inexperienced soldiers have done a fine job, holding off as long as they did.
>
> EMERSON
> They <u>have</u> done splendidly - but the maneuver is not lost yet. One of our patrols hasn't been captured. There's still a possibility those men might reach the objective.

304-B   CLOSE SHOT - MAP

as Henshaw's hand shows the position indicated by his words.

CONTINUED

304-B   CONTINUED

> HENSHAW'S VOICE
> But General, at this time they should
> be <u>here</u> -- The Blue Army has control
> of every road in the vicinity. The only
> chance of reaching the reservoir before
> the Blues arrive is over this range of
> mountains. That's almost impossible.
> I'm afraid your new soldiers aren't
> exactly mountain climbers.

> EMERSON'S VOICE
> (wryly)
> I'm afraid you're right.

                                            DISSOLVE TO:

305   EXT. TOP OF HILL - MED. CLOSE SHOT - RANDOLPH & BOB

panting from their efforts. They look over the crest of
the valley on the other side.

306   LONG SHOT - ANGLING DOWN TO RESERVOIR

Prominently displayed on the bank is a small striped
blockhouse with a colored flag atop it.

307   EXT. CREST OF HILL - CLOSE TWO SHOT - BOB & RANDOLPH

> BOB
> Well, we got through before the Blue
> Army. Get down there and blow up the
> blockhouse.

> RANDOLPH
> So you can tell Judy how you gave me
> a chance to be a hero?

> BOB
> That's better than having her think I
> grabbed off the glory by outranking
> you. Come on - get moving!

Randolph hesitates, then both turn suddenly as they HEAR
marching feet o.s.

308   LONG SHOT - ANGLING PAST RESERVOIR

Approaching at a distance is a small detachment of the
Blue Army.

309   TWO SHOT - BOB AND RANDOLPH

> RANDOLPH
> Quick - give me your pistol.

> BOB
> (puzzled - handing it to him)
> What're you going to do?

309   CONTINUED

RANDOLPH
Surround the Blues with a whole company.

BOB
(completely puzzled)
What?

RANDOLPH
(as he runs off)
Blow up the dam as soon as you
get a chance.

310   GROUP SHOT - BLUE DETAIL

as it moves toward the reservoir.

CORPORAL
Not a White Army soldier in sight.

Suddenly there is a CRACKLE OF GUNFIRE - both rifle and
pistol. The Blues duck for cover at a command from the
Corporal.

310-A   MED. CLOSE SHOT - RANDOLPH

He is lying in the underbrush, firing his own gun and
Bob's to simulate gunfire of a great number of men.

310-B   GROUP SHOT - BLUE DETAIL

The Corporal squints keenly.

CORPORAL
There might be more of them than us --
but we've got to take a chance before
they can get a man through to the reservoir. Up an' at 'em!

They scramble to their feet, CAMERA PANNING WITH THEM, as
they dash toward underbrush from where firing is coming.

310-C   MED. CLOSE SHOT - RANDOLPH

as he continues firing toward the sky. The men of the Blue
detail suddenly break through and surround him. He looks
up and smiles at them.

RANDOLPH
Hello, boys. Looking for me?

The Corporal turns quickly toward the reservoir.

310-D   MED. SHOT - AT RESERVOIR

Bob has just pulled up the lever to explode the charge in
the blockhouse. He pushes it down and the blockhouse explodes.

310-E   GROUP SHOT - BLUE DETAIL AND RANDOLPH

as they duck back from the force of the explosion.

311   MATTE SHOT

The exploding blockhouse as seen through a binocular Matte.

312   EXT. FIELD HILLSIDE - CLOSE SHOT - MAJOR GENERAL EMERSON

as he lowers his binoculars. CAMERA PULLS BACK RAPIDLY
to include the several officers and orderlies comprising
the General's staff.

                    EMERSON
          Gentlemen, the dam is theoretically
          destroyed. The White Army has thrown
          back the invaders and turned the
          tide of battle. We are attacking!

                                        FAST WIPE TO:

313   SERIES OF STOCK SHOTS TO SHOW THE ATTACK
314
315   These shots to include the most spectacular action avail-
316   able. (After selection of stock, we may add scenes of
317   established individuals to inter-cut).

                                        DISSOLVE TO:

318   EXT. RECREATION HALL - NIGHT - CLOSE SHOT - ON SIGN

at entrance, reading:
                         TONIGHT
                WHITE ARMY VICTORY DANCE
                Friends and Visitors Welcome

SOUND of dance MUSIC comes over this. CAMERA PULLS BACK and
we see soldiers entering the hall, some of them accompanied
by their girls. As doors of recreation hall are opened, we
see that it is well-filled.

319   INT. RECREATION HALL - NIGHT - FULL SHOT

320   PICKUP SHOTS - JITTERBUG SQUARE DANCE
321
322   as dance finishes, CAMERA PANS to stage as Patty Andrews
323   enters.
324

325   MED. SHOT - PATTY ANDREWS

MUSICAL NUMBER (#6) - "BOUNCE ME, BROTHER, WITH A SOLID FOUR"

                         PATTY
          Say, what kind'a beat is that,
          Man! That really spins my hat...
          Doesn't sound like boogie woogie,
          But it's really got a beat.

          Seems to me that it's in four.
          Let me hear it just once more
          Whilst I latch on to that rhythm,
          'Cause a solid four's my meat.

                                        CONTINUED

325   CONTINUED

Maxine and Laverne Andrews come INTO SCENE and go into chorus:

> Some folks like to hear eight beat rhythm.
> I don't go for that stuff no more.
> Any time you really want to send me . .
> BOUNCE ME, BROTHER, WITH A SOLID FOUR!
>
> Come on in, - the whole place is jumpin';
> Ev'rybody's out on the floor.
> If you want to keep the rhythm jumpin' ..
> BOUNCE ME, BROTHER, WITH A SOLID FOUR!
>
> The boogie woogie was never like this.
> We've got a new beat that no one can miss.
> If boogie woogie "sent" you like I think it did . .
> Four to the bar .. will flip your lid!
>
> Move the tables and roll the rug up!
> Shut the windows and lock the door!
> While I try to dig the lil' Brown Jug up
> BOUNCE ME, BROTHER, WITH A SOLID FOUR!

326)   PICKUP SHOTS - TO BE INTERCUT WITH ABOVE
327)
328)   When Andrews Sisters are through singing, we go into a spec-
329)   ialty by Patty and Herbie. As their number finishes, or-
330)   chestra starts a dance number.

331   EXT. "K" COMPANY STREET - <u>NIGHT</u> - MED. SHOT

PANNING with Sergeant Collins as he comes along street, looking into the various tents. He is the only man in the SHOT,
the encampment being deserted. SOUND of MUSIC from recreation
hall comes OVER faintly. As he reaches second squad tent
and looks in:

332   INT. SQUAD TENT

as Collins enters. CAMERA PULLS BACK to INCLUDE Randolph
sprawled out on a bunk reading a magazine. MUSIC from
recreation hall OVER.

                         COLLINS
             I've been looking all over this camp
             for you -- Why aren't you with the
             other fellows?

                         RANDOLPH
             They seem a bit allergic to me - or
             hadn't you noticed?

                         COLLINS
             The Captain wants to see you in his tent.

                         RANDOLPH
             Okay.
He rises, starts getting into his blouse.
                                                    WIPE TO:

333   EXT. CAPTAIN WILLIAMS' TENT - <u>NIGHT</u> - MED. CLOSE.

as Randolph approaches it. Captain Williams is standing
just inside the opened flap of the tent.

>   RANDOLPH
>   (saluting)
>   Private Parker reporting, sir.

>   CAPTAIN WILLIAMS
>   Come in.

Randolph enters tent.

334   INT. CAPTAIN WILLIAMS' TENT - <u>NIGHT</u> - FULL SHOT -
CONFINED QUARTERS

In the tent is Mr. Parker.

>   CAPTAIN WILLIAMS
>   (to Randolph)
>   At ease.

>   MR. PARKER
>   Hello, son.
>   (they shake hands)

>   RANDOLPH
>   Hello, dad. It's good to see you...

>   MR. PARKER
>   The Captain has some news for you, Randy.

Randolph turns to the Captain, who picks up a paper from a
desk, hands it to Randolph. Randolph opens the paper and
examines it.

>   RANDOLPH
>   A transfer to the officer's training
>   school --
>   (hands it back)
>   No, thanks.

>   CAPTAIN WILLIAMS
>   Don't you <u>want</u> a commission?

>   RANDOLPH
>   (with a grin)
>   I want it a lot -- but I've heard that
>   it's possible to get an appointment
>   from the ranks.
>   (turns to Parker)
>   Thanks for the string-pulling, dad.

>   MR. PARKER
>   I had nothing to do with that transfer.

>   CONTINUED

334   CONTINUED

Randolph looks at him, a bit confused.

> CAPTAIN WILLIAMS
> (smiling)
> That's right. I recommended you for
> it, along with other men who have
> shown exceptional ability.

The Captain extends his hand cordially to Randolph.

> DISSOLVE TO:

335   INT. RECREATION HALL - FULL SHOT

The soldier orchestra, Dick conducting, is playing for the
dance. The floor is crowded with soldiers in uniform and
their girls.

336   MED. CLOSE SHOT - ON DOOR

as Randolph enters, stands just inside the doorway, looking
around for Judy. Henry and Briggs come in, slap Randolph
on the back.

> HENRY
> Hello, Randy -- How you feeling, kid?

> BRIGGS
> You sure put it over, pal!

Randolph, astounded, turns to look after them as they go.
The Andrews Sisters come INTO SCENE.

> MAXINE
> Nice goin', soldier. Save me a dance
> later.

> PATTY
> (with a grin)
> Remind me to give you my phone number.

The Andrews Sisters exit FROM SCENE. Smitty and Herbie come
up from the other side.

> SMITTY
> Hey, Randy - let me buy you a soda
> or something?

> HERBIE
> Soda, nothing -- buy him a man's
> drink -- a double malted.

> RANDOLPH
> I thought you boys were broke.

> CONTINUED

336   CONTINUED

                         SMITTY
        Broke - ?!!

                         HERBIE
        Does this look like we're broke?

He pulls an immense roll of bills from his pocket. Smitty
also produces a roll.

                         HERBIE
        We practically busted the Blue Army,
        thanks to you. At ten to one!

                         RANDOLPH
        Me -- ?

                         SMITTY
        Sure - Bob's been tellin' us and every-
        body else how you won the sham battle
        for us.

                         HERBIE
        That's really somethin' - overcomin'
        the handicap of bein' a millionaire.
                (as he goes)
        Gee - I wish I was handicapped like that.

Randolph looks after them fondly, as they go off SCENE.
Judy comes up behind him and puts her arm possessively in
his. Randolph turns, reacts.

                         JUDY
        May I have this dance?

Randolph grins and offers his arms - and CAMERA PANS with
them as they dance onto the floor.

337   MED. CLOSE SHOT - ON DANCE FLOOR

as Randolph and Judy dance together happily. Bob comes up
behind them and taps Randolph on the shoulder.

                         RANDOLPH
        Sorry, no cuts.

                         BOB
        Who wants to cut? Captain Williams'
        compliments and the Captain wants to
        see you at once.

                         RANDOLPH
        You and your corny gag! Pal, this is
        my last night in camp -- and my last
        dance with our girl.

                         BOB
        Now - isn't that a coincidence?

                         RANDOLPH
                (reacting)
        You, too?

                                        CONTINUED

337   CONTINUED

                        BOB
              Officers' training school - in the
              morning.

                        RANDOLPH
                        (to Judy)
              We're going to miss you a lot.

                        JUDY
              Oh no, you're not.

                        BOB AND RANDOLPH
                        (together)
              Oh yes, we are.

                        JUDY
                        (airily)
              I don't think so - because it happens
              that I've been transferred.

                        RANDOLPH
                        (astonished)
              Don't tell me they have hostesses at
              the Officers' training school?

                        JUDY
                        (with a grin)
              Now, isn't that a coincidence?

                        RANDOLPH
                        (offering hand to Bob)
              Looks like we're both lucky fellows,
              Mr. Smith.

O.s. the orchestra swings into "YOU'RE A LUCKY FELLOW,
MISTER SMITH" with Andrews Sisters singing it.

338   FULL SHOT

        as everyone present swings into a march, led by the color
        guard and the band. The soldiers, their sweethearts and
        visitors, march to the tune of "YOU'RE A LUCKY FELLOW,
        MISTER SMITH".

339   MED. SHOT (HIGH SETUP) - ANGLING DOWN ON PEOPLE

        as they march through the hall, singing.

        (NOTE: As discussed, these song lyrics will be delivered
        successively by (1) Male chorus; (2) Randolph, Judy and
        Bob; (3) Andrews Sisters; (4) Collins; (5) Smitty and Herbie.)

340   MED. SHOT - SMITTY AND HERBIE

        (Final gag to be worked out).

                                        FADE OUT.

                        T H E   E N D

Special Trailer

Apparently a unique teaser trailer was intended for the film, and is depicted in the still at right and in this continuity script.

OPENING TITLE ON ONIONS

Universal Presents
"A TEARFUL TALE"
with radio's favorite comedians
BUD ABBOTT and LOU COSTELLO

DISSOLVE TO:
A MOUNTAIN OF ONIONS IN
CAMP KITCHEN

CAMERA CLIMBS UP over mountain
and we SEE ABBOTT and COSTELLO
in fatigue uniforms doing K.P. duty.

COSTELLO
(tears running down his cheeks)
Twenty-one bucks a month to mani-
cure onions.

ABBOTT
Look, Costello, your salary is a matter
between you and the government and
shouldn't be discussed.

COSTELLO
Don't worry—I'm just as much ashamed of it as they are. Who started this
draft business anyway?

ABBOTT
I'll explain. Congress convenes in the
Capitol Building in Washington. Now
the Senators meet in the Senate, natu-
rally, and the Congressmen sit in the
House.

COSTELLO
They sit in the house? No wonder it
takes them so long to get things done.
Why don't they come out once in a
while?

ABBOTT
They can't leave the house because a
Congressman just took the floor.

COSTELLO
Then why don't they go out through
the cellar?

ABBOTT
You don't understand. The Congressman is holding the floor.

COSTELLO
Where are the other Congressmen?

ABBOTT
They're sitting on it.

COSTELLO
He's holding the floor, with the other
Congressmen sitting on it? What a
remarkable exhibition of physical
prowess.

ABBOTT
Costello—I'll try to make it clear. The
Congressman is trying to get this draft
bill voted on. If he gets a majority,
then he carries the House.

COSTELLO
First he holds the floor—then he carries the House. What is he, a superman?

ABBOTT
What's the use of talking to you. You
don't listen. Everything I say goes in
one ear and out the other.

COSTELLO
I'M A BAD BOY!

ABBOTT
I'll say you are.

COSTELLO
But what good is the draft?

ABBOTT
'What good is the draft?' —it gets us a
good job in a swell picture, "Buck
Privates" —with some swell people: the
Andrews Sisters - Lee Bowman - Alan
Curtis - Jane Frazee—and, what's
more, it gives us a chance to show the
country how their soldierboys are
doing in the new camps. You ought to
be able to see that.

COSTELLO
Sure I see it.

ABBOTT
Well then, tell the people out there—tell
them something about our picture.

COSTELLO
What am I, a dope?
(faces camera)
If you folks want to know about all the
good things in "BUCK PRIVATES" you
gotta come see the picture. Ahhhhhh!!
(sticks out tongue like a kid)

TITLES SUPERIMPOSED
ON FOOTAGE FROM PICTURE:

YOU'LL LOVE
    THE LAUGHS
        THE MUSIC
THE GRAND STORY
    IN AMERICA'S FIRST FILM
        ABOUT OUR NEW
    "BUCK PRIVATES"

With Lee Bowman
    Alan Curtis
      Bud Abbott and Lou Costello
The Andrews Sisters
    Jane Frazee
      Nat Pendleton

"BUCK PRIVATES"
COMING TO THIS THEATRE SOON.

They're Going to Be Big Stars!

Phil Cahn was editing *Buck Privates* as it was being shot, since Universal raced to be the first studio to release a draft comedy. Dann Cahn explained, "My dad would get the previous day's dailies around eight o'clock in the morning. (Back then they were called the 'rushes.') His assistant would sync up the sound and the picture tracks and right before or right after lunch, my dad would run the dailies for the producer and the production heads. Then, when they finished shooting at night, he'd run the dailies again for the director and get his thoughts. Then his assistant would break everything down and my dad would go to work cutting together a sequence, sometimes having gotten input from the director, sometimes not, depending on what their relationship was and how much trust the director had in the editor."

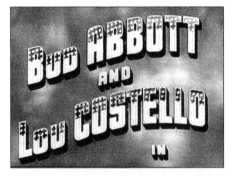

The screenplay suggests opening the film with stock footage of men lining up and filling out draft cards. Instead, a more formal introduction was added using footage from a *March of Time* newsreel. This preamble was probably superfluous in 1941—was there anyone who *didn't* know about the draft? Yet this introduction helps the film travel through the years. It instantly gives new audiences a background brief and suggests that what is about to unfold is rooted in a real event.

On January 17, the day after the stock footage arrived from Fort Ord, the studio screened *Buck Privates* for the Production Code Administration. Breen's staff issued a letter of approval the following day. The picture was also shown to officers at Fort MacArthur and was approved without deletions.

There was also a sneak preview at the Academy Theater in Inglewood, an industrial suburb in the shadow of what is now the Los Angeles International Airport.

"There was a theater in Inglewood about an hour from the studio where Universal often previewed its pictures," Dann Cahn recalled. "They're called 'sneak' previews because they were always secret, and were held some distance from Hollywood so that competing movie studios and the press would not see them until the executives were satisfied with the audience reaction. Universal 'sneaked' *Buck Privates* in Inglewood. The laughs were so great that after the preview my dad had to extend the lengths of the cuts so that the audience could hear the dialogue that was drowned out in the laughs."

After these initial screenings the studio promoted Alex Gottlieb from supervisor to associate producer and told him to start immediately on a follow-up picture placing Abbott and Costello in the navy.

From the newsreel sequence that opens the film: President Roosevelt signs the Draft Bill, and Secretary of War Henry Stimson selects the first random number in the draft lottery, 158.

Arthur Horman was called on again to develop a script. Horman ultimately had *three* service comedies in release in 1941. In addition to *Buck Privates* and *In The Navy*, he wrote *Navy Blues*, starring Jack Oakie and Jack Haley, for Warner Brothers.

Dann Cahn reflected, "To me, Alex Gottlieb was the creative producer. Milton Feld was more concerned with the overall budget and would approve casting and certain things. He also executive-produced other pictures at the same time. Arthur Lubin was the kind of director who didn't consider himself an auteur, but he had some clever ideas. But once the film was off the set, it was out of his hands. I would say the relationship between my dad and Alex Gottlieb was what ultimately put over the Abbott and Costello pictures. It was in Alex's hands, and he relied on my old man."

The *Hollywood Reporter* lauded Gottlieb's initial producing effort: "On the production side, both in conception and execution, [*Buck Privates*] is a distinct tribute to the talents of newcomer Alex Gottlieb."

But most critics—particularly those from the trade papers—acknowledged Lubin's role in the success of the film. The *Hollywood Reporter* wrote, "In his direction, Lubin displayed a brilliant flair for comedy and the spiritual handling of intricate musical numbers, and gave the entire picture a tremendous vitality, while maintaining a fine shading of both scene, situation and characterization." *Daily Variety* was equally effusive: "First, a big credit to Arthur Lubin, directing his first A picture after turning out a steady and dependable quality of more modest budgeters. He has this one in hand at all times, squeezes every bit of fun and entertainment out of the quick-paced succession of close-knit gags and episodes, and generally demonstrates a skillfulness and understanding which qualifies him for continued assignments in the upper brackets."

Lubin, however, was modest about his contributions. "*Buck Privates* was a very, very funny show and, actually, it was very little credit to the director. It consisted mainly of fabulous gags that these two wonderful guys knew from years and years of being in burlesque." Asked what he thought his contribution was to the Abbott and Costello films, Lubin replied, "I think I was very good for them in this respect: not in their routines, but in trying to give them some class. Whenever they got rude or crude, I'd try to soften it, to keep a balance of refinement against the earthiness of some of the routines."

The studio recognized that Lubin and the boys had a special rapport. While Lubin was shooting *Buck Privates*, Cliff Work assigned him to the second Abbott and Costello film, *Oh, Charlie!* (released as *Hold That Ghost*.) Lubin recalled, "I said, 'Even before you've seen this one [*Buck Privates*]?' And they said, 'Yes, we're certain of this.'" Production began on *Oh, Charlie!* on January 21.

On Tuesday, January 28, five months after the Draft Bill was passed, *Buck Privates* was previewed at the Alexander Theater in Glendale, about twenty minutes from Universal. Alex Gottlieb recalled: "We went to preview the picture at the Alexander Theater. Alexander is my real name, so I figured it was going to be good luck. But I was afraid we wouldn't get an audience because this wasn't a big, important preview—Bud and Lou were two unknowns."

(Meanwhile, Universal treated 150 critics and columnists to a multi-day junket to Miami for the premier of *Back Street*.) "Well," Gottlieb continued, "this picture goes on and the audience started laughing and they never stopped! When we came out of the theater into the lobby, Milton Feld said to me, 'You son of a bitch, you were right. They're going to be big stars!' I said, 'Costello will be a big star; Abbott will be who he needs to work with.' That was never meant to be a malicious statement. I think the facts bear me out."

Daily Variety was at the Alexander Theater that night: "Universal has a winner in 'Buck Privates,' first of the crop of pictures dealing lightly or seriously with Uncle Sam's rookie draftees...Bud Abbott and Lou Costello amply justify their stellar rating, establish themselves among the best film comedians of the day, never failing to develop a gag or a situation with precision and sure fire in getting the laughs, from giggles to bellies. Time after time at the preview, the comics were roundly applauded for their adroit clowning. The Andrews Sisters also score with a parade of rhythm and boogie-woogie chanting which fits into and helps make this piece of tuneful funning an outstanding offering..."

(In its review, *The Billboard* referenced the *Argentine Nights* fiasco, noting that in *Buck Privates* the girls are "treated a great deal more kindly by the make-up and lighting departments...[and they] received the benefit of proper handling that shows them in a light that will do much to erase the mistakes of *Argentine Nights*.")

The *Hollywood Reporter* was also impressed that evening: "With 'Buck Privates,' Universal fires a roaring salvo of sock entertainment that is going to have them laughing from coast to coast. At the same time it is tinged with just enough of the patriotic flavor to stir the pulses. On both counts it is a real winner... Bud Abbott and Lou Costello...provide most of [the

humor] themselves, and doing a tremendous job. It is unsubtle to the point of being slapstick at times, but it's swell fun, with the drill sequence close to a classic. The musical numbers, paced by the melodious Andrews Sisters, are about the snappiest the screen has offered in a long time. 'Buck Privates' is great entertainment for the masses, and the masses are going to eat it up. Abbott and Costello, with a set of new routines, are smash hits, far better than in their first successful screen appearance ['One Night in the Tropics']. This round is certain to set them solidly as film funsters of the first magnitude. On the straighter side, Lee Bowman and Alan Curtis get over nicely, with Jane Frazee supplying an intriguing romantic interest and also singing nicely. Nat Pendleton does an excellent job as a hardboiled sergeant, with others in the cast all registering."

Weekly *Variety* chimed in a few days later: "Picture has a good chance to skyrocket the former burlesk and radio team of Bud Abbott and Lou Costello into topflight starring ranks... Picture is studded with several Abbott and Costello routines that are particularly effective for sustained laughs. Tops is a sequence in which Costello is a member of the awkward squad for special rifle drill. Running about five minutes, episode builds quickly for continuous hilarity—with dialog drowned in the audience uproar. A new angle on the oldie money changing routine and a particularly funny dice game also hit high marks for comedy reaction. 'Buck Privates' needs special exploitation to get started in the key spots, but will get immediate word-of-mouth to zoom it to profitable b.o."

Arthur Lubin, who earned $350 a week, received a $5,000 bonus. At the time of the preview, Lubin was a week into shooting *Oh, Charlie!* Editor Phil Cahn was also handed a bonus. Meanwhile, two more Abbott and Costello films were on the drawing

"Maybe Universal had the right idea at that time," Patty reflected, *"because* Buck Privates *was so big, so popular."*

board—*In The Navy* and *Ride 'Em Cowboy.*

Buck Privates was officially released on January 31, 1941, and was an instant hit. The story was panned, of course, but Abbott and Costello were hailed as the comedy find of the decade and enjoyed the best notices they ever received for any of their films. No wonder it remained Bud Abbott's favorite, and probably Lou's.

Dallas Morning News: "The squad drill, with Costello taking the rifle barrel on his kisser, threw us in the aisle. There is a wonderful crapshooting game, followed by the sharp money count-up over the bar. None of it is too new, which is just as well. Suffice to say that Abbott and Costello truck out the oldies for the most irresistible humor seen on the screen in some months...Unless they are badly messed up by corny handling, they will take a place among movie greats."

Philadelphia Evening Ledger: "...'Buck Privates' is one long chuckle and can be classed a perfect anodyne for the alarums and excursions of the headlines. Not since Chaplin interrupted the grim business of Mars with his 'Shoulder Arms' in World War I has the hapless rookie been exposed so merrily. And speaking of Chaplin, he has a rival in pantomime and gorgeous helplessness in Lou Costello, the 'bad boy' of radio and burlesque fame who is presented as Rookie Number One in the new opera."

New York Times: "'Buck Privates' is an hour and a half of uproarious monkeyshines. Army humor isn't apt to be subtle, and neither are Abbott and Costello. Their antics have as much innuendo as a 1,000-pound bomb but nearly as much explosive force."

New York Journal-American: "Thanks to the zany antics of Lou Costello, 'Buck Privates' offers some riotous moments. Whether he's shooting craps, stumbling through a rifle drill, doing his money-changing routine with his partner or just mumbling to himself, the wacky Mr. Costello establishes himself as one of the top comics of the screen."

The critics embraced Bud and Lou as few comedians ever before. But perhaps Costello's most cherished review came from his idol, Charlie Chaplin, who called Lou "the best comic working in the business today." Louella Parsons was gratified. "I am happy, indeed, that Charlie Chaplin agreed with me on 'Buck Privates,'" she wrote in her column. "He was very interested because 'Shoulder Arms,' a comedy about soldier life, was one of his greatest movies. Charlie, always generous to other funsters, paid

Universal ran this double-page spread in Hollywood's trade papers the week the film was released.

Abbott and Costello a compliment on their ability as comedians that should make them very happy indeed."

More amazed were studio executives all over Hollywood. Universal's own trade advertisements trumpeted the film as "The Surprise Comedy Smash." *Buck Privates* outdrew such films as *How Green Was My Valley, Citizen Kane, Here Comes Mr. Jordan*, and *Sergeant York*. The film opened a two-week run on February 27 at the Paramount Theater in downtown Los Angeles, with Bud, Lou, Lee Bowman, Jane Frazee and Nat Pendleton making personal appearances. By April, *Buck Privates* was being held over in cities across the country, including Buffalo, Minneapolis, Sacramento, Oakland, and San Diego. It ran for five weeks in St. Paul. It played in New Orleans for eight, matching the success in that city of *Gone With the Wind*. One theater owner there even dropped short subjects so he could squeeze in an extra showing of *Buck Privates* during the day. In Toronto, Shea's ran *Buck Privates* for thirteen weeks.

Patty Andrews explained, "People kept going back to see it because the laughs were so loud that you missed half the dialogue the first time around."

But the holdovers caused problems for the studio. *Daily Variety* reported that the "rush of bookings on Universal's 'Buck Privates' has caused a sharp shortage of available prints in a number of theater territories around the country. In the Los Angeles area, the film is playing second-run in 14 theaters, forcing the bicycling of seven prints, the only ones available locally, among theaters." A few days later, Universal rushed an additional eight prints to the area, but by then *Buck Privates* was playing in 21 theaters and the 15 prints still had to be shared. Meanwhile, *One Night in the Tropics* was sent back out to theaters to capitalize on the demand for Abbott and Costello.

Buck Privates' gross has been variously reported as $4 million or $10 million. According to Universal's accounting, however, the picture grossed $1,450,000 domestically in its original release. (It was re-issued in 1948 and again in 1953, which may account for the higher figures.) But we must remember that in 1941 the term "box office gross" referred to the money the *studio* made charging rental fees to the theaters; today, it indicates *all* the money taken in at theaters around the country. Since Universal charged exhibitors a 25% rental fee, *Buck Privates'* box office gross by today's definition would have been $5.8 million. According to the Motion Picture Association of America, in 1941 the average movie ticket price was 25¢, while in 2012 it was $8.12. Considering that ticket prices are more than thirty-two times what they were when the film was released, it would be fair to estimate that, with the same number of ticket sales, *Buck Privates* would gross over $185 million domestically today. Yet that does not take into account the fact that the U.S. population has more than doubled since 1941.

How did *Buck Privates* stack up against other films of 1941? It's difficult to compare film grosses from that era because *Variety* did not begin issuing year-end figures for box-office rental grosses until 1946. Before then, a poll of theater managers by *Showman's Trade Review* determined Hollywood's twenty-five "leading productions" of the year. The caveat here is that theater managers tended to vote for the films that made *them* the most money. *Buck Privates* was voted the second "leading production" of 1941, behind MGM's *Men of Boys Town* and ahead of Bob Hope's *Caught in the Draft*. The prestigious war drama *Sergeant York* placed sixth, while Bud and Lou's follow-up service comedy, *In The Navy*, ranked seventh.

But Universal had pre-sold *Buck Privates* to exhibitors at B-picture rates, and the millions of dollars in profit went largely to the theaters and theater chains. The *Saturday Evening Post* mused, "The picture probably financed more new seats, ushers' uniforms, lobby carpets, bank nights and new sets of

Poster when the film was re-issued in 1953.

dishes than any other comedy in history."

Just a few weeks after *Buck Privates* was released, studio president Nate Blumberg hastened to announce that all subsequent Abbott and Costello pictures would be offered at the higher, A-rental rate of 35%.

It's Going to Be a Merry War, Folks

For most Americans, *Buck Privates* was their first glimpse into the rookie army, albeit a rose-colored one. The War Department created one-minute trailers about the new army, but these didn't begin reaching theaters until three weeks after *Buck Privates* was released. Twelve shorts, distributed to movie houses three at a time, covered *The Infantry, The Air Corps, The Armored Force, The Coast Artillery, Flying Cadets* and so on. Thus *Buck Privates* demystified camp training by showing something of what millions of future G.I.'s could expect (the Andrews Sisters and starlet-hostesses notwithstanding).

But from the very beginning, *Buck Privates'* goal clearly was to glamorize Army life. Remember Harold Shumate's first draft, which specified a number "in the spirit of 'Over There' and the feeling of 'God Bless America.'" Before the San Francisco opening of *One Night in the Tropics*, Bud was asked about the team's upcoming service comedy. He was quoted as saying, "The picture will deal with conscription, but don't get the idea we're going to burlesque it. Our idea is just the reverse. We're making the film because we believe it can play a part in helping civilian morale. Its aim is

Truckin' with Nina Orla.

to buck up the mothers, fathers and sweethearts separated from their draftee loved-ones. We'll show the bright side of conscription life; that Army routine and discipline are less arduous than they might have imagined; that cheerful surroundings, healthful recreation and clean entertainment figure in the daily program." (While this probably came from the studio's publicity department and not Bud, it's enlightening nonetheless.)

Buck Privates clearly succeeds in its goals. *Hollywood Reporter* columnist Irving Hoffman noted, "If the United States government could sell the Army to the public as well as Alex Gottlieb has done with 'Buck Privates,' the entire male population of this country would be wrapped in khaki. Besides being a slick piece of press agentry (Gottlieb was once a p.a.), the film...is also a slick piece of entertainment..."

The *Los Angeles News* concurred, "The way 'Buck Privates' has it, Army life is fun." And the *New York Times* agreed, "[Any] foolish notions that training for war is basically a grim business have been largely dispelled. If the real thing is at all like this preview of army life—with the Messrs. A & C dropping gags once a minute and the Andrews Sisters

Mrs. Parker (Nella Walker) asks Captain Johnson, "How can they make a Yale man a private?"

Judy's first lecture, about the benefits of the army, anticipates the army's famous advertising slogan.

crooning patriotic boogie-woogie airs—well, it's going to be a merry war, folks..."

The film works on two fronts to glamorize Army life. There are the obvious enticements of pretty hostesses, boogie woogie concerts, and sympathetic commanding officers. But *Buck Privates'* main appeal is to its audience's sense of patriotism and duty. "You're a Lucky Fellow, Mr. Smith" was particularly effective at this. "Mr. Smith," according to the bouncy tune, should count his blessings as a citizen of the United States, and therefore willingly answer the call to service. The *New York Times* noted, "The songs, especially 'You're a Lucky Fellow, Mr. Smith,' should cause a noticeable increase in new volunteers."

Although a recruit may be inspired by *Buck Privates'* patriotism, he may still be apprehensive. The optimism of a song like "Apple Blossom Time," which promised the resumption of a normal civilian life when a recruit's mandatory year of service was up, was reassuring. Abbott and Costello's broad comedy was also encouraging. After all, even the least confident conscript could feel superior to Costello. But as a comedy, *Buck Privates* also has license to voice (and dispel) many of the objections and concerns of the new soldiers in a palatable way. It's okay to grouse about the army, as Herbie does in "When Private Brown Becomes a Captain." Yet setting his gripes to music helps trivialize them. Eventually, of course, each recruit in the film accepts his responsibility good-naturedly. Each one, that is, but Parker, who sneers, "I didn't ask for this uniform; why should I take it seriously?" While many draftees may have felt the same way, hearing these words from the disagree-

able Parker associates any serious dissent with a spoiled egotist.

The film goes on to say that not only is it a recruit's obligation to serve, but that it will be to his *benefit* to serve. When Parker's mother complains, "How can they make a Yale man a private?" (Sc. 43), Captain Johnson explains to her (and Randolph) that "a year in the Army can do a great deal for any man." Later, in Scene 140, Parker's father joins the pro-Army chorus: "This camp may be a little short on sport roadsters and chorus girls, but it's excellently equipped to make a man out of a playboy."

Even Judy joins the lobby (Sc. 148). She tells Randolph about her father, who was a captain in the Fighting 69th during World War I. Judy says, "He believed army life changed boys into men." (Interestingly, a reference to her father's demise in combat was deleted; it was too early in this rookie army's training to raise the specter of death.)

Furthermore, these benefits are available to every man, because the Army, unlike civilian society, shows no favorites. (*That's* how they can make a Yale man a private, Mrs. Parker.) Judy delivers this message, too. She continues, "He always said [the Army] was the great leveler—it doesn't care how much a man has in the bank or how little. All the army cares about is how much of a man a man can be."

Not only does her line anticipate the Army's famous advertising slogan, "Be All You Can Be," introduced in 1981, but it is also a direct reference to the Depression, which was still felt throughout America. The army was the one place where a man wasn't judged by his wealth, education or connec-

The army as the great leveler: a rich man and his chauffeur have equal opportunity for advancement— and for the affections of the camp's prettiest hostess.

Parker and Bob must set aside their differences and work together as a team to win the war games for their company.

tions. That's why Bob, a chauffeur, is rewarded with officer's candidate school alongside the privileged Parker. The *Philadelphia Evening Public Ledger* observed: "[The] whole film is a lively lithograph in the interests of recruiting and presents our armed forces (with pretty hostesses) as the ideal poor-man's club. War being the great leveler, they meet on equal terms in Uncle Sam's fraternity and the chauffeur obeys the natural impulse to 'hang one' of the chin of his erstwhile demanding employer. He also becomes his ex-boss' rival for the affections of the camp's prettiest hostess."

Bud and Lou were patriotic men who would sell a record $85 million worth of war bonds in 1942 and perform at numerous Army camps. But in 1941, the team had no say in *Buck Privates*' propaganda message—except, perhaps, for Costello's ad-lib about Uncle Sam in Scene 150-A. (Costello was given a more overt flag-waving speech in *Keep 'Em Flying*.) The plot and song lyrics were certainly not in the team's control. Yet the fact remains that the idea for a service comedy was Costello's.

Bud and Lou didn't know it, but the team itself was a propaganda message. A consistent theme running throughout the film is the importance of teamwork. This is overtly stated by Captain Williams in Scene 88, when he says that "a great many people are counting on our success—people from all walks of life who are contributing to this great national defense program just as much as you or I. I refer to the factory workers, the farmers—the citizens whose taxes are paying for this training—the people of

America." He sums up, "If we all work together, I'm certain we'll make 'K' Company a unit of which any regiment can be proud." Later, the reprise of "You're a Lucky Fellow, Mr. Smith" further underscores the importance of teamwork:

The wealthy man, little man, banker and clerk,
They're punching for you so you do your part

and

We're a hundred thirty million strong,
And we're sticking with you right along.

Parker's failure to compete in the rifle match is a direct affront to teamwork and loyalty. Although his efforts to avoid serving have not endeared him to the others, it is only after Parker eschews the rifle match that he is considered a pariah. His transgression infuriates Judy, who rebukes him in a lecture about loyalty (Sc. 164). It is at this point that we see that she starts to get through to him.

During the war games sequence, Parker saves Bob twice, but the first instance (Sc. 291) was cut. During that cut scene, a key piece of dialog from Sc. 292 referenced the "teamwork" theme of the film:

RANDOLPH
Let's get one thing straight, Martin—
I don't like you any better than you like
me, but we've got a job to do and it's
going to take teamwork to get it done.

BOB
Yeah, teamwork—like in a rifle match.

To support this subtext, several teams work to great effect in *Buck Privates:* Abbott and Costello as a comedy team; the Andrews Sisters as a vocal group; Dean Collins and Jewel McGowan as a dance team; and Parker and Bob, whose teamwork wins the war game. Perhaps, as the United States slipped into a teamwork mentality during this period, Abbott and Costello struck a responsive chord. They're two individuals who argue amongst themselves but, when the chips are down, pull together. In the impending world conflict, Americans would have to suppress their prejudices and petty animosities and unite for a common cause. Hollywood films reinforced this attitude during the war. The movies, which previously celebrated lone heroes like the cowboy or the private detective, now glorified the combat *unit*, not the individual soldier. The message was the suppression of personal interest for the good of the squad—i.e., teamwork. Could this help explain why Abbott and Costello and the Andrews Sisters became national crazes during World War II? Did America somehow see in them the teamwork it would need to win the war?

Another appeal of the film not to be underestimated is its nostalgic quality—not for today's audi-ence, but for audiences in 1941. Abbott and Costello's burlesque routines dated from the turn of the century, as did boogie-woogie music. "Apple Blossom Time" was twenty years old. There may have been great comfort in revisiting the past for audiences worried about the future.

Combined with the songs, these overt and subtle messages succeeded in rousing patriotic sentiment among its audience. The *Hollywood Reporter* thought *Buck Privates* "captured completely the spirit of the Army camps and defense-minded America." The *Washington Post* reported the "audience found it alternately hilarious and inspiring."

It also resonated with its subjects—the new recruits. The *St. Louis Post-Dispatch* reported, "Even 2,500 real live soldiers from Jefferson Barracks who saw the picture at a preview last Tuesday night could laugh heartily many times, so 'Buck Privates' passes inspection." Abbott and Costello received a special citation from the Hollywood Post of the American Legion for helping to build morale in the country's training camps. During the war, *Buck Privates* was shown to troops on eight battlefronts: Russian, Chinese, Atlantic, Mediterranean, Middle East, South Pacific, Alaskan, and Western Europe. Just before they landed on Attu, to storm the mountain peaks, G.I.'s were shown *Buck Privates* to ease their nervousness. The film landed in the Smithsonian as an

The two most popular teams of the war years.

187

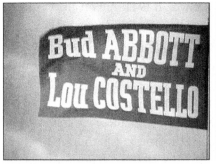

In The Navy *opens with the boys hoisting signal flags that bear the film's credits. When Abbott sees that the title flag reads "Buck Privates," he slaps Costello, who hastily sends up the correct flag.*

example of pre-battle entertainment.

Buck Privates' effectiveness was not confined to the United States. In a 1943 article on the influence of American films abroad, a *New York Times* correspondent reported, "A 16-year-old Beirut boy asked me very seriously how he could join the American Army. It developed that he had just seen 'Buck Privates' and was anxious to join." Meanwhile, the Japanese used the film for their own propaganda purposes to demonstrate the incompetence of American soldiers.

Before Pearl Harbor, isolationists and the Production Code Administration scrutinized Hollywood films for anti-Nazi sentiment or pro-interventionist messages. As the Nazis overran the European continent, war-themed features and shorts proliferated. Isolationists accused Hollywood of attempting to incite America to war. Eventually, a special Senate subcommittee was convened in the summer of 1941 to investigate "war propaganda disseminated by the distribution or exhibition of motion pictures." The subcommittee cited 48 feature films and ten episodes of the *March of Time* newsreel. Yet, as Prof. Don Morlan points out in his paper, *Slapstick Contributions to World War II Propaganda: The Three Stooges and Abbott and Costello*, not one of the targeted films was a comedy.

Of course, *Buck Privates'* message is pro-army and pro-defense, not pro-war or anti-Nazi. Still, Morlan argues that the Three Stooges' war-themed shorts and Abbott and Costello's service comedies were just as instrumental in preparing the country for war as dramas like *Sergeant York* or *A Yank in the RAF*. Morlan writes, "While serious attempts to portray political or military themes were under constant attack, the isolationists allowed slapstick comics to make obvious and direct attempts at molding public opinion positively toward involvement in the war. The financial success of some of those offerings and the millions of people the films played to render them a significant element in forming the mindset of the American public toward the war." The Three Stooges' *You Nazty Spy* and Abbott and Costello's *Buck Privates*, Morlan argues, "deserve the status of classics in American film history as pre-WWII film propaganda."

Army comedies appear to be the genre of choice for comedians just starting out or entering a new phase in their careers. *Shoulder Arms* (1918) marked the first time Charlie Chaplin appeared on screen without his trademark derby and cane. *Doughboys* (1930) was Buster Keaton's first feature at MGM, and his second talkie. Army comedies were the first starring features for Abbott and Costello, Martin and Lewis and Danny Kaye (*Up in Arms*, 1944). It's a tried and true formula pitting the incorrigible comedian against the rigid authority of military life. Bill Murray (*Stripes*), Goldie Hawn (*Private Benjamin*), Steve Martin (*Bilko*) and even Pauly Shore (*In The Army Now*) have tested the waters. What's taking Adam Sandler or Will Ferrell so long?

Buck Privates certainly wasn't the first service comedy, but it was the most successful and influential. Three direct descendants were made by Abbott and Costello themselves: *In The Navy, Keep 'Em Flying*, and *Buck Privates Come Home*.

The first two were released in 1941 after some mad scrambling by the studio. Although *Hold That Ghost* was already in the can, the stunning success of *Buck Privates* couldn't be ignored. According to the *Hollywood Reporter*, "*Buck Privates* is headed to outgross any picture made on the Universal lot since the present organization has been there. And now Universal is planning to shelve [*Hold That Ghost*] temporarily to make a follow-up on the army flicker, titled *We're in the Navy Now*."

The new service comedy, eventually titled *Abbott and Costello and Dick Powell in the Navy*, was released on June 2. Six months later, Universal delayed the release of *Ride 'Em Cowboy* so *Keep 'Em Flying* could be rushed to market. The air corps comedy was in theaters when Pearl Harbor was attacked.

(This was not the first time that the same team made three service comedies in rapid succession. Raymond Hatton and Wallace Beery scored with *Behind The Front* in 1926, and quickly followed up with *We're in the Navy Now* and *Now We're in the Air* in 1927.)

While *Keep 'Em Flying* was in production, the boys performed in a Lux Radio Theater adaptation of *Buck Privates* on October 13, 1941. The Andrews Sisters and their music were missing, but all of the boys' routines were included, although modified for radio. Benny Rubin played Sergeant Collins. Host Cecil B. DeMille welcomed Bud and Lou as two expert comedians "who hit Hollywood with the force of a hurricane less than a year ago. The picture that put them over was *Buck Privates*, which Universal made in the ordinary course of the studio schedule. Suddenly one day, everybody on the lot, from office boy to president, woke up to the fact that gold had been discovered in Universal City. *Buck Privates* had panned out as a bonanza." One thing the radio version had that the film did not was a tongue-in-cheek disclaimer: "Any similarity between this play and life in the armed forces of the republic is purely coincidental."

Other *Buck Privates* cast members also traded in on the success of the picture. The Andrews Sisters made *Private Buckaroo* (1942). Besides the trans-posed title, the film's plot also sounds familiar: a spoiled rich kid ultimately conforms to Army life after he falls for the niece of a retired army officer. The score featured another big Andrews Sisters hit about apple trees and separated lovers, "Don't Sit Under the Apple Tree." And, like *Buck Privates*, the film's finale was a patriotic march.

Nat Pendleton had the title role in Monogram's *Top Sergeant Mulligan* (1941). In this one, pharmacists Frank Faylen and Charlie Hall enlist to avoid their creditors, only to discover that the bill collector (Pendleton) is now their top sergeant.

Of the other draft comedies that were announced in the fall of 1940, only *Caught in the Draft* was in production when *Buck Privates* was released. The others were postponed or replaced by other titles. *Caught*, which barely beat *In The Navy* into theaters on May 29, 1941, received better reviews than *Buck Privates* since it did not have the liability of a corny subplot. Bob Hope plays a vain and cowardly movie star who seeks to marry a colonel's daughter in order to avoid the draft. In a publicity stunt arranged to impress her, he pretends to enlist in the army, but it turns out to be a genuine induction. Hope blunders his way through boot camp but ultimately shapes up and proves himself in a war games sequence.

Even though *You're in the Army Now* was announced weeks before *Buck Privates*, Warner Bros. apparently had difficulty casting the picture. In fact, by January 1941, when another list of forthcoming films was compiled, there was no trace of it. Warners did, however, have a script called *Navy Blues* on its shelves that Arthur Horman had developed before he wrote *Buck Privates*. After *Buck Privates* scored a direct hit, *Navy Blues* was dusted off, revised by other writers, and put into production late in April. Meanwhile, Abbott and Costello were shooting another Horman screenplay, *In The Navy*. When *Navy Blues* was finally released in August, *Variety* was not impressed: "The inevitable comedy team for a picture such as this is Jack Oakie and Jack Haley... [who are] handicapped by the weak gags and situations..."

In January 1941, Republic announced that it was negotiating with the Ritz Brothers to appear in "Rookies Roost." But when they couldn't come to terms, the studio settled for bandleader Bob Crosby and comedian Eddie Foy, Jr. The picture ultimately became *Rookies on Parade. Daily Variety* reported

More comedy teams enlist in 1941: Stan Laurel and Oliver Hardy in Great Guns, *and Phil Silvers and Jimmy Durante in* You're in the Army Now.

that a shortage of the "new style" army uniforms forced a two-week postponement of *Rookies on Parade* because other productions (including *Caught in the Draft*) were using them. Released in April, *Rookies on Parade* follows the boot camp misadventures of two songwriters who look to boost the morale of their fellow draftees by staging a big musical show they hope will land on Broadway. William Demarest plays their tough drill sergeant. *Variety* wrote, "It brings inevitable comparisons to 'Buck Privates,' which it resembles in several ways, but... 'Rookies' has no people even closely approximating [Abbott and Costello and the Andrews Sisters'] talent."

By July, Abbott and Costello had not only released *Buck Privates*, but its equally successful follow-up, *In The Navy*. The other studios began scrambling to jump on what they perceived to be a broader trend. The *Motion Picture Herald* asked, "Are two comedians better than one? Hollywood says yes, pointing to Abbott and Costello as proof positive plus. So Hollywood is going in for two-comedian pictures in a big and quite widespread way, starting forthwith and continuing, per Hollywood custom, until the vein runs out and doubtless a bit beyond." The trade publication counted thirteen upcoming productions featuring two or more comedians in the cast, including rumors of a Bert Lahr-Buddy Ebsen comedy at RKO and a Jack Benny-Bob Hope vehicle at Paramount. Warner Bros., meanwhile, announced it would team Jackie Gleason and Jack Carson for *You're in the Army Now*, but nothing came of it.

At 20th Century-Fox, a Kay Kyser musical comedy called "In The Army Now" was announced but never made. Instead, the studio hastily developed a draft comedy called *Great Guns* for another comedy team, Stan Laurel and Oliver Hardy. The comedians, without a film contract for almost two years, had been biding their time touring with a live revue. According to *Collier's* magazine, Hollywood's interest in Stan and Ollie was rekindled by Bud and Lou's success. The magazine wrote, "Comedy moves in cycles and often in mysterious ways, for Laurel and Hardy, also slapstick comedians, had just been dropped in Hollywood when Abbott and Costello came along with the same sort of material and became sensational. So sensational, in fact, that Laurel and Hardy are now back."

Great Guns is clearly influenced by *Buck Privates*. It includes run-ins with a sergeant, a love triangle, and a war games finale. (Unlike *Buck Privates*, however, Stan and Ollie are a considerable part of their war games sequence.) The screenplay even made a direct reference to *Buck Privates* that was cut from the film. *Variety* didn't think *Great Guns* was all that bad; it was "not overloaded with laughs but funny enough to please the average comedy-seeker."

That fall, nearly a year after it was announced and after twenty-two different pairs of comics were considered, Warner Bros. finally found a couple of comedians for *You're in the Army Now*. Phil Silvers and Jimmy Durante were teamed as vacuum cleaner salesmen who, while trying to interest a recruiting officer in a machine, accidentally enlist. Joe Sawyer was their irascible sergeant. The picture reached theaters a week after *Keep 'Em Flying* and four days before the attack on Pearl Harbor. *Variety* liked it: "Though it is a bit corny in spots and lays the slapstick on heavily...here is a comedy of soldier life that completely entertains." Of course, Silvers had his greatest success playing Sergeant Ernie Bilko on television.

Abbott and Costello and *Buck Privates'* influence was even more conspicuous at RKO, where in 1943 two vaudevillians named Wally Brown and Alan Carney were paired up as the studio's answer to Bud and Lou. At the time, Costello was bedridden with rheumatic fever and the team had been off the screen for months. Following the template established by *Buck Privates* and emulating Abbott and Costello, Brown and Carney made their debut in *Adventures of a Rookie* (1943). *Variety* thought RKO had "potential comedy starring timber in the duo, but they need stronger material...Picture is just a jumble of sequences tied together on a very slender thread, with much of the comedy yanked out from deep down in the bag." A sequel, *Rookies in Burma*, was released just four months later and received similar criticism. Brown and Carney also joined the Merchant Marine for *Seven Days Ashore* (1944). They were teamed in eight films over three years, then parted company.

Columbia finally jumped on the bandwagon with *Tramp, Tramp, Tramp* (1942). This embarrassing bomb was directed by Charles Barton, who later helmed *Abbott and Costello Meet Frankenstein* (1948). "Film does a take-off on Abbott and Costello," *Variety* wrote, "with Jackie Gleason working hard and arduously on the comic end. He fails badly, for his material is dated and the continual repetition of hackneyed clichés tends to arouse resentment rather than good-humored sympathy. His partner, Jack Durant, at times imitates Edgar Kennedy."

Barton and Columbia fared better in 1944 with *Hey, Rookie*. Based on a stage musical that had run in Los Angeles, the plot owed more to *Rookies on Parade* than *Buck Privates*, with Larry Parks as a musical comedy producer assigned to put on a camp show for his fellow soldiers. "His trials in staging the show, hindered by the antics of Joe Besser and [his straight man] Jimmy Little, form the nucleus of the plot," *Variety* explained. Thus there was plenty of slapstick to go around, including Besser's own drill routine as a whining misfit. *Variety* called it "a pleasant vaudeville-type film that will fit snugly into the lower rung of double bills."

Several years and another war later, Martin and Lewis duplicated Abbott and Costello's path through the branches of the service. Like Bud and Lou, Dean

RKO's ersatz Abbott and Costello, Wally Brown (left) and Alan Carney (right), drilling in Adventures of a Rookie *(1943). They dashed off a sequel,* Rookies in Burma, *then joined the Merchant Marine in* Seven Days Ashore *(1944).*

and Jerry's first starring vehicle was also a service comedy, *At War With the Army* (1950). (They had supporting roles in *My Friend Irma* a year earlier.) The correlation would be even more striking had Arthur Lubin, who was approached to direct the film, agreed. (He was busy with *Francis the Talking Mule*.)

Martin and Lewis followed up with *Sailor Beware* (1951) and *Jumping Jacks* (1952). *Sailor Beware* has several sequences that recall *Buck Privates*. At the enlistment center, Dean and Jerry squabble with a civilian tough guy (Robert Strauss) who turns out to be their chief petty officer. Later, at the base, Jerry tosses his bag and hits the C.P.O. in the back of the head, then lands on top of him. During an outdoor calisthenics drill, Lewis falls hopelessly out of sync with the rest of the men. In a similar boxing sequence, a more imposing man replaces Jerry's original opponent, yet Lewis wins the bout by accident. These and other parallels may have been due to a tangible *Buck Privates* connection: John Grant was hired to contribute "additional dialogue" to *Sailor Beware*.

Jumping Jacks also has an Abbott and Costello pedigree: Universal rejected a similar storyline submitted by Robert Lees and Fred Rinaldo for *Keep 'Em Flying* in 1941. Two years later, Lees and Rinaldo reworked their script for Paramount but the studio had a hard time casting it. The screenplay sat on a shelf until Martin and Lewis came along.

After Buck Privates

In October 1941, after directing five Abbott and Costello pictures in just ten months, Arthur Lubin called it quits. "I asked to be released after the fifth film [*Keep 'Em Flying*] because they came on the set late, they didn't know their lines, and they were beginning to get tired of one another."

Lubin blamed the grueling pace for the change in the boys. "The studio felt that maybe they needed a new director to give them some incentive. But it was five fabulous pictures with those boys. They were very good for me. They gave me a reputation. I learned everything about timing from them."

Lubin was rewarded with the opportunity to direct *Eagle Squadron*, one of the studio's prestige dramas of 1942. "It was a big chance for me to break away from slapstick," he said. "I don't regret leaving the boys. I wanted to leave them at a high point in my life with them and a high point in their career. I was never asked to direct them again, and I wanted to keep the memory of them the way I originally knew them. It was a sad parting for me. I loved those guys very much. But I don't think any of their later pictures ever equaled the five that I directed."

Lubin, who spent thirty years at Universal, was also entrusted with the studio's lavish remake of *Phantom of the Opera* (1943), starring Claude Rains. But high-camp opuses followed, including *White Savage, Ali Baba and Forty Thieves,* and *The Spider Woman Strikes Back* (which Lubin detested).

In 1949, Lubin became enchanted with David Stern's novel "Francis," about a talking mule, and wanted to make it into a film. In order to persuade Universal's skeptical front office, Lubin offered to cut his salary and accept a percentage of future profits. "They loved the story," he recalled, "but there were technical problems getting a mule to move his mouth in sync with the dialogue. At the same time, they had a deal with Donald O'Connor—they had to find a script for him by a certain date or else they had to pay him anyway."

By trial and error, a well-guarded technique was developed to make Francis "talk." When *Francis the Talking Mule* became a hit, Lubin shared the windfall. He directed six of the seven sequels and Francis, like Abbott and Costello before him, joined every branch of the service.

In the early 1950s Lubin directed Clint Eastwood's screen test and helped the inexperienced actor to receive a contract with Universal. Lubin cast him in bit parts in four films, including *Francis in the Navy* (1955) and *Lady Godiva of Coventry* (1955).

In 1961, Lubin adapted Francis for TV as *Mr. Ed*. He produced and directed the series, which ran for five years. Lubin's friends Mae West and Clint Eastwood made guest appearances as themselves. Bud Abbott was reportedly asked to do a guest spot, but never did.

Lubin often lamented that he'd be remembered for talking mules and horses, but his sixty-odd credits also include *Rhubarb* (1951, about a cat that inherits a baseball team), *Thief of Baghdad* (1953), *The First Traveling Saleslady* (1956), *The Incredible Mr. Limpet* (1966), and *Hold On!* (1966) with Herman's Hermits.

In December 1994, Lubin suffered a stroke and entered a nursing home. When his condition deteriorated he was moved to Glendale Adventist Medical Center, where he died on May 11, 1995. A respiratory therapist at the facility was later convicted in a series of mercy killings, and Lubin's cause of death will always be uncertain. Arthur Lubin was 96.

Arthur Lubin directs Bud and Lou for the fifth and final time in Keep 'Em Flying *(1941).*

Alex Gottlieb stayed with Bud and Lou through 1942, producing six of their next eight films at Universal. In 1943, when Costello became ill with rheumatic fever and the team was idled for a year, Gottlieb moved to Warner Bros. "I finally realized I was going to be marked as just making Abbott and Costello pictures," Gottlieb explained. "I wanted to get away from Abbott and Costello, because when they went down, I'd go down with them."

At Warners, Gottlieb produced *Hollywood Canteen* (1944); several Ronald Reagan films; and the Dennis Morgan-Jack Carson comedies. In 1946 he married Billy Rose's sister, Polly.

In 1951, Abbott and Costello began producing films outside of their Universal contract. They hired Alex, who had left Warners, to produce their only color films, *Jack and The Beanstalk* (1952) and *Abbott and Costello Meet Captain Kidd* (1953). During the same period, Gottlieb was put to work producing the first few episodes of the team's classic TV series, *The Abbott and Costello Show*. It was Gottlieb's first foray into the medium in which he was to have his greatest success. He wrote or produced over fifty TV shows, including *Dear Phoebe, The Gale Storm Show, The Tab Hunter Show, The Bob Hope Chrysler Theater, The Donna Reed Show,* and *The ABC Movie of the Week*. In 1966 he produced the first Smothers Brothers series, a sitcom that cast Tommy as an angel and Dick

as a publishing executive with a boss named "Mr. Costello."

Gottlieb also continued writing for the stage. His biggest theatrical success came with "Susan Slept Here," which he adapted for a film starring Dick Powell and Debbie Reynolds in 1954. Gottlieb's other film credits include producing Doris Day's film debut, *Romance on the High Seas* (1948); Fritz Lang's *The Blue Gardenia* (1953); and the screenplay for Elvis Presley's *Frankie and Johnny* (1965).

Alex Gottlieb died at the Motion Picture Country Home and Hospital on October 9, 1988. He was 81.

When *Buck Privates* wrapped, the Andrews Sisters were reportedly set to star on Broadway in "Screwballs of Swing," with songs by Don Raye and Hughie Prince. Although this never materialized, the sisters appeared with Bud and Lou again in *In The Navy* and *Hold That Ghost* in 1941. Maxene recalled, "We knew Lou better than we knew Bud, so we would spend Saturdays and Sundays at his house. On the set we never saw them because Universal gave them a big trailer, and they sat in there and gambled between every scene. They let me watch, and there was never less than $30,000 in the pot with nothing less than $100 bills."

In 1942, the girls started their own series of C-budget quickies at Universal. Maxene explained, "When *Argentine Nights* played in Argentina [in May

1941], the Castillo regime took it as a personal affront and banned the picture. Well, from all the publicity, the picture caught on in the states. So, Universal started chasing after us to pick up our option, and foolishly we let them. We signed to appear in three pictures a year. Universal was terrible, really terrible. They never spent any money on our pictures. We had to do them in ten days, which is ridiculous. You just worked your tail off and you got nothing, not even a thanks." Their films included *What's Cookin', Private Buckaroo, Give Out Sisters, Always a Bridesmaid, How's About It?*, and *Swingtime Johnny*.

Alex Gottlieb recruited the girls to appear in *Hollywood Canteen* (1944) for Warner Bros. Meanwhile, the sisters racked up even more hit records, including several with Bing Crosby: "Pistol Packin' Mama," "Is You Is or Is You Ain't (My Baby)," "Don't Fence Me In," and "Ac-cent-tchu-ate the Positive."

During the war, the Andrews Sisters played more army, navy, marine and air force bases than any other vocal group, and were affectionately dubbed the three "jive bombers" by servicemen. "I did a lot of growing up back then," Maxene reflected. "I realized that what we were doing back in Hollywood was playing, and what these boys were doing was real. It made me think of the folly of war." One of their most memorable concerts was in a dirigible hanger in Naples. The commanding officer asked the girls to announce to the 5,000 G.I.'s that the war had ended in Japan.

As the 1940s ended, the Andrews Sisters closed out a solid decade as unrivaled hit makers, but were embroiled in personal and professional turmoil. In the space of a few years the girls lost both parents; Patty divorced her first husband, Marty Melcher; Maxene and Lou Levy split; Jack Kapp, who founded Decca records, died; and Vic Schoen, the group's longtime arranger, left the fold. "We had been together nearly all our lives," Patty explained in 1971. "Then in one year our dream world ended. Our mother died and then our father. All three of us were upset, and we were at each other's throats all the time."

Patty branched out in 1951 and did some records without her sisters. She also married her second husband, Walter Weschler, a pianist in Schoen's band. By the end of 1954, Weschler was managing the trio, and insisted on a larger salary for Patty. After thirty years together, the Andrews Sisters split up. Patty continued to work solo, while Maxene and LaVerne toured as a duo. By then the trio had recorded 1,800 songs,

amassed 113 chart singles, sold 75 million records, earned nineteen gold records including eight number ones, and appeared in twenty-two films. They were easily the most popular, versatile, and successful female vocalists of the pre-rock era.

The sisters reconciled in 1956 and signed with Capitol Records, where they covered many of their previous hits and recorded some new material. In the early 1960s they recorded for Kapp and Dot Records. In the mid-1960s, however, LaVerne became ill with cancer and was forced to leave the act. One of the trio's last appearances was on a *Dean Martin Show* broadcast on September 29, 1966. LaVerne died on May 8, 1967, at her home in Brentwood. She was 55. Her husband of nineteen years, trumpet player Louis A. Rogers, was at her side.

In 1968, Maxene was offered the position Dean of Women and instructor in speech and drama at

The Andrews Sisters and Abbott and Costello, together again in In The Navy *(1941).*

Far left: The Andrews Sisters from their Dot Records greatest hits release early in 1962. Left: Lee Bowman with Rita Hayworth in Tonight and Every Night *(1945).*

Paradise College in Lake Tahoe. She left her post in 1974 to join Patty in the Broadway musical *Over Here!* Newcomers John Travolta, Treat Williams, Marilu Henner, Samuel E. Wright, and Ann Reinking were also in the cast. The show was a hit with critics and the top-grossing production of the season. But it closed after nine months (and on the eve of a national tour) because of bitter salary disputes between the Andrews Sisters and the producers, and between the sisters themselves. Patty and Maxene became estranged and never sang together again. They reportedly only saw each other twice after 1974—once in 1982 when Maxene had a heart attack, and again in 1987 when the Andrews Sisters received a star on the Hollywood Walk of Fame.

Maxene released a solo album, *Maxene: An Andrews Sister*, in 1990, and a memoir, *Over Here, Over There*, in 1993. The following year she sang "Boogie Woogie Bugle Boy" in Normandy at ceremonies marking the fiftieth anniversary of D-Day. In 1995, she sang "America The Beautiful" for thousands of veterans in Honolulu at ceremonies marking the fiftieth anniversary of V-J Day.

In 1991, "Company B," a ballet by choreographer Paul Taylor, premiered at the Kennedy Center in Washington, D.C. The soundtrack consisted of nine Andrews Sisters numbers, including "Boogie Woogie Bugle Boy," "Bei Mir Bist Du Schoen," "Pennsylvania Polka," "Tico Tico," "I Can Dream Can't I," and "Rum and Coca Cola." On the surface it sounds like a jubilant homage, but the choreography was in dark coun-

terpoint to the songs, and reflected the misery of war. In 1992, when the Houston Ballet performed the piece in Los Angeles, Patty and Maxene attended but did not speak to each other.

Maxene died on October 21, 1995, after completing a four-week engagement in an off-Broadway revue, "Swingtime Canteen." She was 79. In a 1993 interview she reflected, "We sold millions of records, made movies, and had shows on radio, TV and Broadway. I don't think there's much we didn't do. Life has been very full."

Patty became a strong advocate for the National World War II Memorial. In 1998 she wrote an Op-Ed piece in the *Los Angeles Times* entitled "Bugle Boys of Company B Died to Keep America Free." Patty wrote, "Helping to build morale and comfort the wounded through our music changed and fulfilled my life, as it did the lives of my sisters, LaVerne and Maxene. We were privileged to know so many courageous men and women willing to give their lives for freedom. It's ironic that because of their sacrifice, we can use words like 'freedom' and 'democracy' today without having to measure their cost. We must honor those brave young people who paid the price."

Patty passed away in her home on January 30, 2013. She was 94. Her husband, Walter, died in 2010.

Lee Bowman returned to MGM in the spring of 1941, where he continued to appear in supporting roles. There was an occasional upgrade, as in *Washington Melodrama* (1941), *Kid Glove Killer* (1942), and *Pacific Rendezvous* (1942). But following the classic battle drama *Bataan* (1943), Bowman left MGM and signed with Columbia, where he was billed opposite Rita Hayworth in *Cover Girl* (1944) and *Tonight and Every Night* (1945). After two years at Columbia, Lee began freelancing. He returned to Universal to appear opposite Susan Hayward in *Smash-Up, The Story of a Woman* (1947); co-starred with Doris Day in *My Dream Is Yours* (1949) at Warners; and appeared in Fritz Lang's *The House by the River* (1950) at Republic.

In 1948, Bowman played Lucille Ball's bandleader husband in the pilot episode of her radio series, "My Favorite Husband." Richard Denning won the role, however, and the series ran until 1951, when it moved to TV as *I Love Lucy.*

Bowman also appeared on stage in "The Magic and the Loss," and on several television dramatic shows, including *Studio One, Kraft Theater,* and *Playhouse 90.* His personal favorite was a TV adaptation of "The Great Gatsby" on *Robert Montgomery Presents.* He also spent three years as TV's *Ellery Queen* (1952-55), and a year on *Miami Undercover* (1961), with Rocky Graziano playing his partner. In 1962 he returned to Broadway in *Mary, Mary.*

After his last film, *Youngblood Hawke* (1964), Bowman, a staunch Republican, became a consultant to the party, coaching candidates and corporate executives in the art of public speaking. He coached Eisenhower, Nixon, and Ford and countless other politicians. Asked if he missed acting, Bowman once replied, "Not a bit. The only thing my job lacks now is billing. The rest is all there—famous people, travel, and some egos that would put my contemporaries to shame." He emceed the Republican national conventions in 1968 and 1972. In 1976, he produced and narrated *Threads of Glory: 200 Years of America in Words and Music* (Decca), a six-record boxed-set featuring Henry Fonda, Burt Lancaster, Jonathan Winters and others. It flopped, and it was a great disappointment to him.

"Hollywood was one part of his life, but I think my father would prefer to be remembered for his dedication to his country," his son, Lee Jr., told the *National Enquirer.* "My father was the kind of guy who wouldn't leave the house unless he was impeccably dressed, just like the men he used to play on screen. He wouldn't even go to the market unless he was wearing jacket and tie."

Lee Bowman died of a heart attack on December

Top: Alan Curtis and Ilona Massey on their 340-acre farm on the Northern California coast. Above: Curtis and Anne Gwynne in The Enchanted Valley *(1948).*

25, 1979, three days short of his 65th birthday. He and Helene Del Valle had been married 38 years. She had been ill for several years, and he took loving care of her. She died in 1993.

Alan Curtis married Ilona Massey on March 26, 1941. Later that year, the couple appeared together in

Left: Jane Frazee around 1951. Right: Jane as Easy Williams, on the cover of her 1957 album. (Courtesy Tim Tryon)

the musical bio-pic *New Wine* (1941). Curtis played composer Franz Schubert, and Ilona sang "Ave Maria." A year later, however, they were divorced.

Beginning with *Remember Pearl Harbor* (1942), Curtis appeared in a string of war dramas, including *Hitler's Madmen, Two Tickets to London,* and *Gung Ho* (all 1943). These last two were made under contract to Universal, where Curtis shot ten films between 1943 and 1945. He also turned up in *Crazy House* (1943) and *See My Lawyer* (1945) opposite Olsen and Johnson; The *Invisible Man's Revenge* (1944); and perhaps his best role, in Robert Siodmak's film noir *Phantom Lady* (1944). In 1945 he played period gamblers in both *Frisco Sal* and Abbott and Costello's *The Naughty Nineties* (1945).

After *The Daltons Ride Again* (1945) and *Inside Job* (1946), Curtis began freelancing at poverty-row studios like Screen Guild, PRC, and Eagle-Lion, in films like *Renegade Girl* (1946) and *Flight to Nowhere* (1946). In 1947 he starred in the last two Philo Vance mysteries, *Philo Vance's Gamble* and *Philo Vance's Secret Mission.* Three of his last four films were made in Italy, for foreign studios: *I Pirati di Capri* (*Pirates of Capri,* 1949), *Amore e sangue* (*City of Violence,* 1951) and *Schatten uber Neapel* (*Camorra,* 1951)

Between 1946 and 1952, Curtis married and divorced three more times. He wed model Sandra Lucas in Las Vegas in 1946; Elizabeth Sundmark in 1950; and Betty Dodero in 1952.

On February 1, 1953, Curtis had a kidney stone removed at St. Clare's Hospital in Manhattan.

Sometime after the operation (accounts vary), his heart stopped. His doctor, who happened to be in checking on him, made an incision and massaged Curtis' heart by hand for four minutes before it started beating again. But Curtis had suffered irreparable brain damage from oxygen-deprivation. He died a few days later, at age 43.

Universal kept Jane Frazee busy after *Buck Privates.* She immediately went into a two-reel musical short, then appeared in 14 features between 1941 and 1943. Many were low-budget musicals with Robert Paige for director Charles Lamont. Jane had the distinction of working with all three of the studio's comedy teams when she made *Hellzapoppin'* (1941) with Olsen and Johnson and *Hi'ya Chum* (1943) with the Ritz Brothers. In 1942 she was reunited with the Andrews Sisters in *What's Cookin'?* That year, Jane married the first of her four husbands, Glenn Tryon. The former cowboy star was a producer at Universal. (He co-produced *Hold That Ghost* and *Keep 'Em Flying.*) Tryon was almost twice Jane's age. Her only child, Tim, was born in 1946.

Jane's reviews always suggested that she was meant for better things. When Glenn Tryon moved to Columbia in 1944, Jane followed, but things weren't much better there. She appeared in *Cowboy Canteen, She's a Sweetheart, Swing in the Saddle, Beautiful But Broke* and *Ten Cents a Dance.* At Republic she starred as one of the era's most iconic figures in *Rosie the Riveter* (1944).

Frazee and Tryon divorced in 1947. That year she

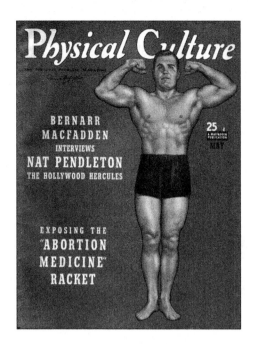

Left: Nat Pendleton on the cover of the May, 1940 issue of Physical Culture. *Above: reprising his role as Sergeant Collins in the sequel,* Buck Privates Come Home *(1947).*

made the first of five appearances in Roy Rogers westerns at Republic. In 1948, Jane married Rogers' stand-in, Whitey Christensen, in Las Vegas.

"She took her work seriously and worked hard," her son, Tim, reflected, "but she admitted she really didn't have the ambition it took to become a big star. It's an infamous road, so perhaps she didn't care to pay that price, because it really would have conflicted with how she felt about how one should conduct one's life. She worked hard and she lived with integrity, and that's what she tried to instill."

Jane's last feature was *Rhythm Inn,* in 1951. (In *The Honeymooners* episode "TV or Not TV," Ralph finds *Rhythm on Ice,* with Kenny Baker and Jane Frazee, in the TV listings. There is no such film.) The following year she joined the cast of the TV series *Beulah.* Jane replaced Ginger Jones as Beulah's employer, and Louise Beavers replaced the sitcom's star, Ethel Waters. (Bud Harris, who played the train porter in *Buck Privates,* played Beulah's boyfriend in the first season.) Jane turned up in an episode of Bud and Lou's TV series ("The Paperhangers") and in two episodes of *The Adventures of Superman.* She also sang regularly on Leo Carillo's local TV variety show.

In the mid 1950s she appeared opposite George O'Hanlon in several of Warner's *Behind The Eight Ball* (a.k.a. *Joe McDoakes*) shorts. O'Hanlon, who wrote more than sixty of the domestic sitcoms from 1942 and 1956, was later the voice of George Jetson.

In 1957, Jane recorded an album for Dot Records under the name Easy Williams. "She tried to make a little comeback," Tim explained, "not to change her persona—she would have just as soon remained Jane Frazee. But some record producer had a better idea and he made up 'Easy Williams,' of all things. It was an album of torch songs. It was pretty good for what it was. But they didn't let her sing her best tune, 'Baubles, Bangles and Beads.' The album didn't sell very well; it didn't have distribution."

Jane left show business soon after and began selling real estate in Newport Beach. Author Richard Lamparski once asked her if her clients recognize her. "Yes," she replied. "They say, 'Don't you sing in the movies? Aren't you Doris Day?'"

Jane Frazee died on August 30, 1985, in a Newport Beach nursing home of pneumonia following a series of strokes. She was 67.

Although Nat Pendleton appeared in about 110 films in his career, only nine were made after *Buck Privates.* He appeared in three more *Dr. Kildare* films, and then reprised his role as Sergeant Collins in *Buck Privates Come Home* (1947). By some accounts, Pendleton, an economics major at Columbia, had invested well and didn't need the work.

Most fans thought Nat's best role was as Lieutenant Guild in the *Thin Man* series. But according to his widow, Pendleton' favorite parts were as a convict who produces a prison musical in *Jailhouse Blues* (Universal, 1942), and as the dumb wrestler in *Swing Your Lady* (Warner, 1938).

Nat Pendleton died of a heart attack on October 12, 1967, in LaJolla, Calif. He was 71.

Thank God for Abbott and Costello!

When Abbott and Costello were filming *Buck Privates*, Lou rented a home on Crescent Drive in Beverly Hills while Bud rented a small house on Alcove Street in the San Fernando Valley. But as production wound down on the film, Abbott sold his house in Stony Brook, New York, and Costello sold his home in Paterson and they each bought houses in the San Fernando Valley. Bud's was on Woodley Avenue in Encino, and Lou's was on Longridge Avenue in Sherman Oaks.

Lou Costello's third trip to the coast was the charm. This time, he was in Hollywood to stay.

Bud and Lou's remarkable comedic timing has been acknowledged and acclaimed for seven decades, but their career timing was just as perfect. They arrived in Hollywood when the door was open for new comedy talent. The critic for the *St. Louis Post-Dispatch* observed, "With the fading of Laurel and Hardy, the disinclination of the Marx Brothers to keep up to standard, and the shabby work of many seasoned comics of the screen, a new pair of clowns is a valuable addition."

Bud and Lou also arrived in precisely the right kind of picture at the right time. *Box Office* noted,

Deanna Durbin was Universal's biggest star in 1940.

"Timeliness is *Buck Privates'* greatest asset. As the first of an impending large number of pictures dealing with the draft and other phases of national defense, it will doubtlessly strike a popular chord and register revenue scores of husky proportions."

The boys' timing couldn't have been better for Universal as well. Bud and Lou started at the impoverished studio just when the Deanna Durbin series started to lose its luster. Although each of her wholesome musicals had grossed an average of about $2 million, they had become increasingly expensive to produce, cutting into the profits. *Nice Girl?*, which was in production at the same time as *Buck Privates*, was budgeted at $885,000. Although the film grossed approximately $1.9 million, Universal's return on its investment was only 211%, which in turn was sunk into her next picture, *It Started With Eve* (1941). Another factor in the series' decline was Durbin's age. She was no longer the virgin ingénue of her early films; she turned nineteen on December 4, 1940, and announced that she was engaged to be married in April 1941. The final blow to the series came after *It Started With Eve*, when her producer, Joe Pasternak, moved to MGM,

Abbott and Costello are crowned Hollywood's No.1 Box Office Stars of 1942.

and her director, Henry Koster, followed soon after. This left Deanna, whose stock was slipping, seeking more control of her pictures, and led to a brief rift with Universal in the fall of 1941. "There was a time when Miss Durbin's revolt would have provoked a crisis in Universal's affairs," the *New York Times* explained, "for she was their outstanding personality. Since the Nate Blumberg regime took over, however, dividends have been paid and the studio holds commitments on the services of such people as Irene Dunne, Charles Boyer, Margaret Sullavan and Abbott and Costello."

The early Abbott and Costello films also grossed around $2 million apiece, but because the pictures were made on much smaller budgets (and, critics complained, with less care), Universal earned an additional $500,000 per film. More significantly, Bud and Lou could churn out films at a faster pace, releasing up to four pictures a year to Durbin's two. The four Abbott and Costello films released in 1941—

Buck Privates, In The Navy, Hold That Ghost, and *Keep 'Em Flying*—cost only $1.4 million to produce. Yet these four films grossed over $7.6 million, accounting for 25% of Universal's gross on fifty-eight releases that year.

In the *Showman's Trade Review* poll of the twenty-five "leading productions" of 1941, the only Universal releases on the list were Abbott and Costello films. A poll of exhibitors by the *Motion Picture Herald* voted Bud and Lou the country's No. 3 Box Office Stars of 1941. (*Variety's* poll named them No. 2.) They were the first Universal stars and the first comedy team to appear in the Top Ten since it was introduced in 1932. For all her success at the box office between 1937 and 1940, Deanna Durbin never made that elite list.

Blumberg and Cliff Work realized that if each Abbott and Costello film earned $2 million and the budgets were kept low, the boon would be unprecedented. It was. The team's films in 1942 outdid those made in 1941 and, true to Alex Gottlieb's original prediction, exhibitors crowned Abbott and Costello Hollywood's No. 1 Box Office Stars. In *The Hollywood Studio System*, Douglas Gomery wrote, "Wall Street analysts noted the trend, upgrading their appraisal of Universal as a stock purchase as a result of this one pair of stars."

Bud and Lou continued to appear in the Top Ten through 1944, and fell to eleventh place in 1945. Meanwhile, the average budget on their first eight films at Universal was just $375,000 per picture. It wasn't until 1946 that the budget of an Abbott and Costello film approached that of Durbin's earlier films; *The Time of Their Lives* exceeded $900,000. But the studio decreed that the Abbott and Costello films continue to be made inexpensively throughout the team's 14-year tenure at Universal. These budgets precluded color; the boys' only color films were the two that they produced themselves outside of their Universal contract. With a budget of $750,000, *Abbott and Costello Meet Frankenstein* was the studio's second cheapest production of 1948, yet the film was Universal's third highest grosser that year.

For eleven years, Abbott and Costello were the studio's single greatest source of income. The only Universal releases to appear on the *Showman's Trade Review* lists of "leading productions" in 1941, 1942, 1943, and 1944 were Abbott and Costello films. After a two-year lull, the team returned to the upper ranks of the Top Ten Box Office Stars in 1948, 1949, 1950 and 1951. Again, they were the only Universal stars to appear on the list.

In *The Genius of the System*, his incisive study of the golden age of Hollywood, Thomas Schatz explains, "Abbott and Costello were a genuine movie industry phenomenon and a tremendous windfall for Universal. Durbin's Depression-era impact may have been more dramatic, given the studio's desperate financial shape at the time, but she had nowhere near the economic and popular success, nor the longevity, of Abbott and Costello."

Eventually the studio got around to acknowledging Bud and Lou's contribution to its history and its very survival. In 1999, numerous buildings and streets on the Universal lot were renamed after famous studio and company personnel. One of the large production office buildings on the lower lot was named the "Abbott and Costello Building."

As Universal's president, Nate Blumberg, once put it, "Thank God for Abbott and Costello."

Cast and Crew
and Pressbook

Production Start..............Dec. 13, 1940
Production End.................Jan. 11, 1941
Copyright Date...............Jan. 28, 1941
Released..........................Jan. 31, 1941
Running Time...................82 minutes
Reissued......Nov. 1948 and Oct. 1953*
(*with *Keep 'Em Flying*)

Directed By......................Arthur Lubin
Produced By...................Alex Gottlieb
Screenplay By.........Arthur T. Horman
Special Material for Abbott & Costello
.........John Grant
Director of Photography............
Milton Krasner, ASC
Jerry Ash, ASC
Art Director...................Jack Otterson
Associate.................Ralph M. DeLacy
Film Editor.......................Philip Cahn
Dance Director.................Nick Castle
Sound Supervisor.......Bernard Brown
Sound Technician................Paul Neal
Gowns...............................Vera West
Set Decorator...............R. A. Gausman
Assistant Directors.................Gil Valle
Vernon Keays
Military Advisor.......Capt. Jack Voglin
Musical Director.........Charles Previn

"Boogie Woogie Bugle Boy," "Bounce
Me Brother With a Solid Four," and
"When Private Brown Becomes a
Captain," by Don Raye and Hughie

Prince and Sonny Burke; "I Wish You
Were Here," by Don Raye, Hughie
Prince and Vic Schoen; "I'll Be With
You When It's Apple Blossom Time"
by Albert Von Tilzer and Neville
Fleeson.

Vocal Arrangements..........Vic Schoen
Music Supervisor.................Ted Cain

Slicker Smith.....................Bud Abbott
Herbie Brown...................Lou Costello
The Andrews Sisters.........Themselves
Randolph Parker, III........Lee Bowman
Bob Martin........................Alan Curtis
Judy Gray.........................Jane Frazee
Sgt. Michael Collins.....Nat Pendleton
Dick Burnette........................Don Raye
Miss Durling.................Dora Clemant
Capt. Williams......J. Anthony Hughes
Henry...........................Hughie Prince
Briggs.........................Leonard Elliott
Hostesses........................Jeanne Kelly
Elaine Morey
Kay Leslie
Nina Orla
Dorothy Darrell
Sgt. Callahan.................Harry Strang
Harmonica Player.............Frank Cook
Maj. Gen. Emerson....Samuel S. Hinds
Cook...........................Shemp Howard
Mrs. Parker......................Nella Walker
Mr. Parker....................Douglas Wood

Edmunds.................Charles Coleman
Captain.......................Selmer Jackson
Announcer...............Mike Frankovich
Sergeant..........................James Flavin
Instructor.............................Tom Tyler
Sergeant...................Herold Goodwin
Supply Sergeant...............John Butler
Medical Examiner..........Jack Mulhall
Major...........................William Gould
Sergeant..................Stanley Blystone
Porter..................................Bud Harris
Tough Fighter.....................Al Billings
Corporal..........................William Hall
Supply Sergeant.........Carleton Young
Sgt. Marks.....................Frank Penny
Fighter..............................Bob Cason
Corporal.......................Jerome Harte
Fighter.............................Frank Dolan
Fighter..............................Lloyd Frank
Small Boxer...............Frank Grandetta
Sergeant..........................Ken Duncan
Corporal........................James Lucas
Lt. Albright.......................Bob Wayne
Lt. Poole..........................Lyle Moraine
Corporal........................Stanley Smith
Lieutenant................William Morgan
Lieutenant............................Tom Reed
and
The World Champion
Boogie WoogieDancers
as Themselves

LEADING THE *BIG* PARADE OF PATRONS!

- **BLOW YOUR BUGLE...ROLL YOUR DRUMS**
  ...and watch 'em come marching in to see the laugh-show they've been waiting for...the FIRST Army Camp Comedy!

- **TRAIN YOUR SHOWMANSHIP GUNS** on the great army of Abbott & Costello and Andrews Sisters fans! Give it Air-Ploitation to reach the radio huggers!

BUD **ABBOTT** and LOU **COSTELLO**
in

BUCK PRIVATES

with

Lee **BOWMAN** Alan **CURTIS**
Jane **FRAZEE** Nat **PENDLETON**
and
THE ANDREWS SISTERS
and 24 world champion
boogie-woogie boys and beauties!

'Buck Privates' Star-Spangled Farce

SYNOPSIS

(Not for Publication)

Slicker Smith (Bud Abbott) and Herbie Brown (Lou Costello), his shill, sneak into a theatre to elude Michael Collins (Nat Pendleton), a cop. But the theatre is a converted enlistment center, and in less time than it takes to tell, they're in the army of the U. S. A.

With them bound for the training camp are The Andrews Sisters (themselves), who are hostesses; plus Randolph Parker, III (Lee Bowman), a good-looking rich boy with a superiority complex; Bob Martin (Alan Curtis), a darn nice guy who used to be Parker's chauffeur, and Judy Gray (Jane Frazee), also a hostess.

At camp, Slicker and Herbie discover that their sergeant is an old enemy, Collins.

Despite her fondness for Bob, Judy finds herself falling for Randolph, who has turned camp "heel."

In the war games Randolph saves Bob's life and turns the trick to victory for their outfit.

Everybody is happy. Even Collins relents with Slicker and Herbie.

CREDITS

Universal Pictures
presents
BUD ABBOTT & LOU COSTELLO
in
"BUCK PRIVATES"
with
LEE BOWMAN, ALAN CURTIS
Jane Frazee, Nat Pendleton, Samuel S. Hinds and
THE ANDREWS SISTERS
Original Screen Play......................
Arthur T. Horman
Special Material for Abbott
*& Costello ....*John Grant
*Cameraman ....*Milton Krasner
*Art Director................*Jack Otterson
*Gowns ....*Vera West
*Sound Supervisor..*Bernard B. Brown
*Musical Director........*Charles Previn
*Musical Supervisor............*Ted Cain
*Dance Director ....*Nick Castle
*Director ....*Arthur Lubin
*Associate Producer......*Alex Gottlieb

THE CAST

*Randolph Parker, III..*Lee Bowman
*Bob Martin ....*Alan Curtis
*Slicker Smith..................*Bud Abbott
*Herbie Brown................*Lou Costello
Patty
Maxene }........The Andrews Sisters
LaVerne
*Judy Gray....................*Jane Frazee
*Sgt. Michael Collins..*Nat Pendleton
Major General Emerson..............
Samuel S. Hinds
*Sergeant Callahan........*Harry Strang
*Mrs. Parker, II..........*Nella Walker
*Henry ....*Leonard Elliott
*Chef ....*Shemp Howard
*Announcer ....*Mike Frankovitch
Camp Hostesses
Miss Durling   Dora Clemant
Jeanne Kelly   Elaine Morey
Kay Leslie   Nina Orla
Dorothy Darrell
and
The World Champion Boogie-Woogie Dancers as themselves

The Andrews Sisters and Abbott and Costello in Universal's "Buck Privates." (Left to right) Maxene Andrews, Patty Andrews, Lou Costello, La Verne Andrews and Bud Abbott.

(Mat 24)

Claim Fat, Thin Contrast Aid to Abbott and Costello

(Current)

The long and short of it and the fat and the thin of it are the starting off points for successful comedy combinations.

Andrews Sisters Philanthropists

(Current)

There is a dramatic story behind the cute American clown dolls which now are nationally on sale bearing the name and photo of The Andrews Sisters, currently appearing with Abbott and Costello in "Buck Privates," the Universal comedy at the .... Theatre.

Was Vaudeville Star

Not long ago, Larry Rich, who drew $4,500 per week in vaudeville, suddenly died leaving his wife, Cherie, $30,000 in debt. She started fashioning the clown dolls to sell to her friends to eke out a living.

The Andrews girls and their mother gave her a few hundred dollars and made a tieup with the Cripple Institute of New York to manufacture the toys.

Reduces Indebtedness

Mrs. Rich has now virtually paid off every dollar she and her husband owed, and the business, thanks to the Andrews, is thriving like the green bay tree.

In "Buck Privates" The Andrews Sisters are seen as army camp hostesses. The colorful roles offer numerous opportunities for the introduction of the many new swing tunes which were composed especially for the picture.

Arthur Lubin was the director of "Buck Privates" and Alex Gottlieb the associate producer.

Even the Jack Bennys and the Bob Hopes say there is no definite set of rules for being funny—you just are, or you just are not, they say—but with two-team funsters, there is at least one "must" that has been proven almost without exception during the past fifty years of American entertainment.

Extremes Essential

It is that the "straight man," or foil, be long and lean, and the comic be short and stubby.

No exceptions to that rule are Bud Abbott and Lou Costello, currently starred by Universal at the .... Theatre with The Andrews Sisters of boogie-woogie fame in "Buck Privates," first of Hollywood's pictures about Uncle Sam's conscriptees.

Bud Abbott is very, very much the "toothpick" type, and his partner weighs 200 pounds, is only five feet, four inches tall, has three chins normally and five when he bends over.

Seen in Reverse

Stan Laurel and "Babe" Hardy reverse the general rule in that the latter is long and hefty, and Laurel is short and skinny.

But down the rest of the list, they nearly all conform to physical pattern. Amos 'n' Andy, Olsen and Johnson, Weber and Fields, "two black Crows" Moran and Mack, and Charlie Murray and George Sidney of "the Cohens and the Kellys" fame all prove the rule.

And that, in a "nut" shell, is the sum and substance, the Mutt and Jeff of it.

Battalion of Talent is Recruited for Laugh Film

(Advance)

Lead-off picture from Hollywood about the funny side of camp life of the conscriptees in Uncle Sam's fighting forces, "Buck Privates" comes to the .... Theatre on ....

Bud Abbott and Lou Costello, the serio-comic battlers of radio and the stage, who were immediately signed to a long term contract following their hit in "One Night in the Tropics," share prominent spots in the Universal hit with The Andrews Sisters, the boogie-woogie girls of rhythm, who also hit the boxoffice jackpot in their first film, "Argentine Nights."

Lee Bowman, recently opposite Lana Turner in a series of films; Alan Curtis, last in "High Sierra," and Jane Frazee, vivacious new film leading lady, form a two-boys-and-a-girl romantic combination. Nat Pendleton has one of the main supporting comedy roles.

Glamour Girls

In addition, there is a whole galaxy of glamour girls, including Dorothy Darrell, producer Joe Pasternak's newest "find"; Kay Leslie, one of the "13 baby stars of 1940"; Jeanne Kelly, Nina Orla and Elaine Morey.

The Andrews Sisters sing several new songs in "Buck Privates," all of them written by Don Raye and Hughie Prince, composers of "Rhumboogie," "Beat Me, Daddy, Eight to the Bar," and a score of other hits. Their new numbers are, "You're a Lucky Fellow, Mr. Smith," "I Wish You Were Here," "Bounce Me Brother With a Solid Four," "When Private Brown Becomes a Captain" and "Boogie-Woogie Bugle Boy."

Old Hit Revived

In addition, the girls revive an old number, "I'll Be With You in Apple Blossom Time."

Arthur Lubin directed the picture from the screenplay by Arthur T. Horman. Alex Gottlieb was the associate producer.

SONGS

Sung by The Andrews Sisters
"BOOGIE WOOGIE BUGLE BOY"
*Words and Music......*Hughie Prince
Don Raye

(Pub., Leeds Music)

♦ ♦ ♦

"YOU'RE A LUCKY FELLOW, MR. SMITH"
*Words and Music......*Hughie Prince
Don Raye
Sonny Burke

(Pub., Leeds Music)

♦ ♦ ♦

"BOUNCE ME BROTHER WITH A SOLID FOUR"
*Words and Music......*Hughie Prince
Don Raye

(Pub., Leeds Music)

♦ ♦ ♦

"I'LL BE WITH YOU IN APPLE BLOSSOM TIME"
*Music by................*Albert von Tilzer
*Lyrics by..................*Neville Fleeson

(Pub., Broadway Music Corp.)

♦ ♦ ♦

Sung by Bud Abbott & Lou Costello
"WHEN PRIVATE BROWN BECOMES A CAPTAIN"
*Words and Music......*Hughie Prince
Don Raye

(Pub., Leeds Music)

♦ ♦ ♦

Sung by Jane Frazee
"I WISH YOU WERE HERE"
*Words and Music......*Hughie Prince
Don Raye
Vic Schoen

(Pub., Leeds Music)

Bud Abbott and Lou Costello in Universal's hilarious army-life comedy, "Buck Privates."

(Mat 11)

♦ ♦ ♦

Army Life Farce Has Alan Curtis

(Current)

When pretty boys were stamped passe by advertising artists and commercial photographers, and the agencies started looking for two-fisted masculine punch, Alan Curtis started posing for the cameras.

The handsome young romantic lead currently is seen with Abbott and Costello and The Andrews Sisters in Universal's "Buck Privates" at the .... Theatre. Previously he was a loan collector, chewing gum salesman, assistant clerk in a brokerage house—and a veteran member of the army of the unemployed, he ruefully admits.

His first screen experience happened when he met a fascinating Russian beauty. She couldn't speak English, he couldn't talk her language. But through interpreters and their own improvised sign language, they signed contracts together, and starred together in a commercial movie.

Following release of the film, Curtis was sought by several studios, and since has been featured in a score of pictures.

Barrage of Laughs in Timely Comedy

'Buck Privates' Funniest of Army Life Productions

(Review)

If army camp life is just a fraction as enjoyable as "Buck Privates," Uncle Sam's quota will be as crowded as the ticket line at the .... Theatre was yesterday when the Universal fun-film began its engagement.

Radio-stage's Abbott and Costello, who were roaringly funny in their first picture, "One Night in the Tropics," completely out-top themselves in this new hilarity-hit. The audience had a difficult time keeping its feet still when The Andrews Sisters of boogie-woogie rhythm got "in the groove" with their new songs.

Comedians in Khaki

Abbott and Costello are a couple of misfit kids in khaki in the army of "Buck Privates" and everything happens to them from K. P. duty to "solitary" in the guard-house, with Nat Pendleton their nemesis in the role of a hardboiled sergeant.

There is a nice thread of romance, too, in the picture, framed by a young "Sergeant Quirk," "Captain Flagg" rivalry, played by Lee Bowman and Alan Curtis, over the affections of a pert and pretty hostess, enacted by Jane Frazee. Incidentally, Miss Frazee, who has made only one picture before this one, exhibits the most pleasing sort of personality and a whale of a lot of ability.

Song Hits Enjoyed

Every one of the new songs registers hit rating. Included are "You're a Lucky Fellow, Mr. Smith," "Bounce Me, Brother With a Solid Four," "Boogie-Woogie Bugle Boy," "When Private Brown Becomes a Captain" and "I Wish You Were Here." In addition, the Sisters revive an oldie, "I'll Be With You in Apple Blossom Time."

Arthur Lubin has given "Buck Privates" topnotch direction, and Arthur T. Horman is certainly entitled to a bow for his ingeniously funny screenplay. Alex Gottlieb was the associate producer.

Lou Costello and Nina Orla in Universal's "Buck Privates."
(Mat 13)

Compose Boogie Music for Farce

(Advance)

Five new songs and one old one are featured in "Buck Privates," the new Universal hit starring Abbott and Costello, coming .... to the .... Theatre. Lee Bowman, Alan Curtis, Jane Frazee and The Andrews Sisters are other headliners in the film.

The eight-beats-to-the-bar tunes introduced in the comedy about army camp life are "I Wish You Were Here," "Boogie-Woogie Bugle Boy," "You're a Lucky Fellow, Mr. Smith," "Bounce Me, Brother With a Solid Four" and "When Private Brown Becomes a Captain."

They are written by Don Raye and Hughie Prince, writers of "Rhumboogie," "Beat Me, Daddy, Eight to the Bar" and a score of other top hits. Vic Schoen, musical director for The Andrews Sisters, collaborated.

The old hit sung by The Andrews Sisters is "I'll Be With You in Apple Blossom Time," first popular right after the last war.

Army Officers Become Actors

(Current)

Every one of the 53 commissioned and non-commissioned officers appearing in "Buck Privates," the Universal fun-film about the army starring Abbott and Costello with Lee Bowman, Alan Curtis and The Andrews Sisters now at the .... Theatre, is of actual military experience comparable to his rank.

But there is one exception. He is Selmer Jackson, who plays the Colonel and has done more than a score of high-ranking officers of the army and navy in pictures. Jackson has never served a day in real-life uniform.

Star Swing Trio In Army Comedy

(Advance)

The story of The Andrews Sisters, featured with Abbott and Costello, Lee Bowman, Alan Curtis and others in Universal's "Buck Privates," coming .... to the .... Theatre, is a story of three girls who believed in each other, two years, and one song.

The song was "Bei Mir Bist Du Schoen." The girls, Patty, LaVerne and Maxene, were an obscure trio on starvation street in vaudeville and radio who were kept together by one thing—they knew they were right, and the world was wrong. The tune and the trio got together, and soon the Andrews were in the four-figure income brackets.

All three girls were born in Minneapolis. They started as kids on the stage with the late Larry Rich in variety, but never got out of the small-time until they introduced "Bei Mir Bist Du Schoen" and it became a best-seller. Since then they started the rave for boogie-woogie music with such songs as "Rhumboogie" and "Beat Me, Daddy, Eight to the Bar."

Bud Abbott (left) with Lou Costello and Nat Pendleton in Universal's army life comedy, "Buck Privates."
(Mat 22)

Andrews Sisters Soar to Fame With Boogie-Woogie

(Current)

If the international situation has you troubled and your rheumatism has you down, just forget your cares and worries and try a little boogie-woogie. It's a cure-all for the blues.

That's the prescription of The Andrews Sisters, who have made boogie-woogie what it is today—just about a national institution.

In Current Comedy

Currently at the .... Theatre with Abbott and Costello in Universal's "Buck Privates," the Andrews, Maxene, LaVerne and Patty, are the girls who first sang "Rhumboogie," "Beat Me, Daddy, Eight to the Bar," "Scrub Me, Momma, With a Boogie Beat," and a half-dozen others that have topped the half-million mark. They say:

"Everybody goes for boogie-woogie. They can't help it. All you've got to do is hear it, and your feet won't let you keep still. Once you've got the rhythm, boogie-woogie does the rest."

There's nothing new about the kind of music that the Andrews sisters sing. Nobody seems to know for certain, but it's supposed to have originated about 100 years ago, down in the deep south.

Heard at House-Warmings

There the colored folk used to have house-warmings, each of the guests bringing his contribution to the party. The musicians brought their talent, but they seldom had pianos, so the basic rhythm was that of the bass or drums, eight beats to the bar.

And just as symphony has its Stokowski, boogie-woogie has its maestros, including such picturesque gentlemen of color as "Pinetop" Smith, late of Chicago, "Crippled" Clarence and "Jellyroll" Martin.

But it never really hit its stride and became a world-wide vogue until the Andrews sisters sang "Well, Allright" a few years ago.

Lou Costello and Nat Pendleton in Universal's "Buck Privates."
(Mat 12)

Lou Costello Seeks Niche in Hall of Fame

(Current)

Mr. Lou Costello, of the firm of Abbott and Costello, caterers of comedic engineering, is a very frustrated gentleman these days.

Mr. Costello, currently engaged on the screen of the .... Theatre with his estimable associate, also Lee Bowman, Alan Curtis and The Andrews Sisters in "Buck Privates," Universal's tune-filled fun-film, ordinarily suffers no defeatist complex.

Looks Into Future

But he wants to be remembered by posterity. He wants future generations to think of him as a great man. And in the face of this burning, all-consuming ambition, it seems to him he is too late. He tells the story in his own words:

"A fellow's got to figure out a boon to humanity to be a famous man. But what boons are left? I had the idea of the hot dog when I was just a little kid. But somebody beat me to the punch.

"Now look what they've got. Hamburgers, nutburgers, cheeseburgers, wimpies, barkies and bowwowsies."

Popular Invention

"Then there was the idea of the chocolate ice cream soda. A fellow came along, slipped a couple of scoops of hokey-pokey into a high glass, tossed in a slug of syrup, gave it a couple of whirls, and there it was. I can't think of the fellow's name right now. But though we may forget his name, shall we ever forget the monument to his genius—the chocolate ice cream soda?

"Pink popcorn, two cookies with every cup of hot chocolate, even doughnuts without the hole. Somebody's already thought of 'em all.

"It makes me feel bad."

Song Writers Seen in Film

(Current)

The Universal casting office found itself on a spot one day during the filming of "Buck Privates," the comedy about army camp life starring Abbott and Costello with Lee Bowman, Alan Curtis and The Andrews Sisters, now at the .... Theatre.

They needed two young fellows to play songwriters, and they needed them in a hurry—but right now! Don Raye and Hughie Prince got the jobs.

Don Raye and Hughie Prince are the boys who wrote all the songs—actually, that is—in the picture.

Home Towns, Birth Dates of Players

Bud Abbott	Atlantic City, N. J.	October 2
Lou Costello	Paterson, N. J.	March 6
LaVerne Andrews	Minneapolis	July 6
Maxene Andrews	Minneapolis	January 3
Patty Andrews	Minneapolis	February 16
Lee Bowman	Cincinnati	December 28
Alan Curtis	Chicago	July 24
Jane Frazee	Duluth, Minn.	July 18
Nat Pendleton	Davenport, Ia.	August 9

Boogie Jamboree Has Headline Cast

Lee Bowman (left), Jane Frazee and Alan Curtis in Universal's army life comedy, "Buck Privates."
(Mat 23)

Noted Comics, Swingsters, Score in 'Buck Privates'

(Current)

Take a tip from a blip who is hip, the squares that talk against hepcats just ain't nowhere, and they're just hitting clinkers and beating up their gums. Furthermore, they may come on like Gang-busters, but they go off like Wayne King.

That, in a word, is the way the boogie-woogie kids feel.

Lee Bowman in Draft Comedy

(Current)

There are lots of people who enjoy a good walk in the rain, but on that certain bleak, drizzling morning a few years ago in New York that Lee Bowman set out from his walk-up apartment—rent six weeks overdue—he was far from pleasurebent.

Bowman, currently appearing with Abbott and Costello and The Andrews Sisters in Universal's army camp comedy, "Buck Privates," at the .... Theatre, had the gleam of hate in his eye. He figured most other frustrated young actors would be kept indoors by the inclement weather, and he'd have a free field in the agents' offices. He was right. It got him his first role.

A few years' diligence in stock and "little" theatres led to an important role on Broadway in "Berkely Square" and he was signed for the screen.

♦ ♦ ♦

Ex-Wrestler is Movie Comedian

(Advance)

Although the dumb, hardboiled sergeant that Nat Pendleton plays for Universal in "Buck Privates," coming .... to the .... Theatre, is typical of scores and scores of his parts, he has proved the lie to the character in real life.

Before he came to Hollywood, Pendleton was a successful importer in Europe, and then the head of his own film producing company. He turned professional wrestler, and was a ranking contender for the world's championship when he deserted the tug-and-tussle racket for the New York stage. Later he returned to the screen as an actor.

♦ ♦ ♦

Clowns Teamed By Rummy Game

(Current)

If Lou Costello weren't such a dummy at rummy, there never would have been an Abbott and Costello to howl about in "Buck Privates," the Universal comedy about army camp life now at the .... Theatre.

Abbott was a cashier in a theatre. Costello was a vaudeville comic. They started playing rummy backstage, with Abbott furious at Costello's fumbles. Somebody suggested that they try squabbling on the stage.

That's all it took.

In plain language, what they mean is this: "Anyone who is informed will tell you that the longhairs who disparage jitterbugs are just off-key and talking too much. And they usually start off like a lion and end like a lamb."

Well Known Spokesmen

Spokesmen for the irate swingsters are pretty Jewel MacGowan and Dean Collins, world champions, who are featured with 24 other ace jive-kids in "Buck Privates," the Universal comedy about army camp life now playing at the .... Theatre.

For a moment forgetting their "jive talk," Miss MacGowan and Collins say, "Anybody who wants to sound off picks the jitterbugs for their target. But there are a few things on our side, too.

"For one thing, jitterbugging is probably the most exacting dancing there is. People think the steps are done in wild random, but actually they are planned and measured.

Good Health Important

"That's why you don't find jitterbugs in beer parlors and saloons. You've got to be in perfect physical condition to swing, and liquor just doesn't mix.

"Well, we'll plant you now and dig you later."

And that is how a jitterbug excuses himself and says "so long" when the director calls him for a scene.

Abbott and Costello are starred in "Buck Privates." Lee Bowman, Alan Curtis and The Andrews Sisters are other headliners in the cast.

Lou Costello and Bud Abbott in Universal's "Buck Privates."
(Mat 14)

See Movie Fame For Jane Frazee

(Current)

Jane Frazee, Universal's recent "discovery" in support of Abbott and Costello and The Andrews Sisters in "Buck Privates," now at the .... Theatre, breaks all established precedent about being a young Hollywood actress.

She has one interest—becoming famous general and she hasn't been the subject of romantic mention once in the peek-a-boo gossip columns.

She has one interest—becoming an actress, and though she has appeared in only one picture previous to "Buck Privates"—it was "Melody in Moonlight"—she is already regarded as one of the "best bets" among the newcomers.

GLOSSARY OF JIVE-TALK

Take a tip from a blip who is hip—A suggestion from an informed source.

You ain't nowhere—You're a false alarm.

Redneck, roundo—One who doesn't understand, in the wrong.

Hepcat, alligator—Wise in jive.

Beat to the socks—Exhausted.

Square—All in the wrong, a "longhair."

Solid, in the groove, solid murder—Full in tone and rhythm.

Latch on, dig it—To anticipate a particular passage for particular emphasis.

Gutbucket—"Lowdown" swing music.

Beat the shins and hides—Play the drums.

Yip and cluck band—A poor orchestra.

Comes on like Gang-busters, goes off like Wayne King—Starts like a lion, exits like a lamb.

Hitting clinkers—Striking sour notes.

Liverlips—Cracks notes.

Lonesome tenor—Bad musician.

Downdraft jazz—Poor music.

Topcoat—Musical arrangement.

I'll plant you now and dig you later—I'll say "so long" now, and see you later.

I'll cut out here—I'm leaving now.

Chicken dinner—Pretty girl.

Ghost chicken—White girl.

Ofay—White boy.

Early black—Evening.

Early bright—Morning.

All racked out—Dressed in the height of fashion.

Flat—Dollar bill.

Kicks—Uplift, inspiration.

Beating up your gums—Talking too much.

Fight Scene is Movie Surprise

(Current)

It happened in Hollywood. Stage 16, at Universal during the filming of "Buck Privates," currently screening at the .... Theatre.

The set was a replica of an army camp recreation center, and in addition to the stars, Abbott and Costello and The Andrews Sisters, there were hundreds of young "conscripts" at the piano, writing back home, or reading books.

Troupe is Busy

Director Arthur Lubin was busily engaged telling the Andrews girls how to get a little more "oomph" out of their new tune, "Boogie-Woogie Bugle Boy." At the same time, Nick Castle, the New York dance director, was telling them how to frame their routine for the number. Simultaneously, Milton Kranser, was putting in his oar about the camera angles.

In the midst of the rehearsal, Lubin's assistant told him that Lee Bowman and Alan Curtis had reported, ready for their first scene together in the picture, in which they do a young "Sergeant Quirk" and "Captain Flagg."

Introduced by Director

The director went over to them, and said, "You boys know each other, of course?"

They both smiled and shook their heads.

Lubin introduced them.

Two minutes later, in a corner of the recreation hall, they made a "take."

Curtis walked up to Bowman and said, "Hello, fathead, I've got a present for you." And he socked him, smack on the kisser.

"Buck Privates" was filmed from an original screenplay by Arthur T. Horman. Alex Gottlieb was the associate producer.

ACCESSORIES

TIE-UP STILLS

Eight tie-up stills to liven your campaign around town. B.P.1. Camera. B.P.2. Catalina Swim Suit. B.P.3. Sportswear. B.P.4. Beechnut Gum. B.P.5. Bathing Suit. B.P.6. Neckwear. B.P.7. Malted Milks. B.P.8. Swank tie-clips.

ONE 22x28

EIGHT 11x14's

CAMPAIGN HAT

A novelty that will draw in the children and make each one of them a walking street bally. Hat comes on 12 x 18 sheet, with directions for cutting out. Printed on light weight cardboard. Price includes theatre imprint and playdate.

500...$5.00 1000...$8.00 3000...$22.50

LETTER NOVELTY

Here is a gag letter that will incite lots of interest. Written by two Buck Privates, telling the inside of Army life. The letter is carefully deleted in spots to arouse curiosity.

1,000...$2.50
5,000...$2.00
10,000...$1.75
per thousand.

Price includes imprinting.

ECONOMY NOVELTY COMPANY, 225 WEST 39TH STREET, N. Y. CITY

HERALD 7x10 3 Color $3.50 Per M

WINDOW CARDS

BANNER $1.50 **14x36**

6 Hit Songs!

Six pace-setting tunes! Four of them sung by the top trio of the nation, THE ANDREWS SISTERS! That, Mr. Exhibitor, is your cue to make the contacts that will put these potent box-office factors to work for you! Widely publicized in every conceivable music channel in advance of your playdate, they have aroused eager interest in "Buck Privates" throughout the country! Timely as well as tuneful, the music forms a campaign keynote that's powerful in profit-attraction!

★ *"Boogie Woogie Bugle Boy"* ★ *"I Wish You Were Here"*
"You're a Lucky Fellow, Mr. Smith"
★ *"I'll Be With You in Apple Blossom Time"*
★ *"When Private Brown Becomes a Captain"*
★ *"Bounce Me Brother With a Solid Four"*

THE SHEET MUSIC

All of the musical numbers with the exception of "I'll Be With You in Apple Blossom Time" have been published by Leeds Music Corp., 1270 Sixth Ave., New York City. "I'll Be With You in Apple Blossom Time" has been published by Broadway Music Corp., 1619 Broadway, New York City.

THE MUSIC ON RECORDS

Those All-American triple treats of swing, The Andrews Sisters, have recorded "Boogie Woogie Bugle Boy," "Bounce Me Brother With a Solid Four," "Apple Blossom Time" and "You're a Lucky Fellow Mr. Smith" for Decca Records. In addition, all record manufacturers and the country's leading name bands will have discs spinning on the nation's turntables in time for your "Buck Privates" date. Decca, Columbia, Okey, Bluebird and Victor are the brands . . . Glenn Miller, Gene Krupa, Tommy Tucker, Dick Todd, Sammy Kaye, Dick Stabile, Will Bradley, Mitchell Ayres, Woody Herman and Tommy Dorsey have already recorded the rhythm tunes, with other names streaming in, as this campaign book goes to press!

RADIO STATIONS

Arrange for some special "Buck Privates" programs and have them dedicated to "the volunteers and conscripted men from Blank City." Include all the recorded tunes from the picture and make use of the spot radio announcements listed on Showmanship Pages. Make sure, too, that the conductors of Record programs over the local air waves have the records and make liberal use of them.

★ THE JUKE BOXES

50,000,000 nickels can't be wrong! The Andrews Sisters boast the highest percentage for the number of hit tunes spinning in the country's juke boxes! "Queens of the Music Machines" said the ballots of 3000 members of the Coin Machine Operators of America at their national convention!

Don't pass up those juke boxes! With over 600,000 of them plugging The Andrews Sisters and your "Buck Privates" tunes they should prove one of the hottest items in your campaign! See the local concessionaire today! Make sure he has every one of the numbers in his machines. Supply special accessory material on "Buck Privates" and get it spotted on the machines together with a line telling patrons the numbers to play. If possible, promote use of a machine for your lobby so passersby can get a "sound preview" of what's in store for them!

★ THE SONG SHOPS

Every music store, music counter of a department store and record shop is a campaign tie-up waiting for you! Arrange for special window and counter displays of the sheet music and recordings. Supply stores with plenty of stills, cutouts and accessories to enhance their lay-outs. Wherever phonographs or piano players are used as "come-ons" get them to do some extra plugging.

★ THE NIGHT SPOTS

The night clubs, dance halls and other spots where orchestras provide the music should be playing the "Buck Privates" numbers . . . make sure that they are. A few tickets will usually net you the necessary plug on the picture and your playdates.

YOUR EXPLOITATION RECORD

This special campaign record features excerpts from the picture's musical numbers as sung by The Andrews Sisters together with punchy sales copy. It is a double-faced, 12-inch, 78 R.P.M. disc. Use it on your p. a. system and sound ballyhoo truck. Get music stores selling the sheet music and recordings to use it as a special ballyhoo. Plant it on ASCAP licensed radio stations. Play it over your non-sync between shows and incorporate it wherever possible in the stunts suggested on Showmanship Pages. Priced at only $1.00 each at Universal Branches.

YOU'RE IN THE ARMY NOW!
A MILLION LAUGHS AND HOW!

USE '24' FOR MARQUEE AND LOBBY FLASH

The 24-sheet will provide both title and cartoon for above set-up. If you have the space, set up a couple of army pup-tents on either side. Colorful cartoons on other posters will provide great cut-outs for your marquee banner, side-pieces and lobby displays. Consult your local Legion or Army headquarters for proper flag displays. Ordinances permitting, swing loud-speakers out over street and play the music and exploitation records! Check the stills and dress your house personnel in similar outfits!

A LOBBY CANTEEN

Fix up a regular Army canteen in one corner of your lobby. (See stills for suggestions.) Plaster it with signs, pictures, display lines, flags, and provide a wooden counter behind which you can spot a girl dressed as an Army Hostess. Have her pass out doughnuts and coffee promoted from a local commissary. It's a touch of camp life authenticity . . . a gag that'll start plenty of talk.

If you have a candy counter in your lobby —build your canteen display around it!

ANIMATE CARTOONS

Every one of the posters carries a laugh-provoking cartoon. Every one is perfect for cut-out purposes and animation. Set-piece shown below uses cut-out from 3-sheet. Follow suggested layout, mounting cut-out on rocker base and wheel on center axle so that they may be animated as shown in upper diagram. Carry stills and copy as shown.

Page Seven

ADMIT THE DRAFTEES

As obvious as this stunt is, it's one that should net some good newspaper breaks. Your local Army Recruiting Office can provide you with a complete list of men in your local board area, that covers the same district as your drawing area, who have enlisted or been drafted and who are about to report for duty. Invite them to attend a showing of "Buck Privates" as your guests. Plug the stunt in advance and set a special section aside for them. Newspaper will undoubtedly go for copy on the event, especially if they are invited to co-sponsor it. You'll find it well worth the gifted tickets.

BALLY COUPLE!

Here's your street bally! Dress a pretty gal in a tan "Army hostess" outfit including overseas cap . . . and bally man in uniform like a soldier. (See stills for costume suggestions. . . . DO NOT USE REAL ARMY UNIFORMS.) Bally man carries compo-board banner . . . girl hands out Heralds from her kit.

'K.P.' BALLY - CONTEST

The illustration speaks for itself. A top laugh-getter for your lobby or a spot in some restaurant window.

Here's one for the stage! A potato-peeling contest . . . a stunt that's sure to cause plenty of hilarity. Idea is to promote the potatoes from a local restaurant and put the same number of spuds in every basket handed to a contestant. They all start the same time and the one peeling his allotment quickest . . . and BEST . . . wins the prize.

BOOGIE - WOOGIE?

"Boogie-woogie" . . . It's a new phrase that is sweeping the country . . . a phrase that the habitats of the swing palaces and the record fans associate directly with The Andrews Sisters, who made it popular. It denotes a distinct new trend in rhythm music! Be sure to cover the juke boxes and dance-halls. Supply display material and stills showing the huge "boogie-woogie" dance sequence in the film! You may find it profitable to sponsor a "boogie-woogie" dance contest with a "Buck Privates" trophy going to the winners. Of course you'll make sure that the dance bands have the sheet music and the juke boxes contain the recordings of the picture's hit tunes. (See Music page.)

DATE SET? HERE'S YO[UR]

1. Contact every patriotic, civic organization and [ex]plained elsewhere on these pages!

2. Preceding your opening, arrange for a "Buck [Privates Day" by] the Legion "in honor of Blank City's 'Buck Priv[ates']"[—organ]ized, of course! Any father-son angles?—A father wh[o was a] "Buck Private" now—should be good for added s[pace.]

3. Build up additional advance interest for your s[how. Have] service clubs dedicate luncheons to "Blank Cit[y's] draftees guested, speakers from nearby Army Camp[s.]

4. Everybody loves a parade. Why, where and ho[w.]

5. Get busy with advance mailing, radio campaig[ns, explained in] this section. "Buck Privates" is one of the grea[t.]

6. With every campaign item be sure to stress "Bu[ck Privates"] pictures . . . its great entertainment value . . . [the music] and Bud Abbott and Lou Costello, a team that'll set [the town talking!]

GO AFTER LEGION SUPPORT

"Buck Privates," although dealing strictly with Army life in present day camps, will bring back many memories of 1918 camp life to Legionnaires and other ex-Service men. Some of your best exploitation can be done in co-operation with the American Legion, the Veterans of Foreign Wars and their women's auxiliaries. Local posts are to be found in practically every area in the United States and you will find the officers and members ready and willing to work with you in various ways that are a cinch to net swell publicity breaks.

Every Legion Post has its special charities which depend upon them for funds and the posts annually stage many benefits to raise money. In return for their help in your "Buck Privates" campaign . . . give them your cooperation in boosting their program! A lobby board and special trailer or slide on your screen plugging a forthcoming American Legion affair will assure you of the Legion's cooperation.

A PARADE! What's more typical of Army life than marching men . . . a parade with drums rolling, trumpets sounding, flags streaming and martial music filling the air! It's a natural! Enlist the support of your Legion Post, their Drum and Bugle Corps or Band, Color Guard and Drill Team. Send your bally parade right through the heart of town with marchers carrying huge cut-outs from the posters and a banner carrying title and your playdates.

IN YOUR LOBBY You'll want to decorate, of course, for your "Buck Privates" engagement. Your Legion Post will be able to provide you with many Army items, show you proper display of the colors, etc.

A barrage of mirth! A salvo of singing and **DISPLA[Y]** swinging! A parade of top tunes! It's the first and funniest military musical!

Discipline? Drills? A.W.O.L.! K.P.! P.D.Q.! Nothing else but! Leave it to Abbott and Costello as "Buck Privates"!

They're in the Army now! Those radio aces are going places . . . in the merriest military musical ever made!

You'll be caught in a draft of laughter . . . when you see this cock-eyed comedy of two cock-eyed "Buck Privates"!

Mirthful! Merry! Military! The screen goes wacky in khaki as your favorite radio funsters and melody maids offer a hilarious prescription for conscription!

YOU'RE BOUND TO GET RICH IF YOU CAMPAIGN "BUCK PRIVATES"

OUR CAMPAIGN LIST!

your Army Recruiting Offices for the cooperation ex-

Privates'' get-together or dinner. Handle through ates' of 1917 and 1941!" This to be widely public-ho was a "Buck Private" in 1917 and whose son is a space!

showing by having Rotary, Kiwanis and other local ty's 'Buck Privates'" . . . with local volunteers and p, etc.

ow to do it—outlined in paragraph below.

gn, the advance stunts and ballyhoos suggested in test exploitation "naturals" you've ever had.

uck Privates" as the first and funniest of the camp its music and The Andrews Sisters . . . its comedy t the whole cockeyed world laughing again!

ARMY CAN REALLY HELP

You're in the Army now! Well . . . not quite, but "Buck Privates," though filled with the riotous antics of Bud Abbott and Lou Costello, presents present-day camp life in a thoroughly approved manner, showing the recreation program and many comforts which the Army has provided for conscripted men. Your local headquarters of the Army Recruiting Service will undoubtedly be willing to cooperate in many ways on your campaign! Here are a few.

LOBBY RECRUITING Arrange with local Recruiting Office to set up a branch in your lobby during the "Buck Privates" engagement. In addition to the eye-appeal of the smartly dressed officers and men, their equipment and colors, the stunt will be good for a lot of word-of-mouth publicity.

A SUGGESTION If you're contemplating a patriotic motif in your lobby with use of Army material and flag displays, officers from your local Recruiting Offices should be consulted as to proper handling.

PARADE Suggested in column at left is a parade in which American Legion cooperation is outlined. It may prove possible to arrange the stunt with help of U. S. Army Recruiting Office. Marching Army men, Color Guard, Drum and Bugle Corps, banners . . . you can't top it!

AN ARMY TRUCK OUT FRONT! This shouldn't be hard to work . . . especially if you suggest it as a recruiting unit. Several exhibitors have used the angle during past months as a straight stunt for getting additional attention. With "Buck Privates" the stunt **really** ties in!

Y LINES

Pack up your troubles and follow the laugh lines to "Buck Privates"! It's a barrage of mirth . . . a bombardment of comedy . . . a salvo of singing and swinging!

Here's the first Army Camp comedy! It's the big parade of laughs . . . of top stars and top tunes!

Here's a laugh-laden, tune-filled prescription for conscription! Hold tight, boys! The Army goes boogie-woogie with a BANG!

The screen goes wacky in khaki! Those rollicking radio boys . . . and the song-sational creators of boogie-woogie rhythm get caught in a draft . . . and blow into camp with the merriest military musical ever to hit the screen!

SURPRINT NEWSPAPERS

The old gag of running a big red surprint over the front page of several thousand local newspapers and having newsboys hand them out free is always an effective stunt. Should be great for "Buck Privates," because you can use some of those blaring headlines which hit the streets when Military Conscription was first announced and later when draft numbers were drawn: "U. S. TO HAVE CONSCRIPTION! 158 FIRST NUMBER DRAWN! 4,000,000 MEN TO BE TRAINED!" Don't forget to supply the newsboys with the novelty "Buck Privates" campaign hats!

Surprint the papers with: "It's the Big Parade of Laughs! See 'BUCK PRIVATES' Rivoli."

MUSIC BOARD

Swing out with those hit picture tunes right in your lobby! Follow layout for Display board. Cut out cartoon, silhouetting the gals so they may be animated with oscillating fan. Conceal phonograph behind board and play the exploitation record and other recorded music!

'BUCK PRIVATE' PHOTOS

In an empty store window or lobby frame, fix up a collection of photographs of local boys who have enlisted or been drafted into the Army. Label the display **"Do You Recognize These Blank City Boys as "BUCK PRIVATES"? . . . See Abbott and Costello and The Andrews Sisters in This Grand Comedy at the Rivoli."** It's a swell stunt for getting local interest and it may prove possible to tie-up with a newspaper on the stunt. Proud parents will eagerly answer a printed call for the photos.

BUGLER OUT FRONT!

Spot a bugler atop your marquee and have him give-out with all the bugle calls, except "taps," during the peak rush hours. Might even have him wind-up his program with a few hot licks that'll give them a hint of what "Buck Privates" has in store.

SOME REMINDERS

Don't forget to post your accessory material in and around local draft board headquarters, Army Recruiting Offices, etc.

Drum and Bugle Corps contests.

Bugler contest with Boy Scout and high school musicians competing.

Flag-raising and lowering ceremony at your theatre.

Signalling demonstrations on marquee or in front of theatre.

Sound truck—use set-up suggested for marquee and have some boys in uniform whooping it up on the truck. Play the exploitation record!

BUILD A TANK FOR YOUR STREET BALLY

Illustration at right shows the hilarious effect you can get with a "tank" load of "buck privates" and gals touring the town. Local handyman should be able to build the tank of compo-board over an old auto body. Your house artist can decorate it properly to make it look like heavy armor plate. Carry copy banners as shown, using plenty of the Display Lines spotted from stem to stern on the tank!

EQUIPMENT DISPLAY

Your local Recruiting Office will probably be willing to supply you with material that can be used for lobby display. Of interest to everyone would be a set-up of the complete equipment issued to "Buck Privates." The uniforms, shoes, socks, underwear, blankets, the duffle bag and all its contents, the soldier's pack, etc. Label each item and arrange them for an attractive lobby showing.

A display of new Army rifle, machine gun or trench mortar with Army man on hand to explain their intricacies would also prove a real eye-riveter for your foyer.

NEWSPAPER CONTEST

Get the veterans and Army men from nearby camps to tell their favorite funny story about camp life—in fact, ask everyone to send in the best conscription, camp life or war joke they ever heard—to your local paper. Announce that prizes will be awarded for the funniest stories about "Buck Privates." Plant the heading shown and the contest should get a big reader response. Order special 2 Col. Mat . . . Exploitation BP1 . . . from Universal Branches.

NOTICE Do NOT use real Army uniforms as costumes for bally-men. Similar outfits—see stills—can be obtained from costumer or local Army and Navy store.

POSTERS

THE 24 SHEET

COLOR DESCRIPTION

Cartoon figures in full color against white background. Red title with blue star credits. Brown panel across bottom with credits in white.

THREE SHEET

SIX SHEET

ONE SHEET

Printed in U.S.A

The Screen Goes Wacky in Khaki !

It's the first army camp comedy...
with your favorite radio funsters
and melody maids!

The screen's new comedy sensations!

BUD   LOU
ABBOTT *and* **COSTELLO**
in

BUCK PRIVATES

with

Lee **BOWMAN**   Alan **CURTIS**
Jane **FRAZEE**   Nat **PENDLETON**
and
The song-sational creators
of Boogie Woogie Rhythm
THE ANDREWS SISTERS
and 24 world champion
boogie-woogie boys and beauties!

ADDED ATTRACTIONS

Directed by Arthur Lubin • Associate Producer: Alex Gottlieb
Original Screen Play by Arthur T. Horman
3B   Special material for Abbott and Costello by John Grant
A UNIVERSAL PICTURE
Ad No. 3B—3 Col.—Mat 45c

A UNIVERSAL PICTURE 2G

Ad No. 2G—2 Col.—Mat 30c

ADDED ATTRACTIONS

Directed by Arthur Lubin • Associate Producer: Alex Gottlieb
Original Screen Play by Arthur T. Horman
Special material for Abbott and Costello by John Grant
A UNIVERSAL PICTURE 2B

Ad No. 2B—2 Col.—Mat 30c

Directed by Arthur Lubin • Associate Producer: Alex Gottlieb
Original Screen Play by Arthur T. Horman
Special material for Abbott and Costello by John Grant
A UNIVERSAL PICTURE 2C

Ad No. 2C—2 Col.—Mat 30c

A UNIVERSAL PICTURE 2F

Ad No. 2F—2 Col.—Mat 30c

IT'S THE BIG PARADE
OF LAUGHS!

ADDED ATTRACTIONS

Original Screen Play by Arthur T.
Horman · Special material for
Abbott and Costello by John Grant
Directed by Arthur Lubin
Associate Producer
Alex Gottlieb
A UNIVERSAL PICTURE

1E

Ad No. 1E—1 Col.—Mat 15c

3A

Directed by Arthur Lubin · Associate Producer: Alex Gottlieb
Original Screen Play by Arthur T. Horman
Special material for Abbott and Costello by John Grant
A UNIVERSAL PICTURE

Ad No. 3A—3 Col.—Mat 45c

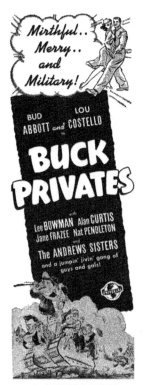

A UNIVERSAL PICTURE

1C

Ad No. 1C—1 Col.—Mat 15c

1A

Ad No. 1A—1 Col.—Mat 15c

Directed by Arthur Lubin • Associate Producer: Alex Gottlieb

Original Screen Play by Arthur T. Horman   Special material for Abbott and Costello by John Grant

A UNIVERSAL PICTURE

3D

Ad No. 3D—3 Col.—Mat 45c

YOU'LL BE CAUGHT IN A DRAFT OF LAUGHTER!

BUD **ABBOTT** and LOU **COSTELLO**
in

BUCK PRIVATES

with

Lee BOWMAN   Alan CURTIS
Jane FRAZEE   Nat PENDLETON
and
The ANDREWS SISTERS
and a jumpin' jivin' gang of guys and gals!

ADDED
ATTRACTIONS

A UNIVERSAL PICTURE

Original Screen Play by Arthur T. Horman · Special material for Abbott and Costello by John Grant
Directed by Arthur Lubin
Associate Producer
Alex Gottlieb   1D

Ad No. 1D—1 Col.—Mat 15c

BUCK PRIVATES
A UNIVERSAL PICTURE
1B

Ad No. 1B—1 Col.—Mat 15c

FUNNY.. ABBOTT & COSTELLO!   SUNNY.. ANDREWS SISTERS!
In the first and funniest military musical!

The screen's new comedy sensations!
BUD **ABBOTT** and LOU **COSTELLO**
in

BUCK PRIVATES

with

Lee BOWMAN   Alan CURTIS
Jane FRAZEE   Nat PENDLETON
and
The song-sational creators
of Boogie Woogie Rhythm
THE ANDREWS SISTERS
and 24 world champion
boogie-woogie boys and beauties!

Directed by Arthur Lubin   Associate Producer: Alex Gottlieb
Original Screen Play by Arthur T. Horman · Special material for Abbott and Costello by John Grant
A UNIVERSAL PICTURE   3C

Ad No. 3C—3 Col.—Mat 45c

IT'S THE BIG PARADE OF LAUGHS!

BUD LOU
ABBOTT and COSTELLO
in

BUCK PRIVATES

with
Lee BOWMAN Alan CURTIS
Jane FRAZEE Nat PENDLETON
and
THE ANDREWS SISTERS
and 24 world champion
boogie-woogie boys and beauties!

ADDED ATTRACTIONS

Directed by Arthur Lubin • Associate Producer: Alex Gottlieb
Original Screen [play] by Arthur T. Horman
Special material for Abb[ott a]nd Costello by John Grant
A UNIVE[RSAL] PICTURE 2E
Ad No. 2E—2 [Col.]—Mat 30c

HERE'S THE First ARMY CAMP COMEDY!

BUD LOU
ABBOTT and COSTELLO
in

BUCK PRIVATES

with
Lee BOWMAN Alan CURTIS
Jane FRAZEE Nat PENDLETON
and
THE ANDREWS SISTERS

ADDED ATTRACTIONS

Directed by Arthur Lubin • Associate Producer: Alex Gottlieb
Original Screen Play by Arthur T. Horman
Special material for Abbott and Costello by John Grant
A UNIVERSAL PICTURE 2D
Ad No. 2D—2 Col.—Mat 30c

HELD OVER!

BUD LOU
ABBOTT and COSTELLO
in
BUCK PRIVATES
with
Lee BOWMAN Alan CURTIS
Jane FRAZEE Nat PENDLETON
and
The ANDREWS SISTERS
and a jumpin' jivin' gang of
guys and gals!

BUD LOU
ABBOTT and COSTELLO
in
BUCK PRIVATES
with
Lee BOWMAN Alan CURTIS
Jane FRAZEE Nat PENDLETON
and
The ANDREWS SISTERS
and a jumpin' jivin' gang of
guys and gals!

The screen's new comedy sensations!

BUD LOU
ABBOTT and COSTELLO
in

BUCK PRIVATES

with
Lee BOWMAN Alan CURTIS
Jane FRAZEE Nat PENDLETON
and the song-sational creators of
Boogie Woogie Rhythm
THE ANDREWS SISTERS
and 24 world champion
boogie-woogie boys and beauties!

Sing and Sway to these Happy Hits!
"Boogie Woogie Bugle Boy" "You're A Lucky Fellow, Mr.
Smith" "I'll Be With You When It's Appleblossom Time"
"Bounce Me Brother With A Solid Four" "When Private
Brown Becomes a Captain" "I Wish You Were Here"

2nd SMASH WEEK!

Ad No. UTIL No. 1—3 Col.—Mat 45c

Bibliography

Costello, Chris with Raymond Strait. *Lou's on First*. New York: St. Martin's Press, 1981.

Doherty, Thomas. *Projections of War*. New York: Columbia University Press, 1993.

Furmanek, Bob and Ron Palumbo. *Abbott and Costello in Hollywood*. New York: Perigee, 1991.

Gomery, Douglas. *The Hollywood Studio System*. New York: St. Martin's Press, 1986.

Hirschhorn, Clive. *The Universal Story*. New York: Crown, 1983.

Izod, John. *Hollywood and the Box Office: 1895-1986*. New York: Columbia University Press, 1988.

Koppes, Clayton R. and Gregory D. Black. *Hollywood Goes To War*. Los Angeles: University of California Press, 1987.

Maltin, Leonard. *Movie Comedy Teams*. New York: Plume, 1985.

Morlan, Don B. "Slapstick Contributions to WWII Propaganda: The Three Stooges and Abbott and Costello." *Studies in Popular Culture,* October 1994.

Mulholland, Jim. *The Abbott and Costello Book*. New York: Popular Library, 1977.

Ruppli, Michael. *The Decca Labels: A Discography*. Westport, Conn.: Greenwood Press, 1996.

Schatz, Thomas. *The Genius of the System*. New York: Pantheon Books, 1988.

Simon, George T. *The Big Bands*. New York: Schirmer Books, 1981.

Thomas, Bob. *Bud & Lou*. New York: J.B. Lippincott, 1977.

CPSIA information can be obtained at www.ICGtesting.com
Printed in the USA
BVOW11*2308140715

408624BV00016B/175/P